When Memory Fails

Helping the Alzheimer's and Dementia Patient

When Memory Fails

Helping the Alzheimer's and Dementia Patient

Allen Jack Edwards, Ph. D.

PLENUM PRESS • NEW YORK AND LONDON

Library of Congress Cataloging in Publication Data

Edwards, Allen Jack, 1926–
  When memory fails: helping the Alzheimer's and dementia patient / Allen Jack
Edwards.
      p.   cm.
  Includes bibliographical references and index.
  ISBN 0-306-44648-0
  1. Dementia. 2. Alzheimer's disease. 3. Caregivers. I. Title.
  [DNLM: 1. Dementia. 2. Caregivers. WM 220 E26w]
  RC521.E43   1994
  616.8'3—dc20
  DNLM/DLC   94-2058
  for Library of Congress   CIP

ISBN 0-306-44648-0

© 1994 Allen Jack Edwards
Plenum Press is a Division of Plenum Publishing Corporation
233 Spring Street, New York, N.Y. 10013-1578

Printed in the United States of America

For Joel,
who still makes
good things happen

Preface

Environmental improvements in the twentieth century have greatly increased the longevity of our citizens. Medical care can frequently control and cure former "killers," allowing more persons to live and to live longer. Nutritional care has made us healthier, stronger, and even taller and heavier. Better housing, cleaner living areas, and elimination of toxic substances such as asbestos have permitted safer and more complete physical and mental development. Recognition of psychological sources of distress (e.g., depression) and the development of therapeutic intervention have enabled us to lead calmer and happier lives. All such elements have catalyzed the increase in average length of life in the United States from 47 years in 1900 to 75 years today. The number of persons aged 75 and over is significant. Indeed, those living to be 100 and older is becoming a sizable and impressive group.

Such blessings are not without their costs, however. The oldest persons in any society are most at risk for debilitating and destructive effects of disease, injury, and abuse. Since we now have greater numbers of individuals living to older ages, the possibilities of more serious and widespread adverse influences are compounded. One result is the increasing incidence of a condition called "dementia," a term coined to signify mental changes in an individual: memory loss, confusion, and disorientation in time and place. The sufferers of dementia may also show various kinds and degrees of personality changes. These kinds of variations interfere with the ability of the person to function normally in our complex world with its multiple modifications and extreme demands. The result is an individual who once acted as a mature, competent, independent, and contributing citizen but who increasingly becomes dependent and ineffectual in normal behaviors.

Such consequences are too serious to ignore. An important human being is lost. The cost is not only personal but deprives family and friends and society as well. Instead of assisting in meeting societal needs and helping to defray expenses, this individual becomes a dependent—unable to reclaim lost abilities. The dementia process from inception to conclusion in death on average takes 8 years or so, and some persons live with increasing dementia for 15 or more years.

There are at least two persons severely affected by these deleterious events—the patient, first, but also the caregiver, who becomes increasingly involved as the patient becomes less competent and more dependent. The devastation to the caregiver's life can be so severe that, in effect, another important human being is lost to society. Children and relatives become involved to a greater or lesser degree in the problems and difficulties caused by the patient's condition. Often, friends and colleagues also become enmeshed in the web that entangles the victims of dementia.

A patient developing dementia experiences increasing numbers of incidents that are mystifying and disturbing. Anxiety, even depression, result when one cannot handle problems effectively. Reactions against those closest and most supportive may occur as these frightening events continue to increase. Eventually, the consequences of dementia affect mental behavior so profoundly that the patient has little awareness and little or no concern. The dependency induced by the sequence leaves a person reacting largely to emotional contexts, with virtually no intellectual ability left to understand the situation. However, *physical* stamina and strength may increase over time.

For the caregiver, the early events of dementia may be perceived as unimportant, or irritating, or even perverse. With time, however, problem behaviors intensify to such a level that they must be confronted. Once aware that the patient suffers dementia, the imposition of stress and burden becomes more pronounced. Without skills to deal with demands, the caregiver may become futile in some efforts, overwhelmed with others, and consequently develop psychological distress. If things do not improve, at some point there most often is an attempt at resolution through contact with others. Education by attending workshops and meetings, reading materials from varied sources, and attending support groups help bridge some of the disparity. Self-sustaining actions become more prominent, although not all of them are pertinent to the problems. Some adjustment to and acceptance of reality often eventuates. One caregiver has spoken of the gamut of emotions she experiences every day. Gradually, the pain is lessening, she says, and she finds pleasure in unplanned places. Kindness from others helps her cope with what otherwise would be a dismal existence. She is finding a way to continue with life—but a life that is largely devoid of the rewarding experiences most of us have.

Dementia, then, has become one of the most serious concerns for adults in this country. Already, as much as 20 percent of our population is affected by the consequences of dementia in some way. If present trends and forecasts are correct, that total may triple or quadruple by the year 2030. There is increasing evidence of worry about oneself or family members as potential victims.

This book has been written with the purpose of informing the general public about present knowledge of causes, effects, and treatment concerning dementia. Further, it has been prepared to assist those who live with the dementia patient to understand what and why events are happening, and to offer means of intervention that may be tried. There are not many answers—not from physicians or other professionals such as psychologists, social workers, and gerontologists—for the many difficult behaviors that caregivers will encounter. In that sense, then, the content of this book is "state of the art."

This book is a singular effort. However, the means to the product required many sources and contacts that yielded varied and enlightening experiences. Chief among these were the many patients and caregivers who patiently schooled me in the realities of lives dominated by dementia. Professionals who have hands-on experience daily—social workers, case workers, nurses, directors of special care units, nurse's aides, activities directors, and social services directors—were of inestimable value to whatever is correct and good about this volume. To the agencies, particularly the Southwestern Missouri Chapter of the Alzheimer's Association, I owe a debt of gratitude. My wife, Jean, has been supportive of all my efforts, even during the times when the writing was not going well. To all, and others I have not mentioned, I offer my heartfelt appreciation and thanks.

Allen Jack Edwards

Springfield, Missouri

Contents

Chapter 4 Psychological Effects of Dementia 71

Chapter 5 Diagnosis of Dementia 105

Chapter 6   Dementia and the Patient   133

Chapter 7   Dementia and the Caregiver   157

Chapter 8   Facing Problem Behaviors   183

Chapter 9   Helping the Caregivers   215

1

What Is Dementia?

There is a condition found throughout the world today that threatens the well-being and the welfare of millions of people. Known by several different names, it has outcomes that cause fear and dread in those who see it in others. Because we believe that physicians are the proper persons to tell us what is wrong, and how to correct it, most people believe this condition is a medical problem, even though it brings severe psychological and social consequences. It is so damaging to the functioning of the individual that personal integrity will be lost as competencies are destroyed. The need for care may become so great, and the length of time that the patient may live may be so long, that the expenses associated with the daily life demands of the victim will erode whatever financial resources are available. The fear of winding up as a dependent, incompetent, unwanted, and expensive ward of the state is steadily growing in the minds of people all over the world. The dreaded condition causing this fear is best described by the term "dementia."

Surely, many people would say, anything this dangerous must be the major focus of scientific research in pursuit of appropriate treatment and cure. Research sponsored by governments and foundations must be underway to determine the cause and find a preventive. Yet the fact is that little or nothing is being done that promises an effective *remedy*, largely because doctors tend to view the condition as progressive, irreversible, and untreatable. This means that changes in behavior will only grow worse with time (progression) and that nothing can be done to treat the patient, either to stop the effects of dementia or even delay them, much less reverse them so that the person is cured (irreversibility and untreatability).

The efforts to find a cure or a preventive are limited by the amount of money devoted to research. With so little known about dementia, very basic studies must be conducted before more in-depth ones can be undertaken. In the United States alone, for example, there was less than $400 million spent by the government in 1992 on research to find the causes of dementia. Though a considerable sum by personal accounts, it is small compared to what was spent on military defense or AIDS (acquired immunodeficiency syndrome) or any number of other "causes" that have greater appeal to the Congress or administration. In fact, the research sum amounted to only about $100 per patient for the number of estimated dementia patients in this country today! By contrast, the recommended appropriation for AIDS research for fiscal year 1993 was more than $1.2 billion, with the number of patients who suffer the condition estimated at 240,000. On average, this means that each AIDS patient had an investment of more than $5,000 for research purposes. Certainly, one cannot quarrel with the justification for such an investment; the discrepancy between the two cannot be ignored, however.

The cost of caring for dementia patients averages to at least $32,000 per year in long-term care settings (i.e., nursing homes), and this is a conservative estimate at best. Medicare and most private insurance plans do not cover the costs of care for dementia patients because the condition is medically classified as a mental condition. Such facts are more than frightening; they show that our goals as a society need reexamination, that our investments from taxation need reappraisal, and that our concerns for the happiness and security of present and future elderly need redirection.

The prevalence of dementia we see currently is merely the tip of the iceberg at that. There are now some 32 million individuals in this country age 65 and older. That figure is expected to grow to 39 million (a 19 percent increase) in less than 20 years. Though there are now an estimated 5 million victims of dementia, the number may increase to more than 17 million in the same time period. If true, within 20 years, over 40 percent of the elderly will suffer some form of dementia compared to less than 15 percent at the present time. These are staggering figures, and they are only estimates because no statistics are kept by any agency of the exact number of persons diagnosed by physicians as suffering from dementia. In fact, doctors resist any imposition of record keeping that would lead to actual numbers and realistic data. It is possible that the figures I have cited are underestimates of the real problem.

The Communication Process

Most Americans are poorly informed about dementia, its causes, and its consequences. Though some organizations are making strong efforts to educate the public, there is greater *mis*understanding than understanding. Indeed, due to the lack of knowledge on the part of professionals (an outcome from the dearth of research), straightforward answers to questions about dementia are seldom given, or even possible. The American public needs to know how to recognize the onset of dementia, what happens in the months and years that follow its onset, and how to avoid the consequences.

What seems to be the usual course of events goes something like this: The person who is developing a dementia will show only minor and widely spread symptoms at first. Some important events, duties, or promises may be forgotten, to the chagrin and dismay of the individual. Particularly if this person is older, there may well be an "explaining away" of the incidents. After all, it is expected that memory will suffer somewhat as one gets older, and because the forgetfulness is infrequent it surely should not be a cause for great concern. Even at this point, however, there may be some telling differences between the "normal" forgetfulness of old age and the loss of memory that is part of dementia. While it is true that one may have some difficulty remembering a name, or whether one turned out the light in the bathroom before leaving home, and so on, incidents such as these do not interfere with a person's ability to cope with significant life events. Functioning is not really impaired so far as awareness and adjustment are concerned. The events affected by dementia may be much more important. For example, the person developing dementia is more likely to forget an important appointment, or be unable to remember how to get to the place of the appointment. Some well-practiced, seemingly simple task may not be done when it is required, thereby causing inconvenience, delay, or even loss for an employer. The *functional* status of the person gradually erodes in the most human of all our traits: thinking, reasoning, calculating, planning, and performing.

It is not unusual for dementia to develop over a period of several years before there is finally a willingness to admit that a problem exists. In fact, by the time the person goes (or is taken) to a physician for an examination and diagnosis, the condition may have developed to major proportions. Not infrequently, the "signs" are ignored or explained away until a critical event of some kind makes it impossible to disregard the problem any longer. On the job, the loyal and once-competent employee may begin to make errors that the supervisor can correct or cover up for a while. As the dementia continues to develop, it will express itself more often and with greater impact. At some point, the supervisor must admit that the employee should be let go before greater damage is done. One might question how the dementia could develop this far without the employee or the employee's spouse noticing that something very worrisome was happening. Indeed, all parties involved may have been aware of at least some of the signs, but it was less threatening to deny them than to face them realistically.

After having been a competent adult for so many years, dealing effectively with a wide variety of situations, it becomes difficult to believe that such extreme changes could be taking place.

When the individual finally seeks medical consultation, all the usual medical tests will be conducted to see if there may be some treatable condition (such as infections or depression) that might be causing the behavioral problems. This step is essential, but, in the case of a dementia, will not often prove helpful; that is, most of the time the tests will be negative, indicating that the search for a cause must continue. At this point, the examining physician may make a referral to a neurologist or psychiatrist. More extensive psychological and physical tests that focus on how dementia may be identified will be used. There may even be the decision to do a brain scan, using new technology that is sensitive to the condition of the brain but does not require any intrusion into the brain. The knowledge gained from such a brain scan will not definitely diagnose the cause of a dementia. It may, however, identify a condition that is not apparent by standard examination techniques. There may be, for example, a brain tumor, operable or inoperable. Most times, again, for dementia patients the results are cited as "negative," which means that such possible causes of the behavior changes are unlikely.

The psychological test data, which screens for mental competence, may include a number of different tests. Each of these provides somewhat different facts that help define the extent of the individual's loss in abilities. Test results also will help to isolate the particular kinds of mental abilities that are no longer functional. Finally, perhaps after several weeks of various examinations, the person's physician may have to admit that there are no definitive causes shown that might be treatable and correctable. Instead, there must be some presumption that a condition that inevitably leads to irreversible dementia is the culprit. The doctor may give the dementia a specific label (the most common of which is Alzheimer's disease) or a more general label (such as senile dementia of the Alzheimer's type) or even a vague label (such as senility). What is really being communicated is that the behaviors cannot be corrected with present medical knowledge, that the cause is essentially unknown, and that the patient will only become worse. Unfortunately, all doctors are not equally capable of communicating such dire news to the patient or caregiver. Instead, they may use some confusing label (such as primary degenerative dementia) and ask if there are questions. At this point, however, neither the patient nor the caregiver knows what questions they should ask. Indeed, they may be so overwhelmed by the implications of the diagnosis that they are unable to think very capably. They may leave the office in ignorance but with a clear understanding that things are worse than ever. Instead of the hope for a cure, they are now burdened by the fact that things will only get worse!

To create the impression that all physicians are uninterested in or incapable of communicating clearly about dementia would be both unfair and incorrect. Caregivers frequently report some displeasure about what was said to them and how it was said. This may be a result of their own anxiety over the realization that there will be no improvement or cure for the patient. The anxiety is only buttressed by their inability to know what questions to ask. Unfortunately, there are not as many resources for understandable and useful information outside the medical profession as might be expected. Organizations such as the Alzheimer's Association* publish a number of pamphlets and other educational materials but only a portion of those who need such information are aware of the resource.

There is an urgent need for understanding that must be met in as straightforward and explicit a manner as possible. This book has been written to meet that need. The topics were chosen to reflect questions to which caregivers say they need answers, in areas where they believe there is a lack of knowledge. To make the book's content as useful as possible, each topic is fully described and relevant questions that caregivers should ask professionals in

*The address is: Alzheimer's Association, 919 North Michigan Avenue, Suite 1000, Chicago, Illinois 60611-1676. Telephone: 800-272-3900; 312-335-8700.

various disciplines are included. It is hoped that the book will aid caregivers during the entire time a patient–caregiver relationship exists.

Defining Dementia

Let's begin at the beginning. Given the significance of the condition, one would think that there is common agreement on the meaning of the term "dementia." Actually, however, there are differences between disciplines (such as between medicine and psychology) and even within disciplines (such as within medicine, where terms such as Alzheimer's or senility may be used). In one case, the outcome (the dementia that develops) is considered synonymous with the cause (e.g., Alzheimer's disease). In another case, the two may be considered separate, with any one of several causes (Alzheimer's, vascular strokes, or Parkinson's) leading to the same outcome (dementia). In still another case, it may be difficult to determine just how the term is being used (e.g., dementia may be said to be due to aging). Even dictionaries do not agree. In one, there is reference to "deteriorated mentality." In another, the definition includes not only mental loss but the "irreversible" nature of that outcome accompanied by "emotional disturbance," all resulting from an "organic brain disorder." A medical dictionary defines dementia as a loss of mental competence with significant "decline" from the person's former mental capability. There is also a mention of frequent instances of "emotional apathy." Which of these best defines dementia is difficult to say. Of course, the lack of agreement in definition reflects the limited level of knowledge about a highly visible, emotion-arousing concept that should be clearer in meaning than it apparently is.

The use of the term in this book will be as follows: Dementia is the *effect* of several medically diagnosed conditions that lead to increasing losses in memory, disorientation in time and place, and confusion even in highly familiar settings. These outcomes are the observable signs of a major problem. It is possible to demonstrate when and how memory loss occurs, how a person may be disoriented in time and place, and the presence of confusion in highly familiar settings. However, it is just as important to know as much as possible about what *causes* these kinds of behaviors to occur.

Demonstrating Dementia

As you read this book, you will find greater detail about both causes and outcomes of dementia. First, however, it may be helpful to describe the general nature of dementia and its consequences.

What Does a Dementia Patient Do?

Since so much emphasis has been put on the negative changes that occur during the progression of a dementia, it might seem that the patient will be unable to do much of anything. Although that may eventually occur, it may take several years. In fact, while some competencies and skills may begin to deteriorate early in the process, others remain intact through most of the course of the dementia. Unfortunately, there is little or no regularity to the progression, and the changes found in one individual may be more severe or occur earlier than those seen in another person. It is impossible to set up a neat list of what to expect to occur when. This inability makes it even more difficult for the caregiver and patient to know what to anticipate and how changes may express themselves. What is a severe problem for one caregiver may never even occur for another. For example, one patient may become a wanderer, keeping the caregiver constantly on the alert to prevent the patient, who is unable to remember locations, traffic laws, or meanings of signs and signals, from leaving the house. Preventing wandering may exhaust the caregiver's time, patience, and strength. Yet, for another caregiver, the patient may be content to remain in the house all the time. In fact, *this* may represent a problem since the caregiver is tied down even when it is necessary to shop, go to the beauty parlor or barber shop, visit the doctor, or the like.

Given these restrictions about how dementia will affect the patient and when, certain generalizations are still possible. To illustrate how abilities may change, let us consider a description of a dementia patient.

Martha Wells is a 69-year-old woman who has spent most of her adult life as a mother and housekeeper. She has been responsible for buying and preparing food, selecting and purchasing clothing for herself and her children, maintaining a comfortable home, establishing a relaxed and warm atmosphere for living—all the kinds of things associated with the popular stereotype of a woman's role for her generation. She was successful at these tasks, and believed that her life was meaningful and worthwhile. Since her children have matured and left to set up their own homes, she has withdrawn from some of her previous roles. In some respects, she performs other tasks less competently than she did formerly, although she seems unaware of the changes and there are no obvious reasons why she should be less efficient.

In fact, Martha seems to behave less efficiently in several behaviors. She herself has noticed some problems in remembering *what* she is supposed to do at specific times. Worse, it seems to her that sometimes she can't quite remember *how* to do things she has done for years. There are days when she has some sense that a period of time has elapsed that she can't account for. Recently, she was supposed to meet her oldest daughter for lunch and shopping. She even noted the event on her calendar, and was looking forward to it. For some reason, she completely forgot about the date and did not consult her calendar as she usually does every morning. Her daughter called that afternoon, angry that she had been stood up. Martha was caught by surprise but kept her wits enough to make up a story that a neighbor had had an emergency and Martha got tied up trying to help her. Her daughter seemed to accept this explanation as reasonable. Martha managed to persuade herself that the neighbor's dilemma had really happened. By the time her husband got home from work, she gave him a detailed description of the event and what she did to help. He seemed impressed, and congratulated her on her neighborliness. That night, Martha slept well, knowing that she had been so helpful.

There have been other indications of forgetfulness that Martha has had to cover up as well. She was driving to the store recently and found that she didn't recognize the neighborhood. In fact, she couldn't remember how to get to the mall where the grocery store was located. She stopped and asked for directions at a gasoline station, and found that she was only two blocks from the mall. Frightened by her confusion, she told herself that she must have taken a wrong turn and gotten into a different area than she usually went through. After shopping, she returned home directly and easily. As she thought about it, she decided not to mention to anyone what had happened. After all, everyone gets a bit confused in new places as they grow older.

One irritating fact to Martha is that she recognizes increasing problems in recalling the names of some common objects. Fortunately, she remembers how to use the object even if she can't recall its name so that she can describe its function to others during a conversation. She also is missing a favorite ring. She believes her husband must have taken it although he denies it and she can't think of any plausible reason for him to have taken it. The ring isn't really valuable; it's just that it was a gift from her parents to her when she was a teenager. Some pieces of their everyday china and silverware are gone also. She has decided not to make an issue of it since her husband is not always understanding if she can't give him specific information about missing things.

Her husband, Sam, is concerned that something is wrong with his wife but he doesn't know what it could be. They both had physical checkups a few months ago. The doctor said that Martha was healthy, with no apparent problems. Sam mentioned to him that his wife seemed pretty forgetful at times. When the doctor questioned him for specific instances, Sam couldn't give him many concrete details since some of them were rather embarrassing. The doctor said that it might be just an effect of her growing older. But Sam is suspicious that it's more than that. After all, he's three years older than his wife and *he's* not having problems. He knows several women as old or older than Martha and they seem all right. However, because he can't put his finger on anything particular, he tries to ignore little problems and not exaggerate them.

It is aggravating, though, when she does things like what she did last night. She had fixed a casserole that they both liked, but it was so salty that they couldn't eat it. She claimed that she had made it as she always had so there must have been too much salt in the ingredients. Since they had some of the same product in a dish the night before and it was not too salty, Sam knew she was just refusing to admit her error. Then, too, last week she had served liver. Neither of them liked liver, and, besides, it has far too much cholesterol, as she had told him several times. When he asked her why they were having liver, she claimed he had asked her to fix it. She became a little belligerent and finally cried when he lost his temper.

The children all see Mom as calmer, quieter, more composed than ever before. She doesn't initiate much conversation or bother them about their business, and they like that. To them, she is better than ever. Her friends don't see as much of her as they used to. When she's invited to participate with them in social events, she usually begs off although her reasons don't always make sense. Several friends have decided to drop contacts because Martha doesn't always keep ideas straight and gets a little uptight when told that she's mixed up.

Martha Wells is behaving, in several ways, like an aging person who is developing dementia. Though *why* she is changing isn't apparent, there is evidence that her mind is not functioning as it once did. The future may hold increasing difficulties and problems for Martha, Sam, and their children if the benign neglect continues.

Using this case study, we can survey some of the changes that occur during the progression of a dementia.

Physical Stamina and Health

Medical conditions and syndromes are most often based on changes in the physical state of the person. Physicians are trained to look for the effects of "disease" on the ability of the individual to function normally. If there is a complaint, the effects described by the patient are used as symptoms to help focus on possible causes of the complaint. Tests of several kinds may be used to eliminate or verify each possible source of discomfort. Today, medicine is able to identify the true cause of, and often to suggest treatment for, most of the conditions that cause us to be ill.

Even where treatment is limited or impossible, medical diagnosis frequently is possible. For example, all of us know something about the deterioration of the body when a disease such as cancer is present. Even in cases where treatment cannot occur, the doctor can prescribe drugs or routines to make the patient more comfortable. For dementia, however, the expectation is much more limited for accurate diagnosis of the cause and especially for treatment and cure. It is necessary to understand that dementia itself is not a *physical* condition. In fact, the patient's physical status and health may remain as good as ever, and sometimes improves, during the time that the dementia is becoming worse; that is, dementia systematically "robs the mind" but not the body. The patient may remain strong, or become relatively stronger, while mental abilities fade. This effect is illustrated by Martha's case study. Notice that Martha had had a recent physical examination and

> the doctor said that Martha was healthy, with no apparent problems.

When her husband mentioned forgetfulness, but was unable to give any concrete examples,

> the doctor said that it might be just an effect of her growing older.

This description is not atypical for dementia patients. It is true, of course, that the person may have other syndromes in addition to the cause of the dementia. However, the two need not be related; that is, the dementia need not be caused by nor itself cause the second condition. As unsatisfactory as this may seem, it is typical for most cases, as it is for Martha's:

> Though *why* she is changing isn't apparent, there is evidence that her mind is not functioning as it once did.

By contrast, the caregiver may maintain mental integrity but show increasing physical problems because of the mounting demands made by the patient. Figure 1.1 illustrates the changes that occur in both patient and caregiver. Just how fast these changes occur is an individual matter—but the general direction of change is almost certain.

Mental Competence and Ability

Even though the central effect of dementia is to reduce mental ability, the change may be gradual for some skills and more rapid for others. The patient may be able to continue doing certain kinds of tasks easily and effectively (and should be allowed to do so, and not "invalided") while other tasks are no longer possible. In Martha's case,

> she had fixed a casserole that they both liked, but it was so salty that they couldn't eat it

and

> last week she had served liver. Neither of them liked liver, and, besides, it has far too much cholesterol. . . . she claimed he had asked her to fix it.

One behavioral enigma for caregivers is the fact that part of a task may still be done while another part of it is no longer possible. The reason for such changes is to be found in the loss of memory. Nerve cells (called *neurons*) in the brain have been and are being destroyed as a result of the cause of the dementia. These nerve cells do not regenerate (i.e., they do not produce new cells) and they cannot be replaced (although there is a certain amount of plasticity so that healthy cells sometimes may be trained to take over the functions of dead cells). Wherever neurons are destroyed, there will likely be an adverse effect on the person's ability to perform some task to some degree. This means that the area of the brain where damage occurs is important to the kinds of abilities that will be affected. The more generalized the cell destruction, the more behaviors affected. With time, large numbers of cells in several locations of the brain will be lost; the effect is the individual's increasing inability to do what was once easy. The practical

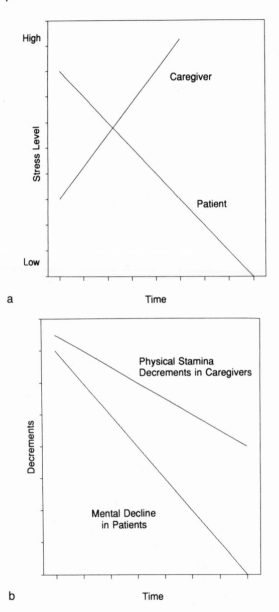

meaning of such changes is illustrated by Martha's behavioral changes. In the general sense,

> she has withdrawn from some of her previous roles. In some respects, she performs other tasks less competently than she did formerly, although she seems unaware of the changes and there are no obvious reasons why she should be less efficient. . . . Martha seems to behave less efficiently in several behaviors. She herself has noticed some problems in remembering *what* she is supposed to do at specific times. Worse, it seems to her that sometimes she can't quite remember *how* to do things she has done for years.

More specifically,

> she was driving to the store recently and found that she didn't recognize the neighborhood. In fact, she couldn't remember how to get to the mall where the grocery store was located.

In a very specific way,

> she recognizes increasing problems in recalling the names of some common objects. Fortunately, she remembers how to use the object even if she can't recall its name so that she can describe its function to others during a conversation.

Such effects are distressing to both Martha and Sam; their experience with the physician did nothing to suggest the possibility of improvement. Justifiably, they are concerned about whether she will show even more (and more distressing) behavioral changes. Yet they do not mention their concerns to one another, much less discuss them frankly.

Social Skills

In many cases, some of the well-rehearsed social skills and competencies will remain virtually intact for a number of years. The patient may remain polite, seemingly interested and involved

---

Figure 1.1. Effects of dementia on patient and caregiver. (a) Changes in mental and physical states; (b) stress expression in patients and caregivers. From Edwards (1993). Reprinted by permission of Plenum Press.

in social activities, and able to carry on a conversation. This apparent discrepancy between a "sound" mind and one that is incompetent confuses those who do not have many contacts with the patient. Friends, neighbors, and even some family members will think there must surely be some mistake in diagnosis because the patient seems so "normal." But much of our social interaction is quite superficial. When a patient is asked, "How are you?" it does not take any great ability to continue to reply, as one has for years, "Fine, thank you. And how are you?" Comments on the weather and other topics are similarly shallow. However, if superficial communication meets the basic rules and seems rational and reasonable, we are apt to assume that *all* communication with this person will be just as rational and reasonable.

In Martha's case, she shows some mixed evidence about social skills, at least as observed by others:

> The children all see Mom as calmer, quieter, more composed than ever before. . . . To them, she is better than ever.

However, in another setting:

> Her friends don't see as much of her as they used to. When she's invited to participate with them in social events, she usually begs off although her reasons don't always make sense.

In fact, she is becoming a "social embarrassment" in some ways:

> Several friends have decided to drop contacts because Martha doesn't always keep ideas straight and gets a little uptight when told that she's mixed up.

Overall, the points on which we judge whether or not a person is "ill" or "incapable" are not very stringent. To understand the difficulties of a dementia patient, the attitude must be assumed that criteria used in the past are no longer particularly helpful for this person. In addition, there must be some willingness to explore more deeply in the mental sphere, to try to understand why behaviors are occurring and what they mean. There must be less reliance on the physical status, since it seems so normal, and more emphasis on the intellectual, which is in the process of deterioration.

What Does a Dementia Patient Not Do?

There have been many articles and books describing what the dementia patient is unable to do. Most of these focus on mental changes that prove worrisome to caregivers, often extending to include social skills and behaviors that are affected adversely. It would be impossible to catalog all of these changes at this point, so a more general discussion follows here. It will be expanded as you read the rest of the book.

Physical Status and Health

As observed in the preceding section, dementia itself is not a physical condition and the causes of dementia do not directly affect body systems. However, the damage done to the brain by a condition that causes dementia (such as Alzheimer's or multi-infarct dementia) is profound and widespread. Particularly affected is the *cortex*, that part of the brain from which arise our abilities to think, reason, calculate, use experience, and the like. It is currently believed that the first area affected by the dementing process is a small, horseshoe-shaped body in the brain called the *hippocampus*. One of the functions of this area is to act as the seat where processes that lead to memory storage and retrieval are begun.

There is no physical pain that accompanies the effects of brain damage. Unlike truly physical conditions (such as cancer), there are not the "signs" that alert the person and others that something is wrong. With cancer, heart attack, or pneumonia, there are noticeable physical effects and definite discomfort (in almost all cases). There is nothing similar in dementia, so the patient may be unaware of any disorder that is causing the behaviors that are making life adjustment increasingly difficult. It is not surprising, then, that so many persons ignore warning signs of impending and increasing problems. The outcome of dementia does not fit our traditional idea of what a *medical* condition is. Sometimes even physicians may be "fooled" by the complaints brought by such a patient. For example, the doctor may hear complaints by the patient that forgetfulness is increasing, but the examples given may seem rather trivial or unimportant. In order not to involve the patient in a series of expensive and inconvenient medical and psychological tests, the physician may decide to wait for six months or so. If the problem persists, then there may be attempts to find the cause. Unfortunately, if there is some condition inducing dementia, another six months may allow progression that reduces the functional abilities of the patient to a significant degree.

Physically, there is a definite process going on that is destructive to parts of the brain and has consequences for behavior. However, this process is not directly observable by any medical test, it does not express itself in the conventional form that we attach to "illness," and its consequences can be confusing even to professionals.

Mental Competence and Ability

Dementia has its most profound and disruptive effects on a person's mental status and mental life. The principal effect is on memory. There is first a loss in short-term memory that continues and worsens. Attending short-term memory loss, other forms of memory may become adversely affected. Some of the memories from the past that have been stored because they are so important will be lost. For example, the patient may hold a job that requires making decisions quickly based on experience. For years, this employee has been successful and it seems reasonable to assume that the skills will continue throughout his or her career. One of the effects of dementia may be that the person can no longer remember the experiences that help in the decision-making process. In fact, the individual may find that at least some job-related tasks are no longer recognized for what they are and mean. Gradually, there will be more error, with the result that the employee is a liability instead of an asset. Sooner or later, the individual must be relieved of the responsibilities that were handled so capably in the past.

As the dementia increases, there may be effects on the most intimate and emotional of contacts. Some caregivers find that their spouse no longer recognizes them, does not know their name, and may even deny that they are the spouse. Such outcomes are heartbreaking in their consequences. Since the caregiver is assuming more and more responsibility for the well-being of the patient, it is ironic as well as distressing that these efforts will neither be recognized nor appreciated in the way they deserve. It is understandable that some caregivers may become bitter and somewhat resentful when their personal lives are sacrificed without reward. Indeed, the patience, love, and kindness displayed by most caregivers under conditions that can only be described as disruptive and devastating are a tribute to human compassion and empathy.

As the person's memory is increasingly adversely affected, a second effect of the dementia will occur: the patient will become disoriented, particularly in terms of time and place. There will be less awareness of *where* one is as well as *when* events are occurring. The importance of orientation is not as appreciated by most of us as it should be. It might be explained on the basis that each of us is a unit in a universe of units. We observe, we react, we accommodate, we influence. At the same time, we are observed, reacted to, accommodated to, and influenced. Reality is a personal matter, so each of us knows reality only in the sense in which we interact with all other units. As my reality overlaps with yours, we can communicate, we can understand each other, we can relate. If my reality is very different from yours, we will have problems.

Imagine for the moment being put into some foreign environment. There are elements you recognize—other people particularly. Suppose, however, that these people speak a different language. Suppose they dress differently than you. Suppose they seem to ignore you. Suppose they do not attempt to understand what you need to communicate to them. In one sense, you would be disoriented in that setting. In somewhat the same way, dementia patients may have lost contact with people around them so there is only a feeling of isolation, rejection, and a lack of understanding. Carried to its extreme, the patient may not know where she or he is or what relationships exist on the temporal basis. The resulting frustration may lead to maladaptive behaviors, perhaps even violent ones. Our case study of Martha Wells illustrates some ways in which these outcomes may occur:

> There are days when she has some sense that a period of time has elapsed that she can't account for.
>
> She also is missing a favorite ring. She believes her husband must have taken it although he denies it and she can't think of any plausible reason for him to have taken it. . . . Some pieces of their everyday china and silverware are gone also. She has decided not to make an issue of it since her husband is not always understanding if she can't give him specific information about missing things.
>
> Last week, she had served liver. . . . When he [her husband] asked her why they were having liver, she claimed he had asked her to fix it. She became a little belligerent and finally cried when he lost his temper.

Such incidents reflect change in the ability to deal with reality. The outcome produces problems for both husband and wife, without a basis for understanding *what* or *why* there is the discrepancy between their two views of reality.

Finally, there will be increasing confusion on the part of the patient. Even in familiar places, the person may not "recognize" what was once easily perceived. In the home in which the patient has lived for many years, he or she may become "lost." Where is the bathroom if one needs to use it? Once there, what is the proper receptacle: the sink, toilet, bathtub, wastebasket? The problem occurs because the patient can no longer *remember* the functions that these objects serve.

Such confusion is apt to be increased if the patient has to be moved to another setting. For example, being placed in a nursing home, no matter how progressive the staff may be, can cause great distress for the patient. Everything is unfamiliar, and the patient has no competence to adapt to the changes. The result may be a change in personality, including abusive language or physical lashing out. Since it is impossible to "explain" why placement is necessary and what the placement will accomplish in a way that can be understood and accepted by the patient, the period of adjustment may be difficult for all concerned.

There is an *irregularity* in the expression of these kinds of changes that is difficult for both the patient and the caregiver to deal with. Some things are remembered and some former actions may still be successfully carried out. Orientation may be present in some situations, not in others. Confusion is not found in all settings. When and how these irregularities will be expressed is unpredictable. They vary from one patient to another, and even within a given patient from one time to another. Caregivers cannot be provided with a list of changes that will occur at a particular point in the progression of dementia for every patient. Still, the dreadful forecast of increasing problem behaviors is realistic and must be understood by the caregiver. Eventually, the caregiver must accept such a disordered sequence if adaptation to the condition is to occur.

Social Skills

Even before severe memory loss, disorientation, and confusion occur, there may be noticeable changes in some "social" skills. These changes are most apt to be reported by the caregiver because of the burdens they create. Some patients become abusive (either verbally, physically, or both) even though they may have been very different behaviorally in the past. Others become unpredictable in their reactions, making it difficult for the caregiver to understand what is happening or what response to expect from moment to moment. Some patients may express unacceptable language—become vulgar and insulting. Sometimes a patient will wander away from home unless constantly supervised; at other times, the patient may demand to be taken "home" even when that is where he or she is. Just what is meant by the expressed wish is not always clear, though seldom is a patient satisfied even when taken to a former residence.

There are some cases where the patient becomes calm, compliant, cooperative—though these cases are rarely reported in settings where caregivers are seeking respite.

The list of behavioral changes could be almost endless, depending on the individual. Again, however, the pattern of change is irregular and thus unpredictable. There also is no systematic relationship between behavioral changes and the losses occurring mentally; that is, the kinds of behavioral changes shown by a particular patient cannot be predicted in terms of memory loss, confusion, and disorientation in time and space. Such inconsistencies in behaviors during the time that progressively deteriorating competencies are notable are the rule in dementia.

To "understand" dementia—and the problems it brings to both patients and caregivers—one must have an open attitude and a very pliable personality. Maintaining such traits even part of the time is difficult. The perfect caregiver would seem to be an impossibility, though some individuals adapt better and quicker than others, and all seem to find their own "best" recourses and adaptations. The picture is one of increasing (to the point of being constant) demands and impositions without being able to anticipate what may happen next and how it may express itself. The skills needed to cope under these circumstances are not well defined. Recent study has helped to isolate some adaptive mechanisms that work some of the time for some caregivers, and these are discussed in the following chapters.

Summary

Dementia is a state that is expressed through increasingly extreme losses in mental competence. It results from any of several conditions that may be medically diagnosed. These conditions (e.g., Alzheimer's disease) cause damage to or destruction of nerve cells in the brain, leading to behaviors that reflect the demented state. Particularly affected are memory, orientation in time and space, and regularity in routine. Effects are most obvious in mental competencies such as thinking and reasoning, creating deficits in social skills and decision making. There is no physical symptomatology in the usual medical sense except for the altering of nerve cells in the brain, making the patient unable to respond and adapt effectively to some portions of environmental demands. The remainder of this book more fully details the conditions and results of dementia, and describes ways of dealing with its adverse effects.

2

What Causes Dementia?

When a condition exists that has detrimental effects on people, one of the first questions that will be asked is: "What causes it?" The question is legitimate because "cause" has certain implications for what happens to the victim, for whether or not treatment is possible, and for prognosis in terms of cure or prevention. If the cause is known, there is the strong possibility that an intervention can be developed, or is already available, although this outcome is not assured. Unless causation can be specified, hope for an intervention is limited, perhaps even impossible, since *symptoms* alone are insufficient evidence on which to base treatment. For example, when a patient complains to a doctor that he or she has trouble remembering important items, and testing indicates that the complaint is true, what might be the cause? The possibilities are so extensive (depression, dementia, infection, poor retrieval skills, to mention just a few) that the doctor has no way to know what steps to take.

Scientists spend much of their research efforts in trying to specify the *source* of an illness or state. The success they have depends on funding to support the research effort. Unfortunately, there has not been much money available for research on the possible causes of dementia. What monies are available may be targeted to finding a means of controlling symptoms (like memory loss), certainly an important issue for patients and caregivers but not of great help in ensuring an end to the problem. Ideally, finding a way to *prevent* dementia would be the best possible outcome from research.

Possible "Causes" of Dementia

The behaviors that characterize dementia (memory loss, disorientation in time and space, and confusion) have been recognized for many years. As a result, there have been attempts to demonstrate what may be the cause(s) for such behaviors. Among the first scientific efforts was that of Dr. Alois Alzheimer, a German physician who described what he considered to be "senile" behavior in some of his patients. He noted that middle-aged persons under his care sometimes showed the effects that physicians expected to find only in the very aged. These effects included memory loss, already described in the medical literature of the time as an outcome of vascular disease (e.g., hypertension). With his middle-aged patients, however, Alzheimer suspected that something other than vascular disease per se was causing the senility.

His suspicion was supported by an autopsy he performed on the brain of one of his "demented" patients after her death. He found an alteration in some brain cells that was atypical of a healthy cell and that suggested to him why such patients might show behavioral changes. Many of the autopsied cortical cells included a fibrous material not ordinarily found in the brain; Alzheimer called this material "neurofibrillary tangles." These fibers were found, in large numbers, in the cytoplasm (the plasma, or living fluid) of nerve cells. They were tangled together, so it seemed to Alzheimer that they must interfere with proper cell functioning. Alzheimer decided these fibers must be the cause of demented behavior. Further, he proposed that such fibers must be the result of some disease process—perhaps vascular since medicine already accepted the principle that vascular disease could lead to dementia.

We must remember that Alzheimer lived and practiced medicine at a time when all physical illnesses were believed to be due to disease processes whether or not there was evidence to support that belief. (Even today, doctors use the term "disease" to apply not only to infectious agents but to environmental causes such as climate or industrial dangers, genetic defects, and even to combinations of these. "Disease" can be defined to mean *any* cause of adverse effects on individual performance.) Later, when the condition he described in his patients was labeled Alzheimer's disease, that label indicated nothing more than a disruptive change in nerve cells that has certain behavioral consequences. Do not assume, then, that Alzheimer's disease is caused by some infectious agent that may or may not be communicable. No one knows, at present, what the cause may be any more than Dr. Alzheimer did.

Since several conditions that lead to demented behavior are of unknown cause, there is good reason to keep an open mind and encourage research that looks in several directions. Among the conditions of unknown cause associated with dementia are Alzheimer's and Pick's diseases, along with "normal-pressure hydrocephalus" (a medical syndrome in which an increase in the amount of fluid in the skull causes some compacting and shrinkage of brain tissue). Though a deficit in a brain chemical called dopamine is known to be associated with Parkinson's disease—another condition associated with dementia—the exact relation is not clear. A rare condition called Creutzfeldt-Jakob disease is believed to be caused by a slow-acting virus, yet there has been no visible evidence of that virus. Obviously, then, there are a variety of conditions that seem to cause or be related to a cause for dementia that are not yet clearly identified.

There are, however, some conditions that will lead to dementia whose causes are well understood. One of these is arteriosclerosis (characterized by hardening of the artery wall, which reduces elasticity and slows blood flow to cells). The adverse effects of arteriosclerotic damage are major or minor strokes. Where there are strokes, there will be brain-cell destruction. If enough cells are damaged in certain areas of the brain, dementia will result. Another cause of dementia is alcohol related. Years of alcohol abuse and consequent poor diet starve and destroy brain cells in sufficient quantity to bring on behavioral changes. Even a head injury may introduce dementia, at least for a period of time. The *sources* of dementia are many, although Alzheimer's disease is certainly the most recognized and diagnosed condition.

Sources Being Investigated

There are a number of possible causes for the conditions leading to dementia and most of them are currently under investigation, although there is no assurance that any of them will prove to be the only and direct cause. There is even the plausible alternative that *none* of them is the answer, that the true basis for such syndromes as Alzheimer's has yet to be suggested. With that in mind, it is still a good idea to consider what scientists believe to be the most likely suspects and the sources of the greatest research activity.

Viruses

One possibility is that dementia results from a virus, an agent that causes infection. At present, we are greatly concerned about the virus that causes AIDS. Scientists know the characteristics of this virus, how it enters the body, and how it attacks white blood cells to change cellular function. A viral connection (not the same virus that causes AIDS, however) for dementia is based on its association with a condition called Creutzfeldt-Jakob disease. It is known that this syndrome is caused by a virus even though the virus has not yet been identified. Viruses grow and multiply only in living cells, so it seems reasonable to investigate the possibility that conditions (including Alzheimer's) that produce dementia may be caused by a virus.

Chemicals

Another possible cause of the conditions producing dementia may be chemical in nature. Two particular approaches are being investigated, one concerning chemicals intrinsic to the body and the other dealing with environmental chemicals, or toxins. One group of chemicals being investigated is the neurotransmitters. A *neurotransmitter* is a natural chemical in the body that works in several ways. One way is to assist the functioning of nerve cells by transmitting an electrical signal representing a stimulus from nerve cell to nerve cell until it reaches the place (usually the brain) where it will be interpreted. There are at least 50 neurotransmitters already identified or suspected, and there may be many more. One of these is the chemical called *acetylcholine*, an agent that assists in the transmission of signals from the ending of one nerve cell to the beginning of the next in a sequence. There is evidence for a deficit of this chemical at nerve-cell endings in Alzheimer's patients. Some scientists believe that this deficiency may be the *cause* of Alzheimer's. Investigations are underway to try to define more precisely the role of this neurotransmitter, what causes its deficiency, and whether or not there is some way to replace the loss with an artificial substitute.

Another "chemical connection" that seems plausible for investigation is the role of toxins. Toxins are substances that may cause a disease that would not normally occur in their absence. Many drugs are toxic, for example, when misused or abused. Chemicals from environmental sources, such as atomic waste or pesticides, can also be life threatening. This relatively new area of study has not produced any definite possibilities to explain dementia so far, but continued research may find a link that will be helpful.

Aluminum

About 20 years ago, when some of the first efforts to find a cause of Alzheimer's began, an early candidate was aluminum. Brain autopsies of patients who were believed to have had Alzheimer's disclosed relatively large amounts of the mineral stored in the brain cells. It seemed logical that a connection existed, and possibly that meant causation as well. Aluminum enters our bodies from a number of sources, and once present the excess is stored rather than being excreted. Among the sources that contain aluminum are most antacids, which many people take for upset stomach and heartburn. Aluminum is also an agent in anti-perspirants, although it is not found in deodorants. There are those who believe that we can ingest sizable amounts of aluminum if we eat food that is prepared in aluminum cookware.

Some caregivers report a history of considerable consumption of antacids over a number of years in some patients. It does not seem illogical to suspect that aluminum intake may account for the abnormally large amounts of the mineral found in the neurons of these patients. Yet, even after years of study, it is still unclear whether the accumulated aluminum is from outside sources, is a by-product of the disease process, or is due to some other unknown and unrelated factor. Research continues today to try to discover specifically what the role of the mineral actually is.

Amyloid

Probably the most active research interest today concerns the possibility that an abnormal type of protein found in the brain cells of Alzheimer's patients is the dementia-causing culprit. Every cell must have nutrients to function effectively, and protein is a major constituent of all cells. This particular form of protein, however—the amyloid—can be harmful to the cell. Called *beta amyloid protein*, it was once believed to be found only in the brain, but recent findings indicate that it may be stored in cells in other parts of the body as well. It is not known how an amyloid is formed although there is evidence for a precursor (forerunner) protein that has its gene on the chromosome involved in a condition called Down's syndrome. Down's is a genetic condition that produces mental retardation along with certain physical abnormalities (such as a fissured tongue and somewhat slanted eyes). Down's patients who live beyond age 35 include a high percentage who develop dementia symptoms much like those of Alzheimer's patients. Yet there is evidence that the two conditions (Down's and Alzheimer's) are not necessarily related. Amyloids are associated in some way with the death of the nerve cell and thus with the development of neuritic plaques (clusters of collapsed nerve cells). Current research efforts are attempting to determine how and why this happens. A more complete discussion of a possible genetic cause for Alzheimer's follows later in this chapter.

A study done in England reveals a possible connection between beta amyloid protein and both Alzheimer's and age. The scientists involved made the assumption that the beta amyloid precursor normally serves a useful function by helping neurons to resprout nerve endings as the body ages and declines occur in brain cells. Further, they proposed that there may be excessive amounts of the precursor protein produced, the excess being converted to beta amyloid protein, thus leading to the development of Alzheimer's. Some older persons may be more vulnerable to this effect than others, for reasons yet unknown. The idea is interesting and deserves further research, at this point being only a set of assumptions, each of which must be proven if the "connections" proposed are valid.

Immune System Deficiency

A different approach currently being tested is the possibility that the immune system develops a deficiency that permits otherwise benign organisms to become virulent. As we grow older, the immune system, which normally protects us against disease from invading organisms, becomes less competent to do so. It may even begin to change its character to *assist* the invading source. Older people are more susceptible to extreme reactions to diseases that they could resist without danger at a younger age. The logic of this explanation, then, is that declining immune function makes us more at risk for disease. This position is not as popular as some of the others but it remains a worthwhile one to continue to pursue with research. There is also an obvious relation of this position with syndromes that cause immune system deficiency (e.g., AIDS) or with treatment that destroys the immune system (e.g., chemotherapy). A more in-depth discussion of dementia symptoms developed in AIDS patients is presented in Chapter 3.

Systemic Disorders

Some scientists believe it is possible that some causes of dementia are not innovative or independent. Instead, they propose that body systems may have been diseased over a number of years. Since these conditions were not identified and/or treated, they continued to develop in the body even though there were no observable consequences. Eventually, they began to attack and affect the cells of the brain, subsequently leading to dementia. Those who take this position advocate investigating the medical histories of dementia patients to discover systemic disorders that might be related to brain-cell destruction. As these scientists accumulate relevant data, there will be increased study of the relationships between diseases and brain disorders, which may lead to methods of treatment for conditions that might otherwise later produce mental deficiency. According to this explanation, the answer, then, is in our bodily histories, not in some separate and unique cause.

Genetics

Because of their concern about future generations, laypersons frequently ask about the heritability of the conditions that cause dementia. When a case of Alzheimer's is diagnosed, for example, family members wonder if there is added danger to themselves and their children. There may even be comparisons with past generations. Someone comments that Aunt Hattie has problems that seem remarkably like those observed in the patient, and another points out that Grandma Sara almost certainly had dementia before she died. Such memories are, of course, probably distorted and certainly should not be taken at face value. However, the concern is genuine and must be given serious attention.

There is agreement that a small percentage of Alzheimer's cases (about 10 percent) occur within families; that is, the incidence of confirmed diagnoses within a given family is greater than chance. Such a "familial" relationship may be due to some environmental source (such as toxins) that affected several members of the same family or to a genetic mutation on a chromosome that is transmissible to children (and future generations). This inheritance figure is estimated to be about 1 in 4; that is, the chances that a blood relative will show the symptoms and receive the same diagnosis is about 25 percent. Even though this figure is a low probability, it is large enough to justify concern. The majority of cases seem not to be familial (the term used is familial Alzheimer's disease, or FAD); most cases (about 90 percent) occur in a sporadic fashion. Whatever causes Alzheimer's is no respecter of education, wealth, status, or any other identified variable. Perhaps one should be more concerned, then, when there is *no* history of Alzheimer's in a family. At least, there seems to be no reason to become overly concerned that other family members will develop Alzheimer's disease simply because one family member has been diagnosed. There are, however, conditions that cause dementia that have a demonstrated heritability rate (e.g., Huntington's disease). The research in genetics is barely begun, but there is some suggestive evidence that is worth description.

Currently, the "suggestive evidence" is based on research of "errors" that have been identified in certain genes. A *gene* is an element that carries the hereditary patterns we receive from our parents at the moment of conception. In most instances, our development is relatively normal so that such characteristics as height, hair color, skin color, and so on, reflect the traits of our parents. These, and other expressions, are encoded in the genes on the 23 chromosomes received from each parent. But there can be mutations in genes (changes from the expected or typical expression of a characteristic). A genetic cause for Alzheimer's is possible, then, based on scientific evidence of some mutation in a specific gene.

To date, there is evidence for mutation in three genes (Alzheimer's Association, 1993). In 1987, a mutation in a gene on chromosome 21 was discovered that appeared to play a role in the development of Alzheimer's. At first thought to be related to Down's syndrome (which *is* due to a mutation of a different gene on chromosome 21), there now appears to be little or no support for such an argument. A relationship *was* found, however, between the mutation and adults who develop Alzheimer's in middle age (called early-onset FAD). About 5 percent of all cases of Alzheimer's are of early onset, and may begin in persons as young as 30.

In 1987, the gene that controls the production of a substance called amyloid precursor protein (APP) was found to be located on chromosome 21. One of the products of APP is beta amyloid protein, found in the neuritic plaques of Alzheimer's patients and believed to be associated with cell death. Further research indicated that only a few Alzheimer's patients had a gene mutation on chromosome 21.

However, in 1991, a mutation was found in the APP gene on chromosome 21. Two families showed the pattern and each family had members with early-onset FAD. Later, another family exhibiting early-onset FAD was discovered with a mutation at a different point on the APP gene. Unfortunately, only a handful of families (less than 15) anywhere in the world has shown either mutation. Obviously, mutations on chromosome 21 are only tangentially related to FAD.

In 1992, scientists discovered a second gene that displayed evidence of mutations. A number of early-onset Alzheimer's patients showed an unidentified mutation on chromosome 14. Currently, research is directed toward isolating the specific gene involved, and that result should be achieved in the next several years. Even so, there are still many cases of early-onset FAD that show no abnormalities on either chromosome 21 or chromosome 14.

The third gene to be implicated in Alzheimer's is associated with those who are diagnosed after age 65 (late-onset Alzheimer's). The culprit is a gene mutation on chromosome 19, and a number of families with late-onset cases have been found with the defect. Indeed, there is evidence that a gene mutation on chromosome 19 is more than three times more common in those with late-onset FAD than in persons without Alzheimer's (Alzheimer's Association, 1993, p. 5). The altered gene occurs in 15 percent of the general population but in 50 percent of cases of late-onset FAD. Since it can occur in those *without* Alzheimer's, the mutation is a "risk" factor rather than a direct cause.

Such research is critical to finding the cause (or, more likely, causes) of Alzheimer's disease. The efforts have only begun but they will eventually produce answers and suggest treatment or prevention if sufficient funding continues. It seems reasonable to believe that not all cases of Alzheimer's are due to genetic errors of the types disclosed so far. Eventually, however, it may be discovered that gene mutations account for virtually every incident. The answer to whether or not the current balance of sporadic to familial types remains (with most instances now being sporadic) lies somewhere in the future.

Other Possibilities

There are several other potential links with dementia that are being investigated without the extensive involvement found for those areas discussed above. One possible cause is the toxic effect of calcium in cells. When the amount of calcium needed by the cell is exceeded, destructive effects on cell functioning occur. Research here is too recent to claim any definite causal role for calcium even though the adverse effects of excess calcium on cell functioning are well established.

Nutritional deficiency may play a role in the development of dementia. When the body has inadequate or inappropriate nutrition, nerve cells may starve and damage to them may occur. Because the nerve cells are unable to function as they should, one result may be dementia. If the connection proves to be central, or even important, it should be possible to prevent the occurrence of dementia in some persons by providing adequate nutrition throughout life.

As a final example, some scientists are investigating the function of mitochondria in the health of nerve cells. A *mitochondrion* is the power plant of the cell, so to speak, and all cells have a number of them. Some cells have less than a hundred, while others may have several thousand. The number is determined by the needs of the cell. If more mitochondria are needed, those already present can generate their own duplicates. These power plants extract energy from oxygen and nutrients. If there are insufficient mitochondria in the cell, or if there are none at all, the cell cannot function. Given this state of affairs, scientists are looking at mitochondria in the nerve cells of dementia patients to determine if there are changes that might explain the behavior changes noted in the patient. This research is a recent and focused area of investigation that is only in its beginning stages.

Summary

As you can see, there are many, many possibilities for "causes" of dementia that are under investigation (and this survey is only a sample of the total number). At present, the most definitive statement that can be made about the reason why a person develops dementia is that knowledge is limited. This means that many areas of research must be investigated until some definitive answer (or, more probably, answers) is reached. An analogy to a puzzle is appropriate. No one knows what the finished puzzle will look like. Research may disclose a piece of the puzzle, but where that piece fits will remain something of a mystery until most of the pieces are found. Agencies speculate on a breakthrough that will provide *the* answer. Writers speak of "promising leads" but are unable to say when the promise will be fulfilled. The answer will come if the research continues—but the research can only continue if there is money to get the job done. The answer, then, may be a matter of only months or of many years.

Diagnosis and Dementia

There are several conditions that may produce the behaviors of dementia. Some of these are treatable, allowing the competencies lost to be regained. Others, however, are not treatable at present, permitting the mental incompetence to become greater as time passes. Since a doctor may tell a patient and caregiver that the dementia is due to any of several causes, the principal ones are described more completely.

Alzheimer's Disease

There are reports from throughout history that people have suffered from the medical syndrome that today is called Alzheimer's disease. However, medical and scientific knowledge about this disease has been restricted largely to the twentieth century. The doctor credited with first describing the changes in the brain that represent the syndrome was the German physician Alois Alzheimer. He published a journal article in 1906 that described his microscopic study of brain tissue from a woman patient who had developed the symptoms of dementia while she was still in her fifties. Alzheimer assumed, as most physicians of the time did, that if one lived long enough senility or dementia was inevitable. His interest was aroused by this unusual case, where his patient showed senile behaviors expected only in the very old. *Why* this should happen was the important question. After her death, he performed an autopsy on her brain and found structural changes in many of the nerve cells (see Figure 2.1).

One of these changes was the presence of a large number of fibers in the cytoplasm of the neurons. In fact, these fibers were tangled, altering the appearance and the apparent function of the cells. Alzheimer labeled them neurofibrillary tangles and declared that they must be the reason his patient had become prematurely senile. This case, he said, demonstrated a form of *pre*senile dementia (i.e., occurring before age 65 or so) that he assumed must occur in other cases as well. As time passed, doctors did report confirming evidence of early senility and, where autopsies were performed, evidence of neurofibrillary tangles.

Dr. Alzheimer reported a second feature of these diseased neurons. Some neurons seemed to shrivel, their dendrites (branched processes of neurons that conduct impulses to the cell

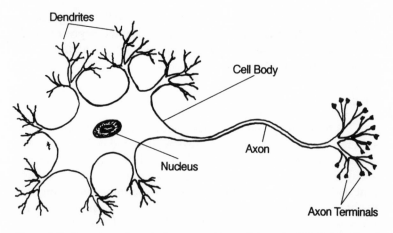

Figure 2.1. Drawing of typical neuron. From Edwards (1993). Reprinted by permission of Plenum Press.

body) deteriorating to the point where the cell could no longer perform in a healthy way. The deterioration of dendrites caused the cells to collapse. In the autopsy, Dr. Alzheimer found sections of the brain where there were clusters of these collapsed neurons, now called neuritic plaque. He believed that the occurrence of these two structures (tangles and plaques) was evidence that detrimental changes had occurred in the brain, causing dementia. Since Dr. Alzheimer was the first to point to this dreadful consequence, the syndrome was named for him.

For the next several decades, some research was published but the importance of the disease was not realized. In fact, the condition received prominent attention only as the number of aging people in our society increased and there were more and more complaints about mental problems. The emphasis, however, was shifted from middle-aged individuals with an unusual change in the structure of the brain to older persons in whom memory loss, confusion, and disorientation were more or less expected.

The apparent discrepancy between what Alzheimer meant by his description of cellular changes in a middle-aged person's brain and the presence of similar effects in old age has caused some confusion in terms. Diagnoses now may be "senile dementia," "Alzheimer's disease," "senile dementia of the Alzheimer's type," or "dementia of the Alzheimer's type." The difference between these is supposed to be related largely to the age of the patient, but in fact more and more doctors and other professionals believe that such distinctions are neither necessary nor helpful. With the present state of knowledge, all these diagnoses seem to mean the same thing. Eventually, there may be evidence that the process can be differentiated in certain meaningful ways. For now, if you hear any one of these labels, you should simply accept it as a descriptor to indicate that neurons are systematically being destroyed by a process that causes neurofibrillary tangles and neuritic plaques. The result will be the outcome we call dementia.

In addition to the loss of nerve cells, atrophy (shrinkage) of the brain is common in Alzheimer's disease. Autopsies have shown that half or more of the neurons have been destroyed, at least in certain parts of the brain. Some studies report that up to 70 percent of the cells were affected. Generally, with time, the brain atrophies, particularly in the front and on the sides of the brain (frontal and temporal lobes). Remember, though, that these findings are reported only after the death of the patient, an event that may have occurred 10 or more years after diagnosis of Alzheimer's. Brain atrophy is probably a gradual process and how far it progresses will depend on the patient's age at death. What this degeneration means is not clear but it is suspected by some scientists that it has significance for the behaviors of the patient.

The cause of Alzheimer's is not known. Among the possibilities are several of the conditions described in the preceding section. These include aluminum toxicity, a virus, amyloid protein, toxins, or neurotransmitter deficiencies. Other possibilities include a familial or genetic factor. In fact, almost any reasonable argument has to be considered until proven inaccurate. Eventually, we should like to ensure that no person need fear the destruction of Alzheimer's, just as we wish to prevent cancer, heart disease, and other conditions that threaten the well-being of citizens. Since there is no treatment at present, prognosis (the prediction of what will happen to the patient in the future) is for continued mental deterioration and eventual physical decline. Over some period of time, differing somewhat from one person to another, there will be continued gradual degeneration in mental competencies until the patient is totally dependent on a caregiver. As the brain becomes more diseased, physical deterioration will eventually set in also.

Of course, it is possible for a patient with Alzheimer's to have cancer or heart disease or some other condition that does have direct physical effects. Where only Alzheimer's is involved, the patient may not show physical decline until years after the onset of mental decline. The individual appears to be healthy to most observers, even family members who do not have close contact. Since health is so often associated with physical status, it is difficult for those who do not deal directly with the patient to understand why the caregiver is experiencing so much distress.

Death eventually results from the more conventional causes in the elderly, such as pneumonia, and is only indirectly due to the disease itself. This means that Alzheimer's disease is not a "killer" in the usual sense. Once again, however, if the patient also suffers some terminal disease like cancer, death may occur from that cause before the dementia has completed its process.

Course

With Alzheimer's the key word is *degeneration*. In terms of neurons, cells are increasingly invaded and destroyed in various parts of the brain. Apparently, the hippocampus (the place where memory functions begin) is the first area to be involved. Memory loss, particularly for recent events, is frequently reported as the first "sign" of a problem. Such problems with memory are not the transitory and relatively unimportant ones experienced by most of us (regardless of age). For example, there will be times when we will be unable to recall someone's name when we see him or her. The fact is, though, that we can still carry on a conversation without difficulty. The dementia patient, however, is unable to carry out routine behaviors that depend upon interpreting experience accurately. Thus, there would be no reasonable conversation regardless of whether or not the name could be recalled, or if introductions are accomplished in some way. The essential mental processes that permit normal social interaction are no longer available.

With time, more memory loss occurs and there is an increasing inability to deal with ordinary aspects of life. The capacity to reason, to make judgments that are accurate, to use experience in order to produce wise and judicious choices erodes. Gradually parts of the brain where the higher mental processes occur may suffer disease, adversely affecting abilities such as reading and writing.

Only a general description of both the course of the disease and the outcome (the dementia) can be given because the disease progresses at irregular or different rates in various patients. Some patients will show greater effects earlier than others. There is no way to predict what behaviors will be affected because there is no way to trace the progression of the disease in the brain cells that are being affected. (It would be impossible to predict behavioral changes anyway since the relationships between locus of cells and functions served are largely unknown.) Many caregivers ask about stages of Alzheimer's—when they may expect certain behaviors to occur and particular abilities to be lost. It would be helpful to know that after a year the patient will become abusive, or that wandering will begin in the third year of the disease, or that confusion will be greatest during the initial six months. However, realistically, there are no such patterns, and professionals who describe stages will make predictive errors. Such inaccuracies may cause caregivers to believe that professionals are poorly informed, or that the patient must not suffer from Alzheimer's, or even that the whole diagnostic procedure has been a mistake. Since caregivers wish desperately for things to improve, they may even assume that there is some other, treatable cause for the adverse changes they see in the patient. The fact is that Alzheimer's disease is unpredictable in its *specifics* even though we know what will happen to the patient in the general sense.

The general pattern may be described in this way. In the early part of the disease process, the patient will have difficulty doing routine tasks of certain (but not all) types. The patient's reaction may be frustration and irritation, an understandable response since this person has performed well on these tasks in the past. Social skills probably will initially remain unaffected, allowing the patient to continue to engage in activities such as church services, shopping, visits, parties, and the like.

As the disease progresses, however, significant and detrimental changes will occur. Any *new* demand or task may prove impossible for the patient. Disorientation increases to the point that the individual does not seem to recognize places and time frames. This disorientation distorts awareness of the relationships that keep the person in contact with the environment and others in that environment. Confusion, even in very familiar places, becomes intense and more generalized, causing the patient to forget specifics of well-rehearsed behaviors.

Because memory is increasingly affected, repetition will be a common need for the patient. At the same time, the demented person will tend to repeat things over and over since there is no encoding of what has been said or done already. Some memories of the past will be lost or altered, resulting in clarity in some thoughts and error (called "confabulation") in others. When this level of dementia is reached, dependency is great. The caregiver must provide constant, close supervision. There must be some anticipation of what the patient may do next, even though no one can help the caregiver in making the right guesses. Dressing often becomes a major chore because the patient may no longer remember which clothes are undergarments and which are outer garments. Patients may "cross-dress" due to confusion over what is appropriate even as they realize that clothes are to be worn. Patients may want to wear the same clothing constantly and may refuse to bathe so that hygiene becomes a problem. If the patient is stronger than the caregiver, the problem is intensified.

As life continues for the patient, there will eventually be a regression to the infant level in some respects. There may be no memory for how to walk or talk, and there may be increasing incontinence. Memory may be so altered that the patient may not even be able to swallow, with resulting problems in nutrition. Malnutrition may result along with other physical consequences as well. Now the patient is totally dependent, unaware of the ordinary happenings of life. Not infrequently, the caregiver will no longer be recognized even though he or she is a spouse or child of the patient.

The course of Alzheimer's disease, with its consequent dementia, involves the medical, social, and psychological realms. Though these elements may be considered separately, it is more important to consider their interactions. For example, what are the psychological effects on the patient and caregiver of medical decision making? What are the effects of cultural attitudes (psychological judgments) on the willingness of patients and caregivers to continue to be socially involved with other people? Questions such as these may be more important than obvious ones such as, How is Alzheimer's diagnosed? This is particularly true for those most closely involved with the disease process—the patient and caretaker.

Outcomes

The inevitable consequences of Alzheimer's disease are the loss of all mental competencies and eventual physical decline and death. The disease process from beginning to end is a varied and complex one. Indeed, *how* persons are involved and *what* the progression of the symptoms mean to all those involved can vary from patient to patient and family to family. Yet there are some general trends that may be described.

For the patient, the pattern probably begins with some awareness that something is wrong. There may be some bizarre behaviors that the patient cannot account for. During the period before diagnosis, even though it cannot be documented, there almost certainly will be events involving memory lapses that will be noticeable to the patient if not to others. However, the events may be isolated and well separated in time so that it is plausible for the aging person to explain them away. The stereotype of an aging mind losing its sharpness is still accepted and will be used if it helps the person avoid confronting a frightening reality. These events may be self-explained, then, as just a little forgetfulness that happens to all of us as we age. (This kind of behavior was described for Martha Wells, the case example in Chapter 1.)

With time (the exact amount differing from one patient to another), these incidents will occur more often and be more noteworthy in their impact. It is reasonable to expect certain reactions to such events: fear, perhaps terror at times; denial; irritation; oversensitivity to reasonable mistakes; even projection of problems onto other persons, blaming them for what is happening. (Again, the description of Martha Wells in Chapter 1 reflects some of these reactions.) Eventually, there will be some incident that is critical to the recognition of a severe problem. Once the doctor is consulted, the various tests run, and a diagnosis made, what was a threat of a major difficulty becomes a reality. Since there often is no treatment medically, intervention in the conventional sense is impossible.

The decision-making burden now shifts to the caregiver, at least in part. The patient may be placed in an institutional setting (a nursing home, or, as it is euphemistically called today, a health care center). This is not the usual step, however. Most caregivers prefer to keep the patient at home, primarily because the relationship is long standing, but also because they feel a responsibility to the patient that goes beyond the medical reality. A part of the decision may rest on economics since placement means major expenditures not anticipated in one's planning for retirement. Also, the caregiver may have little or no notion of the problems that lie ahead. Or, there may be some belief that the diagnosis is wrong, or that the patient will not develop the severe problems that others have reported, or even some dogged adherence to duty. Whatever the motives and their interactions, caregivers become a part of the problem, as well as part of the solution, in terms of care.

Caregivers may become involved with a support group at some point in the disease process, although many are not ready to do so at the time of diagnosis. Others persevere without respite until the patient is finally placed in an institution or dies, or the caregiver collapses or dies. With a decline in mental competence, patients will become less likely to experience stress and may become physically stronger than the caregiver. There do seem to be a few caregivers who manage to escape the tangles and perplexities of the situation but they are rare and unusual personalities indeed!

The tone of these comments may give the impression that little or nothing can be done for or with the Alzheimer's patient. Such a cynical viewpoint must be resisted. There is an awareness of the kinds of problems caregivers will encounter and techniques have been developed to help deal with them (with varying degrees of success). Later in this book, such problem behaviors as wandering, dressing and eating difficulties, and abusive language will be described and ways of dealing with them discussed. Unfortunately, few of these interventions are foolproof. Most will have to be adapted for individual situations. However, they do offer at least the possibility of turning a defeating situation into one that can be lived with. General techniques for problem solving and coping will also be discussed since they will be beneficial in situations where a specific intervention is unavailable.

Multiinfarct Dementia

Considered the second most common cause of dementia, multiinfarct dementia results from vascular disease that leads to strokes. The strokes cause damage to the cells in the affected area of the brain. There may be many cells damaged (major stroke) or only a few ("silent," or small, stroke). In either event, the destruction is permanent. When enough neurons have been damaged in the parts of the brain that control mental competence, mental changes that identify dementia will begin to occur.

The principal predisposing condition identified with strokes is arteriosclerosis, a chronic disease that causes thickening and hardening of the walls of the arteries. As the arterial walls lose their elasticity, blood flow may be slowed or interrupted. Neurons are highly susceptible to insufficient blood supply because they have higher metabolism and energy requirements than other cells. Inadequate blood flow starves cells of oxygen and nutrients and destroys them easily and rapidly. Insufficient oxygen supply to the brain leads to a stroke, with the complete destruction (called an infarct) of some amount of tissue.

The location of the damage is crucial to its effects. Strokes may occur wherever there is insufficient blood flow. To produce dementia, however, there must be damage in cells where mental processes occur. This usually means in the frontal lobe of the brain. Strokes occurring in the motor cortex, for example, lead to an inability to use associated muscle groups (at least for some recovery period). Yet the patient might not show interruption or decline in mental abilities. Unfortunately, knowledge of the brain is so limited that specific functions of many areas of the brain are undefined.

When the strokes are so small that they are not diagnosed or even noticed by the patient, the chances that multiinfarct dementia will eventually occur seem to be increased. Of course, arteriosclerosis is potentially preventable. Usually, persons who suffer multiinfarct dementia have a history of diseases associated with high stroke risk: hypertension (high blood pressure), diabetes, heart disease, and the like. Often, these patients will have a history of transient ischemic attacks (TIAs, caused by temporary blockage of an artery) or strokes. There may also be neurological signs that can be measured, such as exaggerated reflexes or defects in the visual field. A number of these specific disorders are treatable and even preventable. Doctors have placed greater emphasis in the last 20 years or so on identifying conditions like hypertension as early as possible in adulthood. Patients are then advised on ways to reduce the high-pressure readings. Treatment includes a modified diet, with controlled intake of fat and cholesterol, and weight reduction as needed. Exercise programs can assist in controlling blood pressure as well as ensuring physical fitness. If blood pressure remains too high with these interventions, medications are used as well. Following these measures should reduce the risk of stroke and may even ensure that no strokes of any intensity will occur.

Since infarcts may occur anywhere in the brain, the result of a stroke (or even of a series of strokes) may not be dementia. Where dementia occurs with stroke, a stepwise deterioration of mental competencies may be noted (see Figure 2.2). In a small (silent)

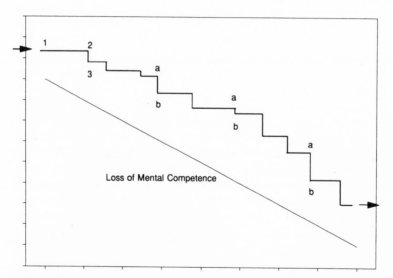

Figure 2.2. Progression of multiinfarct dementia. (1) period of life without strokes; (2) occurrence of "silent" stroke; (3) degree of loss of competence; (a) recurrent strokes; (b) loss of mental competence. From Edwards (1993). Reprinted by permission of Plenum Press.

stroke, there is usually only brief blockage of one or more arteries, leading to physical symptoms that may be muted. The person may feel numb for a period of time, or unable to use some part of the body effectively, or show speech defects with problems in thinking. There may be dizziness and nausea. *What* effect is felt depends on the place where the stroke occurs and the degree of brain tissue involvement. Since the episode is temporary, perhaps only seconds, and will not reoccur until another stroke is experienced, it may be dismissed as unimportant. It is even possible that the person will simply feel bad for a few hours and wonder whether it was something she or he ate or a result of being overly tired. The symptoms may be *so* mild that they are not even noticed.

However, any damage done to cell bodies in the brain is permanent so that, over time, reoccurrence of strokes in critical areas may bring on the behaviors of dementia. Predicting when the next "step" will occur (see Figure 2.2) and the depth of that step is impossible. Untreated, the process may move rapidly but even with treatment there may still be progression to dementia. There is evidence to indicate that multiinfarct dementia is more common in blacks than whites, probably due to environmental conditions, including poor diet over many years, as well as discrimination in a variety of forms, which increases stress levels. Some scientists believe that there is a strong case to be made for a genetic factor. Blacks also show a higher incidence of dementia resulting from alcohol abuse over many years.

Multiinfarct dementia seems to result from conditions that are medically identifiable and either preventable or treatable. As more persons assume responsibility for healthier lives (in terms of nutrition and exercise, particularly), there should be fewer cases.

Cause and Prognosis

There is increasing evidence of a connection between high blood pressure and the occurrence of multiinfarct dementia resulting from silent strokes. Cardiac disease and hypertension (high blood pressure) are found commonly in the medical histories of persons who develop such a dementia. The relationship may not be a direct one; that is, there may be some other factor intervening between the two conditions. By contrast, there is no strong evidence of any relationship between high blood pressure and the occurrence of Alzheimer's disease. So, it seems reasonable to assume that vascular disease is involved in multiinfarct dementia.

Prognosis for the patient with multiinfarct dementia is poor, suggesting even more strongly the need for us to take appropriate care of ourselves. A diet low in fat and cholesterol, proper aerobic exercise, and weight control are more than just "good" for us. They may actually prevent a later mental problem that cannot be corrected after it occurs.

Multiinfarct dementia is more commonly diagnosed in men, and particularly black men, than in women. It occurs earlier in life (usually beginning in the late 50s or early 60s because of the connection with vascular disease) and has a more rapid course of decline than does Alzheimer's.

Course

Since strokes occur in an irregular pattern, the course of multiinfarct dementia is irregular also. Nevertheless, there is a certain predictability to the process since each stroke may have a negative effect on mental functioning. Whether the amount of mental decline is directly related to the severity of the stroke, or even if every stroke (in certain areas of the brain, at least) will cause greater incompetence, is unknown. What *is* accepted is the fact that stroke and dementia are related, with progression of mental decline as more brain cells are destroyed.

The risk factors center on hypertension but there are other conditions that may cause multiinfarct dementia. These include heart disease, cigarette smoking, and diabetes mellitus. The presence of these factors seems to lead to multiple small infarcts of the brain also. It is essential to remember that the neuronal damage must occur in areas of the brain where mental processes occur if dementia is to result. For this reason, a person may have a major stroke that incapacitates that person physically (say, by paralysis on one side of the body) and yet that person will not suffer dementia as a result. It is not, then, *how much* brain damage is done as it is *where* damage, even in small amounts, is done.

Outcomes

Multiinfarct dementia seems to progress more rapidly than Alzheimer's, with the eventual cause of death being either a sudden cerebrovascular attack or one of the conventional causes such as pneumonia.

There is evidence that during the course of the disease, speech and language may be affected. However, there are some differences in how these effects are shown when compared to Alzheimer's. In multiinfarct dementia, there is greater likelihood of abnormalities in *motor* aspects of speech, such as difficulties in producing the sounds and ideas that the patient desires to express. This causes frustration since the patient may know what he or she is trying to say but simply cannot get it said. By contrast, Alzheimer's patients seem to have much less awareness of what is relevant or correct and thus they are apt to be satisfied with a statement whether it is appropriate or not.

In multiinfarct dementia as in Alzheimer's, patients may make errors in naming objects because they cannot recall the appropriate label, indicating destruction of neurons where the concepts were stored. However, multiinfarct patients seem to retain their *learning* abilities better than Alzheimer's patients because they may continue to acquire some new information and skills.

Multiinfarct dementia seems to present a relatively clear picture. Cause is well agreed upon, intervention is recognized and strongly advocated, and diagnosis is increasingly accurate. If persons accept the responsibility for maintaining health, the incidence of multiinfarct dementia should decrease markedly in the future. There is even the possibility that the condition can be prevented under ideal conditions.

Summary

Dementia is characterized by memory loss, disorientation, and confusion. Research is attempting to isolate the factors that contribute to these behavioral symptoms of dementia. Among the many possible sources being tested for causality are viruses, an immune system deficiency, neurotransmitter deficits, environmental toxins, aluminum toxicity, and excess beta amyloid protein. There is also interest in and investigation of a possible causal role for systemic disorders and gene mutations. To date, no definitive answer has been found, so the research continues.

Destruction of nerve cells in certain parts of the brain lead to the demented behaviors that prevent an individual from coping effectively with the environment. The process responsible for the destruction may be a disease caused by one or more of the variables referred to above. Dr. Alois Alzheimer was the first to describe the brain-cell alterations—the presence of neurofibrillary tangles and neuritic plaques—that seemed responsible for behavioral degeneration. Later, the condition exhibiting these brain alterations was named for him. Today, Alzheimer's disease is the most common diagnosis made by doctors when demented behavior is found in patients.

Vascular disease has also been observed to be a primary cause of dementia. Small strokes (called silent strokes because of their relatively mild symptoms) result in damage (infarcts) in brain tissue. After a number of such strokes, dementia may appear and increase as strokes continue. This condition, called multiinfarct dementia, is the second most commonly diagnosed cause of brain-cell loss.

3

Irreversible and Reversible Causes of Dementia

Professionals, including physicians, agree that most cases of dementia are due to Alzheimer's disease. Since there is no governmental agency that gathers data to provide a true census of the actual incidence in this country, we depend on estimates from various sources. Of all the persons suffering dementia today, it is estimated that half of them (50 percent) have Alzheimer's disease. An additional 20 percent have multiinfarct dementia, and another 15 percent have *both* syndromes. If accurate, these two syndromes account for 85 percent of all cases of dementia. This means that all other causes together represent minor contributions to the social and medical problems that come with dementia. However, even though rare, these remaining sources for dementia assume importance for those in whom they occur and for their families.

One matter of concern is the "age connection." Alzheimer's disease may occur at any point in adulthood, but as originally described, should only be diagnosed during middle age. In fact, however, the disease is principally diagnosed *after* age 65. With increasing age, there is a heightened possibility for a dementing process to be found and ascribed to Alzheimer's disease. By some estimates, the group over age 85 will show a 40 percent incidence. This is a frightening suggestion when we consider that more people are living longer; currently, the fastest growing proportion of the population is the group over age 85.

Multiinfarct dementia is more likely to be expressed somewhat earlier in life, usually in middle age. The conditions producing arteriosclerosis may have already been present for two decades or so by this time. The consequences (small, silent strokes) have been expressed and have had their cumulative effects long enough that the patient may begin to show behavioral changes. Still, the progression of the dementia depends on continued strokes with accumulating cell destruction. In the individual case, the dementia may show its stepwise advances for another 10 years or more. (Potentially, as well, the process may be interrupted if appropriate action is taken: exercise, diet, weight loss, perhaps medication.) Generally, however, survival rates are shorter (perhaps by several years) for multiinfarct than for Alzheimer's dementia.

The age connection is even more diverse for the rare conditions that have been associated with the development of dementia, some of which proceed so rapidly that death will occur within a year or so after diagnosis. Other conditions develop more slowly and produce their effects over many years. In addition, treatment is possible in some instances, with real potential for reversibility and cure. A major factor in intervention is the level of knowledge about the various conditions, some of which have been widely studied and are well understood, while other conditions are little known and remain a major mystery.

Irreversible Causes

There are several conditions that produce dementia in which the prognosis is considered at best poor and at worst hopeless. Such syndromes, when diagnosed, are presumed to produce increasing loss of mental competence because there is no treatment or intervention. Further, the condition is considered progressive: it will not run its course at some point in time; it will not reverse its effects if one changes one's lifestyle; it will not be cured by any presently known drug or agent. For these reasons, the diagnosis implies that things must only get worse, though no one can say how quickly or how completely. Essentially, then, all of these syndromes are irreversible and untreatable.

Pick's Disease

This disease is a very rare brain condition. Though only a guess, there probably are less than 80 thousand persons in this country with Pick's. This amounts to less than three-tenths of 1 percent of the total population. Of course, if you or someone close to you suffers the condition, such statistical estimates are of little consolation. The cause of the disease is unknown, and a diagnosis of Pick's disease indicates a hopeless future for the patient.

One of the outcomes of Pick's is atrophy (shrinkage) of the brain. As the condition progresses, the structure of the brain changes, with a loss of brain tissue particularly in the frontal and temporal lobes. Using a CAT scan (computerized axial tomography), this structural change can be identified without intrusion into the cranium. Such evidence helps in diagnosis although there are reasons other than Pick's disease for shrinkage in these areas of the brain.

Even if the evidence favors a diagnosis of Pick's, the effects are difficult to distinguish from other sources of dementia. For example, there is the usual memory loss, though Pick's patients show greater emotional apathy than is found in dementia from other causes. These patients also present problems expressing their ideas and thoughts. Consistent with Alzheimer's is an increasing carelessness in behavior stemming from the loss of memory stores that permitted distinguishing the socially acceptable from the unacceptable. These patients present problems with speech and communication, particularly in expressing their ideas and thoughts.

There is some evidence that sufferers of Pick's do not use their remaining intellectual abilities in a very constructive way. By contrast, Alzheimer's patients are left with little mental ability to use.

Pick's disease occurs most often in those between the ages of 40 and 60 years. Rarely is Pick's a diagnosis of old age. Once diagnosed, the patient usually dies within five or six years. It is almost unknown for a Pick's victim to live more than eight years after diagnosis. Although studies done at autopsy are limited in number and scope so far, unusual chemical changes have been reported from diseased cells in the frontal and temporal lobes, with some evidence that these changes are affecting other cells. However, there is as yet no evidence of a connection between the disease and these chemical changes.

Overall, our knowledge of Pick's is too limited to make definitive claims or statements. More study and research of cause, progression, and effects are needed. At present, a diagnosis of Pick's is more educated guess than medical fact.

Creutzfeldt-Jakob Disease

This condition is so rare that it has been estimated to occur in only one of every million persons. This means that there are no more than 250 cases in the United States currently. Though very rare in incidence, the cause is known: a virus that incubates for a long period of time before being expressed. Once the virus becomes active, the life of the patient is usually very brief. Most victims die within a year or two after diagnosis, and the maximum period of continued life is eight years.

The virus that causes Creutzfeldt-Jakob disease is one of a group of infectious agents that can be seen only with an electron microscope. They are composed mostly of genetic material and can grow and multiply only in living cells. How the virus is transmitted is unknown. The fact that a virus causes Creutzfeldt-Jakob is known only because diseased brain tissue from a human transplanted into a chimpanzee caused the chimp to develop the symptoms of Creutzfeldt-Jakob after a long incubation period. These symptoms include irregularities in muscle control (ataxia), muscle spasms, seizures, incontinence, psychotic behavior, and visual symptoms. After death, an autopsy discloses a brain that is atrophied (shrunken) and somewhat "spongy."

If the cause is, in fact, a virus, how it is transmitted becomes an issue. Some scientists have argued for a genetic transmission of the disease, with or without a connection to a viral agent. Others point out that there is little evidence for a hereditary link. Further, there seems as much reason to believe that environmental conditions are involved as that a genetic defect is responsible. There have even been attempts to identify a relationship with diet for those who develop Creutzfeldt-Jakob. It has been speculated that the eating of brain, kidney, tripe, and the like might introduce the virus into the human body. However, the results of such studies have been fruitless.

Clinically, patients show an insidious onset of symptoms, usually without any fever or illness that can be identified. They show increasingly confused behavior and gradual loss of muscular coordination, often accompanied by depression and withdrawal. Given the unexplainable physical and mental changes, it seems reasonable that the patient might become depressed and attempt to withdraw from normal contacts and problem-solving situations. Increasing fluctuations in emotions (called emotional lability) also occur, making certain reactions seem extreme or out of place. The dementia progresses slowly and is characterized by structural changes in the brain that can be identified using a brain scan.

There is an urgent need for extensive research to identify the nature of the virus that causes the dementia associated with Creutzfeldt-Jakob disease. Only when that step is achieved will there be the possibility for treatment or prevention. Unfortunately, the condition is seen as not important enough (particularly since so few individuals are diagnosed) to warrant funding at a time when monies are in short supply.

AIDS (Acquired Immunodeficiency Syndrome)

The increasing evidence that a sexually transmitted disease may lead to demented behavior may be frightening. What must be remembered is that *many* conditions produce outcomes that are identified with dementia: memory loss, confusion, and disorientation in time and space. These are the universals of dementia that may also be accompanied by personality changes and emotional instability. The emphasis should be placed on the results, not the cause, so far as understanding the dynamics are concerned.

Scientists are increasingly reporting the fact that AIDS patients develop and display the signs of dementia. The number of patients being studied is increasing so that documentation of the outcome of dementia is now possible. The key to the relationship, based on current evidence, seems to be an immune deficiency that causes the many physical problems and eventual death of the AIDS patient. In recent years, those who study the causes of dementia, and particularly Alzheimer's, have suggested the possibility of immune system decline as an important factor in leaving the brain cells susceptible to the disease process.

The immune system protects us from invading organisms, including germs and viruses that would cause us to become ill or perhaps even die. This system includes what are called T-helper lymphocytes, a particular kind of white blood cell. The T-helper cells activate other cells, which produce antibodies to fight whatever infectious agent has entered the body. In our youth, the system is normally competent enough to protect us even though we may become sick to some degree during the process. With age, however, and increasingly with old age, the immune system shows decline. In fact, in some ways, the system may come to actually assist the invading organism rather than activating cells to block it. As a result, elderly persons are more at risk for becoming ill. In fact, they will become ill more easily and suffer longer than they would have at a younger age. The most common causes of death in the elderly (e.g., pneumonia) become exaggerated cases that the young adult would not encounter under normal conditions.

The "normal conditions" are not always met, however. When a person of any age is infected with the viral agent that leads to AIDS, the eventual result will be destruction of the immune system. This viral agent is called the human immunodeficiency virus (HIV). Once in the body, the virus attacks only certain types of cells but particularly the T-helper lymphocytes. The body slowly but certainly loses its resistance to diseases as the HIV takes over and converts the function of the T-helper cells to its own purposes.

If AIDS inevitably leads to dementia, a plausible case could be made for the role of immune system dysfunction in the conditions related to Alzheimer's and other causes of dementia. Certainly, the availability of research funds is much greater for AIDS than for Alzheimer's. Research into the characteristics of AIDS could yield results useful to those studying dementia from other causes. This may be a backdoor approach but the possibilities should not be ignored or refused. Even if the immune deficiency connection proves to be a false lead, one theory about causes of dementia will have been disproved. At the same time, other data may suggest alternative explanations that may be researched.

Down's Syndrome

One of the arguments presented to support a genetic basis for dementia is a connection with Down's syndrome. Down's is a genetically determined condition that presents distinctive physical symptoms (such as fissured tongue, some slanting of the eyes, a tendency to short stature and overweight) and retardation in intellectual development characterized by slow learning and some problem-solving deficiencies. In the past, persons with Down's syndrome rarely lived beyond the age of 30 years but recent developments in care now permit many of them to live to age 40 and beyond. What has been noted in such cases is that a large percentage (estimated to be anywhere from about 40 percent to 100 percent) show the symptoms of dementia as they grow older.

Down's syndrome occurs because of a genetic error. At the moment of conception, the human-to-be receives 23 chromosomes from each parent. These chromosomes contain the genetic pattern that will determine features such as hair color and amount, skin color, general body build, biological sex (male or female sex organs), and probably general intellectual competencies and perhaps even personality traits. The Down's patient, however, receives part of an extra chromosome attached to chromosome 21. As a result, the child will show the typical symptoms and effects that denote Down's.

Since there is demonstrable evidence of dementia in older Down's patients, scientists have pursued the possible case for Alzheimer's to be the result of a genetic error. There is some evidence that the expression of dementia in the Down's patient differs somewhat from that in Alzheimer's.

Normal-Pressure Hydrocephalus

At birth, the skull within which the brain is encased is not completely joined. There are actually four portions of bone that will knit over time to form the hard protective covering. Since the bones have not joined completely, there is the possibility that they may be prevented from doing so. Some children have a rare condition—called hydrocephalus—where the fluid in the brain forces the portions of the skull to remain unjoined. They may even become further expanded, exposing the brain tissue to potential damage. In most of us, of course, the amount of cerebrospinal fluid around the brain is normal, the skull knits as it should, the head size is proportional to the rest of the body, and only a severe head wound or disease represents a danger to brain tissue.

When normal development has occurred, we do not expect an adult to develop hydrocephalus. However, there is some shrinkage in brain tissue with aging even in normal individuals. The space in the cranium created by this shrinkage is then occupied by additional fluid. Though the proportion of tissue to fluid is altered in this case, the level of *pressure* between the two remains normal. This condition is called normal-pressure hydrocephalus.

The principal symptoms of normal-pressure hydrocephalus include some memory loss, difficulty in thinking, and changes in behavior. Physically, early in the process the patient begins to show problems in standing (station) and walking (gait). Urinary incontinence also occurs. The *early* occurrence of these physical changes helps to distinguish normal-pressure hydrocephalus from other conditions and, when accompanied by evidence of dementia, assists the physician in making a diagnosis.

The cause of normal-pressure hydrocephalus is unknown. Treatment has been restricted to a procedure called "shunting," where a plastic tube is placed in the brain to carry the excess cerebrospinal fluid into the jugular vein. A dangerous procedure, the operation is not as common today as it was some 30 years ago, and its success rate, in the sense of relieving both physical and mental symptoms, has not been very good. Still, it remains a viable option that may be tried in a few cases.

The normally aging brain shows evidence of shrinkage (disclosed through the use of brain scans) and a consequent increase in fluid. Yet the results need not be the physical problems of gait disturbance and urinary incontinence, nor the degree of mental difficulties, that characterize normal-pressure hydrocephalus. This disorder, then, must be a distinct and unique condition that requires knowledge both of cause and intervention. Since shunting has not been as successful as hoped in resolving patient difficulties, there is a need to determine why the systems responsible for removing fluid from the brain are not functioning properly.

Huntington's Disease

Huntington's is a hereditary disorder that affects the nervous system. In this case, the genetic trait is highly predictable. If a person inherits the gene responsible for Huntington's from one parent, there is a 50 percent probability that the gene will be expressed and the condition will occur in that person. Huntington's disease may develop at any time during adulthood but is somewhat more likely after age 40.

Not all Huntington's patients develop dementia. The exact

incidence is unknown; estimates range from 20 percent to 80 percent although some authorities claim that all cases of Huntington's will become demented if the patient lives long enough. Where dementia does develop, the prominent sign is memory loss. Reasoning is also adversely affected but there are not the losses in the functional ability to recall the name of an object or person (semantic memory) that are found in Alzheimer's patients. In fact, such wide differences in the amount of intellectual decline are reported for Huntington's victims that eventual total loss of competencies is not certain by any means. The chief physical symptom is abnormal muscle movement, usually in the trunk and lower limbs. There is no treatment for the condition. Usually, there are accompanying emotional problems and personality changes. Some physicians report psychotic disorders in some patients.

When dementia does occur, the symptoms that distinguish this syndrome from others include slow thought processes, problems of recall from memory, and some loss of control involving judgment. The slow thinking (called bradyphrenia) is characterized by the long (and sometimes agonizingly long) time it takes a patient to express a thought. Although the patient may eventually be able to communicate an idea, others may lose patience while waiting and either attempt to express the patient's idea themselves or simply give up on understanding what the patient is trying to say. Not infrequently, Huntington's victims also disclose increasing difficulties in spatial relations. This may be expressed as an inability to perceive depth in, for example, a drawing or blueprint, or the relationship among parts in a diagram. Some patients become apathetic, uninterested in the events going on around them, and unaffected by the things that happen to them or others. Depression is a likely state, understandable as the circumstances of life deteriorate. There is evidence that persons with Huntington's often have a history of major affective disorders (emotional difficulties). This suggests the possibility of a systematic relationship between the psychiatric conditions and the later emergence of Huntington's. To date, no one has been able to clarify what the "systematic relationship" is.

Parkinson's Disease

Parkinson's is known to be related to a deficiency in one of the neurotransmitters (in this case, dopamine) needed in the brain to ensure appropriate functioning of the neurons. Many scientists believe a dopamine deficit is the *cause* of Parkinson's. In recent years, with the explosion in the use of drugs by young persons, there have been reports of increasing numbers of persons who show parkinsonian symptoms from the toxic effect of certain drugs. Parkinson's most commonly occurs in middle to old age and progresses gradually, often over many years. About 1 percent of the population over age 50 suffers from the disease, indicating about 2.5 million cases in this country. The percentage of those who display the symptoms of dementia has been estimated at anywhere from 20 percent to 80 percent.

A deficit in the neurotransmitter dopamine is the significant physical feature. One of the functions of the chemical is to control complex movement. Where there is insufficient dopamine present in the brain, muscle movements cannot be adequately controlled, leading to the muscle tremor and weakness characteristic of Parkinson's patients. There can be partial though temporary relief by administration of a drug called L-dopa, which the body uses to produce dopamine. However, this treatment does not alter the course of Parkinson's or influence the development of dementia. In fact, L-dopa and other drugs used for treatment of the physical symptoms produce side effects that exaggerate the dementia symptoms. Some physicians report that the use of even small doses of drugs with a Parkinson's patient who suffers dementia can bring delirium, agitation, and psychotic states.

In Parkinson's patients, language function is adversely affected with increasing difficulty in thinking abstractly. This leads to uncertainty in planning and poor problem-solving skills. Abilities needed to deal with visual stimuli may be affected. Yet memory may be only partially reduced so that mental competence seems unaffected as measured by mental status tests used by professionals.

It appears that the later in life Parkinson's occurs the more likely that severe cognitive impairment (and consequent dementia) will occur. There will be particular problems with the ability to express oneself verbally. This is most likely due to the patient's inability to retrieve material stored in memory in order to communicate. Short-term memory (used to store information for use within a few seconds to a minute or two) is particularly poor while long-term memory (experiences stored for use over long periods of time) is affected only when there is significant mental decline. Parkinson's patients with dementia show more specific patterns of memory dysfunction than Alzheimer's patients. This is shown behaviorally by the kinds of material that interfere in memory retrieval. In Parkinson's patients with dementia, events occurring after onset will interfere with recalling some particular fact (retrograde amnesia) while events preceding onset (anterograde amnesia) do not interfere with recollection. In contrast, with the Alzheimer's patient it appears that *everything* interferes with recall. Such differences can be identified in psychological examinations for use in making decisions about a diagnosis.

All the conditions described in this section are untreatable. This means that the progression is inexorable, that nothing can be done to stop or reverse it, and that dementia will become worse with time. Yet there is no way of predicting *when* the dementia will start, *how rapidly* it will progress, or *specific ways* in which it will express itself. Treatment will be symptomatic only—a kind of "band-aid" to make worsening conditions as comfortable as possible.

Reversible Causes

Since the principal effects of dementia involve memory loss, confusion, and disorientation, it is reasonable to assume that such symptoms may be caused by treatable conditions as well as untreatable ones. Such is indeed the case although many professionals are concerned that misdiagnosis may occur in some cases.

Certainly if the proper cause is identified, and correct treatment made available, the dementia should disappear with improvement in the patient's condition. There are so many potentially reversible causes of dementia that only a survey of some of the more prominent ones is possible. So far as number of cases go, it is probable that the majority are properly diagnosed and treated. The result is that *most* long-term examples of dementia are from irreversible causes. Still, there is a need to examine those conditions where a costly mistake may be made. Certainly, physicians are concerned with eliminating the possibility of a treatable condition before assuming irreversibility.

Functional Disorders

There are several psychiatric syndromes that are treatable but if neglected or misdiagnosed may mimic or even induce dementia. The principal one of these is *depression*, which often affects the memory of the sufferer. The depressed individual, who finds life hopeless and futile and who has lost enjoyment in all activities, may present a picture to a physician or clinician that resembles dementia. Particularly if the person is elderly, and there is some predisposition on the part of the physician toward a belief that older individuals are susceptible to developing dementia, the mistake is more likely to occur. However, depression is treatable. As a result, professionals are likely to check for this functional disorder whether or not an eventual diagnosis of dementia is made. One can understand that a person developing dementia may, in fact, also become depressed. The suffering associated with depression, however, should be correctly evaluated and treated.

Although not so apt to be confused with dementia, other functional disorders may accompany dementia and need to be correctly diagnosed and treated. One of these disorders is *anxiety*, a common occurrence in the lives of all of us. In the elderly, anxiety often becomes generalized (called free-floating anxiety) because so many things may appear to be threatening to the person. As with depression, a patient developing dementia may be expected to feel generalized anxiety resulting from an inability to understand and deal with the behavior problems that are occurring more frequently. There are certain drugs (called anxiolytics) that can help control anxiety without some of the side effects that drugs may bring. When the use of drugs is accompanied by the teaching of coping mechanisms and education about the dementia process, the patient can become less anxious and more functional.

Dementia patients may also develop *delusions* (alterations of reality) if they cannot cope with changes and are not aware of the realities of their condition. The delusions may reassure patients by placing the blame for their problems on some other person. This often will be the caregiver (the spouse or child usually). Although unfair and stressful to the caregiver, through delusions the patient finds some means of living with the frightening changes and some hope that things may change for the better. All such behaviors are adaptive in the sense that they are intended to help "explain" circumstances that are unacceptable. True, outsiders will not understand and may even be offended by unfair accusations and reactions. Yet the behaviors of the patient are understandable and are treatable, leading to better adaptive behavior in most instances.

Head Injuries

Blows to the head may cause a person to develop memory loss and confusion. You may have suffered an accident—say, in your car—that caused you to be confused for a short period of time. Maybe you could not quite remember what happened (and may still be unable to do so). Your "dementia" was temporary but real.

Perhaps the most notable dementia associated with head injury comes from the sport of boxing. Fighters receive multiple blows to the head over a number of years. Damage occurs to some cells with each blow and over time the fighter becomes what is known as "punch drunk." He will be forgetful, confused, and disoriented. In some cases there may be treatment that will allow some recovery, but not always.

The expression of dementia from head injury will depend on the extent and location of brain damage. Remember that some portions of the brain can take over functions lost in other portions. Where the damage is not progressive or compounded further, this possibility is more likely. It seems that injury occurring to the frontal lobe of the brain, where the higher intellectual processes take place, may lead to the expression of dementia. This rationale fits the effects found in professional boxers as well as in others who have sustained head wounds from other sources.

Brain tumors may cause dementia. If the tumor is operable, removal usually will bring reversal in the condition. Current technology has greatly increased the chance that tumors will be identified. Use of the CAT scan (or other brain scans) makes it unnecessary to cut into the brain to identify a tumor, a much safer procedure than was formerly available. Although not all tumors are excisable, or even diagnosable, with today's technology, medicine is in a much better position to find tumors and to correct the problem by surgical intervention in some cases.

Systemic Disorders

The various systems in the body may be associated with eventual brain damage and consequent dementia. Among the agents that are capable of adversely influencing systems of the body and the brain are *infections*. There are several that are found in the brain itself, such as meningitis and encephalitis. These infections, which are caused by various agents (e.g., bacteria, viruses, or fungi), are often treatable. The resultant dementia may be reversible with the appropriate treatment in some cases, and arrested but not reversed in others.

Toxins may also produce dementia. A principal toxic effect comes from medications that are taken in an inappropriate dosage. There are several categories of drugs particularly associated with the possibility of toxic effects, and potential dementia. These include psychoactive and neuroactive agents, opiates, and adrenocortical steroids. However, there may also be a negative case made for more frequently used medicines intended to arrest or reduce the symptoms of other conditions. For example, L-dopa is helpful in controlling muscle tremors in Parkinson's patients but it may complicate and increase dementia symptoms as well. It may even be that such substitute chemicals induce dementia.

Side effects from drugs needed for life-threatening syndromes have been associated with dementia as well. For those with high blood pressure, antihypertensives are often prescribed. Certainly appropriate for controlling blood pressure, these medications may cause dementia symptoms. Drugs used to reduce allergic reactions and those prescribed for diabetics have also been implicated.

The so-called recreational drugs are even more dangerous. There is evidence that the symptoms of Parkinson's, and eventual dementia, are increasingly being found in drug users. Glue sniffing is hazardous behavior because of adverse effects on the brain. Of course, drugs such as cocaine and heroin may bring a variety of changes, physically and mentally, and can result in dementia.

Though all these toxic sources may have permanent effects, the behavioral consequences may be arrested or reversed if the drug involvement stops. One possible source of dementia that is increasingly of concern to doctors is the effect of interactions between several medications, either prescribed or across the counter. Sharing drugs with others and taking drugs under unsupervised circumstances is a dangerous practice.

Dementia may result from *metabolic disorders* as well. Metabolism refers to the chemical changes that occur in the cells of the body by which they absorb and use nutrients to remain healthy and viable and provide energy for vital processes. If the glands involved in this system (thyroid, parathyroid, adrenals, and pituitary) are diseased and left untreated, dementia may be one of the severe effects. Kidney and liver failure not only have their terrible physical effects but can be involved with mental incompetence and dementia as well. Even dehydration (more common in the elderly than is generally recognized) has metabolic consequences. With diagnosis and treatment, most of these conditions can be corrected. Whatever dementia symptoms have been shown by the patient should clear up as a consequence.

Finally, there are a number of *nutritional disorders* that have been shown to be associated with at least temporary dementia. Anemia is a central one of these. If the body's cells do not receive sufficient or appropriate nutrition, they will die. This effect is illustrated among those who abuse alcohol over a number of years. In cases where dietary needs are unmet, because alcohol contains sugars that cause the patient to feel nourished and lose appetite, slow starvation of brain cells may result. Dementia is a likely result.

Pellagra, a disease caused by niacin and protein deficiencies, is commonly found in countries experiencing famine. Still, there are instances in this country where families are so deprived that they are unable to maintain an adequate diet. An outcome may be dementia that can be reversed by including niacin in the diet.

All systemic disorders are not reversible and mental changes that may have occurred may only be partially correctable. The point is that dementia occurs in many circumstances that are controllable and preventable under proper medical and social conditions. It is probable, however, that only a small percentage of cases of dementia are due to such causes. This means that cases involving the reversible causes of dementia are in the minority, as important for the individual as each may be. The problem is most severe and most complex for those conditions where a treatable cause goes undiscovered or treatment is possible but unavailable.

Summary

Dementia may result from either irreversible (untreatable) or reversible (treatable) conditions. The major recognized sources (Alzheimer's and multiinfarct) are not the only ones. There are several other irreversible syndromes. Though rare in occurrence, they are just as devastating in their effects on patients and families. Among these conditions are Pick's and Creutzfeldt-Jakob disease, AIDS, Down's syndrome, and normal-pressure hydrocephalus. Huntington's (a hereditary condition) and Parkinson's diseases include a certain number of cases resulting in dementia although that outcome does not always occur. There is some overlap of symptoms from these irreversible causes with Alzheimer's. But it is the differences between these diseases that can help doctors make more accurate diagnoses.

Reversible (treatable) causes may also produce dementia if ignored or improperly treated. The emphasis, then, should be on identifying the characteristics that distinguish these conditions from irreversible ones. Sometimes, the behaviors of treatable patients are so like those with untreatable syndromes that physicians confuse the diagnosis. However, physicians are increasingly aware of the need to discriminate clearly and treat completely. Reversible conditions are depression, anxiety, and delusions. Head injury may also bring dementia, although usually of limited degree and for a brief time period. Infections, toxins, and drugs have been implicated in leading to demented behavior, and both metabolic and nutritional deficiencies can produce dementia unless corrected.

4

Psychological Effects of Dementia

Few, if any, caregivers and patients are prepared for the presence of dementia, which introduces trials and demands for which neither has the knowledge and tools to cope. Yet, there is no choice: coping is necessary and unavoidable. The result is an attempt at adjustment that may be positive and rewarding (at least in some instances) or defeating and negative (at least in others). Understanding what observed behaviors may mean and how they may be faced underscores the psychological nature of the effects of dementia. These behaviors are not induced by the dementia itself, but represent the personality of the caregiver: a personality that has a history of trying to cope, sometimes with success, at other times not. In other words, we use the tools of coping available to us regardless of their relevance. What is important to remember is that we are always trying to adjust so that the coping devices we use are attempts to deal with problems. It is not a matter of "good" or "bad" decisions but a matter of the means we have available to us. In this chapter, I describe some of the *psychological* adjustments that humans commonly make and apply them to the patient and caregiver, both of whom are dealing with all the stresses and strains that result from dementia.

Encountering the Unexpected

Dementia may be the source of frustration, stress, anxiety, and disorganization. Such outcomes are based on the fact that we are not prepared for such an adverse event when it occurs. The behaviors that result from dementia begin only in adulthood, usually after a person has served a useful and meaningful life. When forgetfulness occurs in one who is 70 years old, say, it is easy to assume that the stereotype is true—that as we get older, we have to expect some changes that reflect "slippage" in our mental competencies. Even if forgetfulness occurs in a 50-year-old, it is still likely that some excuse may be found. Usually, the instances of memory loss occur only seldom and are often restricted to less important behaviors. There may be some uneasiness in either the patient or caregiver that "something is wrong" but the potential is too frightening to accept. Unfortunately, if the dementing process has begun, the instances will occur more often and closer together in time.

The Critical Incident

Eventually, something will happen that cannot be ignored. Most caregivers report that some signs of dysfunction had been noticed for at least a year or two. But these signs had been ignored or explained away by both the patient and caregiver. Then, an event may have occurred that was too important to permit further avoidance. There is now a firm sign that something must be done to identify what is wrong and what may be done about it. The result very well may be an appointment with a physician, and a subsequent diagnosis of one of the causes of dementia.

The critical incident may not be detrimental to the well-being of the person but may cause problems that indicate the need for a doctor's opinion. You will recall that in Chapter 1, Sam Wells commented to the doctor about memory problems that were occurring in his wife, Martha. Though the case report does not indicate that a diagnosis was made, it is apparent that Sam is concerned because he sees some behaviors in his wife that he cannot explain. Given the other circumstances reported in the case study, it seems likely that Martha will soon need a thorough examination to find what is causing her problem behaviors.

Diagnosis

When problem behaviors become too frequent or too damaging, a physician will be consulted. Unfortunately, this step often happens only after some compounding of problem behaviors and some long period of time (perhaps years). The doctor will check all possible causes for the changes, and perhaps even refer the patient to specialists for specific tests. In most cases, the efforts will yield only the conclusion that there can be no treatment and that the condition is both irreversible and progressive. Such a decision will be very difficult to understand, much less to accept, by both patient and caregiver. A second opinion may (and should) be sought, although the chances are slim that the outcome will be any different. The finality and meaning of the diagnosis may be accepted by both parties intellectually, but the emotional impact will still be overwhelming. There is usually some period of time during which the caregiver and patient attempt to achieve some psychological acceptance of the fact that the future must bring only more serious difficulties. During this time, the caregiver may seek out sources of information to gain a better understanding of what has happened, will happen, and why. There may be an element of grasping for hope in such efforts. One caregiver, whose mother has only recently been diagnosed with Alzheimer's disease, has attended several support group meetings, each in a different place. Her questions have always focused on what to expect, how to handle problem behaviors, how satisfied others are with their arrangements in caregiving (e.g., placement in a nursing home), and the like. To date, she has found no answers that she can accept psychologically as she works through the process of acceptance.

Accepting the Inevitable

With time, caregivers will begin to accept the fact that life can no longer be what it was for them or for the dementia patient. They then begin to adapt, to develop ways to protect themselves and their patients, and live with a reality that is unpleasant but certainly genuine. Successful caregivers begin to find ways to handle the many burdens, even if they cannot reduce them, and to find the "bright" side in circumstances. For example, many caregivers are eventually able to find humor in what is certainly not humorous. Instead of reporting instances of behavior in anger and frustration, they can describe them with wit. A caregiver who had lived with dementia for 11 years reported that her spouse still dressed himself correctly until one morning recently. It seems he had dressed, but only with his undershirt, shirt, and tie. From the waist down, he was nude. He went for walks in the mornings so he left the house without her seeing him. Very soon, she heard a scream: her neighbor was in the yard when he came out! The patient's action was not intentional and the consequences were less than funny, but she (and the other caregivers) was able to see the humor, besides the tragedy, in the situation. It takes time and *considerable psychological growth* to reach such maturity, however.

Increasing Pressures

The upshot of what has been said so far is that detrimental changes in behavior will continue and increase, which bring increasing pressure on both the patient and the caregiver, though not in the same ways or at the same time.

Patient Changes and Reactions

The chronology of events for patients begins when there is some incident that is discomforting, at least momentarily. The incident may represent a kind of "lost moment"—and truly be only momentary. In the case described in Chapter 1, Martha Wells was reported to have had such experiences. She became lost on her way to the grocery store, and had to have help in locating the mall. However, *she returned home without error or incident*. How can one explain such a paradox? Martha did by persuading herself that she had merely taken a wrong turn into a neighborhood that was new to her. This confabulation (an invention of an explanation to cover up faulty memory) is not unusual in persons developing dementia. The most common "explanation" for behavioral errors of this sort is that one is "just getting a little older."

As such events increase, there may be greater concern by the patient but continued cover-up of the events. When more critical incidents start to occur, the psychological effects may become disturbing and damaging. Without necessarily expressing any ideas to others (including the caregiver), the person may wonder: Why is this happening to me? The rhetorical answers may range from "I'm being punished for past actions" to "Someone is putting something in my food." The particular answer chosen will influence the way the patient reacts to everything that follows, from diagnosis to interaction with the caregiver.

Inevitably, in the many lucid moments that will remain, the patient may also ask: Can't someone help me? It is psychologically too threatening and potentially damaging to accept the idea that one is experiencing mental decline that will continue and expand. After all, the patient does not have any physical symptoms, there is no pain, life is still worth living. Why doesn't the doctor do something? There are all those wonder drugs; operations are performed to correct causes of illness; doctors are healers. Why can't I be healed? An example of the demand that something be done is the actions of AIDS patients, who have said they want treatment and cure *now*. Demonstrations, marches, and demands have not led to the achievement of effective intervention, even though research is ongoing. These patients have even said that they care little about others who need a cure and treatment for their illnesses. One may call the plaints sad or self-centered, but they illustrate the fact that those who are terminally ill or whose way of life is threatened want and even expect help immediately.

(On television recently, I personally saw a note of maturity in a young AIDS patient who said, "We were wrong to demand immediate use of experimental drugs and total focus on a cure for our problem.")

Once a diagnosis has been made, the patient must adjust his or her concept of reality. What has already happened may have been seen as unreal, an aberration that can be cleared up. That outcome is now no longer possible, although some patients may persist in seeking a solution anyway. In collaboration with the caregiver, there may be trials of so-called drugs that have been used in other parts of the world and found "successful." Sometimes there will be a search for a "healer," someone with more or less divine powers (at least by the healer's report). Obviously, such attempts are a waste of money—sometimes considerable amounts of money—but, even more importantly, there is a heavy investment of psychological energy that could be more realistically invested.

Whether or not some intervention is sought, the months following diagnosis will include movement toward acceptance. The patient has some advantage in this respect since he or she will become less mentally competent over time. This loss of capability reduces awareness, and the patient may become less concerned about matters that formerly caused stressful reactions. With the passage of time (perhaps years), those things that disturb the patient and lead to undesirable behaviors will center on creature comforts. The patient may become quite upset because there is no ice cream but be oblivious to any difficulties about finances.

The general perspective has changed to an increasingly self-centered one, even to taking advantage of the caregiver. One of the painful experiences that some caregivers have is that the patient does not realize how demanding he or she is, how unappreciative of the caregiver's efforts. Even if the caregiver expresses some feeling about such matters, the patient is not very likely to interpret it correctly and may be unconcerned within moments.

This general perspective reflects an altered reality on the part of the patient. From our external view, it may seem that the patient lives in an unreal world—and it is as compared with our world view. But the patient will continue to experience a reality that seems regressive to the outsider, in certain ways childlike and simplistic and in other ways demanding and self-centered. An area of research needed in psychology is investigation of the limits and meaning of reality to dementia patients. Once understood, there may result a comprehension that will allow communication at the patient's level of reality. This would permit interventions currently unknown with better direction of the competencies still remaining to the patient.

Caregiver Changes and Reactions

Though there will be some overlap and congruence in reactions of patients and caregivers to the dementing behaviors, there also will be some distinct differences. The experiences of the early period of the developing dementia will be interpreted differently by the two, in all probability. Those "lost moments" that the patient interpreted as unimportant or reconstructed to be psychologically more acceptable may have a different meaning to you, the caregiver. When behavioral errors are made by the patient, you may see them as deliberate attempts to create problems, to be perverse, to cause difficulties, or to evade responsibility. When Martha Wells "forgot" the appointment with her daughter, she confabulated a reasonable excuse. You may remember that she made up, on the spur of the moment, a story that a neighbor had needed help. Her daughter accepted this report, and as the day wore on, Martha persuaded herself that the story was factual. By contrast, when Martha fixed liver for dinner, her husband became angry since neither of them liked liver. Martha's reaction was to become belligerent and to cry.

The *interpretation* of events, then, is a personal matter. Since there has not yet been a diagnosis, either viewpoint may be defended and accepted. Until such time as the "critical incident" occurs, there may be many incidents where misunderstanding and disagreement are the norm. Unless the two persons are willing to discuss the behaviors and what they mean, there will be no resolution. When the critical event does take place, the psychological implications are profound. Both parties begin to reassess and reinterpret, although the conclusions drawn may not be beneficial.

After consultation with a physician and a diagnosis that points to dementia, caretakers are apt to experience increasing uneasiness about the future. For one thing, the normal order of life may have to change. Perhaps the patient has taken responsibility for certain elements in the relationship, such as keeping home accounts and paying bills. If there has already been a problem in bookkeeping, the caregiver will have to take over such a duty at once. Even if there has not been a problem in this area, eventually there will be. The caregiver has to undertake an assessment of the skills still remaining to the patient and those that are undergoing loss. This task is ongoing since, with time, most or all competencies will be lost.

The meaning of dementia to the caregiver focuses on the developing and expanding burdens of caring for a dementia patient. Finding the resources and energy to cope with such demands will be a considerable part of reality for you. Instead of continuing to have some life of your own, there will be an increasing need to protect and provide for the patient. The nominal tasks of life, once shared, will be forced on you. This means that you must take care of all matters of living: shopping, transportation, housekeeping, and the rest. In addition, the fabric of life will become more stinted: social relationships must decrease, perhaps end; supports will evaporate to some degree; personal intimacy will be lost; and so on.

Reality to the caregiver becomes congruent with patient demands. The patient's psychological losses may cause a perspective that increases stress and frustration as time goes on. The day may be too short to accomplish everything that needs to be done and take care of the patient at the same time. Physical strain, even exhaustion, may result and lead to illness. Emotional turmoil may impair even the strongest relationship and make it more difficult to feel concern for anyone else. The caretaker must develop means to cope with such distressing circumstances. Reality may become defined as simply making it to the next moment, literally.

If the caregiver was not already persuaded, there now comes the awareness that the inevitability of dementia is burden and loss. Handling such an inevitable outcome requires psychological resources that the caregiver may possess only in a limited fashion. The caregiver must develop from somewhere within some added capabilities, but how can that be accomplished? Most caregivers do not have the background of experience or education to do so. Though some caregivers may become dejected and defeated and give up hope, most seek help. These efforts may take several directions (support groups, counseling, education, and so on) but the outcome, when successful, is greater psychological strength, capacity, and proficiency.

The picture presented thus far may seem brutal and disturbing. It may appear that things are hopeless and that achieving some measure of success in coping is at best only a product of chance—luck at finding the right source for help. However, the very fact that you are reading this book is an indication that you believe in the positive possibilities even in the worst of circumstances. In the remainder of this chapter, I consider the kinds of *psychological* variables that operate in the caregiving of a dementia patient, what these variables mean, and how they may be controlled, if negative, and used, if positive.

Stress

The study of stress has been going on for over 40 years. It began as research on physical changes in the body that occur under conditions that may be labeled physically stressful. These investigations, which were conducted on animals, yielded the fact that *all* stressors elicited the same set of physical signs. Psychologists soon became interested in the possibility of such changes in human beings placed under psychological stress. By and large, the same results have been obtained as those found with animals.

We may define *stress* as the result of exposing a person to stressors (any event which causes stress). That is, if you are put into a situation where you feel fear (such as seeing a bear), you may feel stress as a result. You are just as likely to feel stress if you are in a setting where you feel incompetent (such as being asked to perform a difficult task). Thus, stress results from sources that threaten either physical or psychological harm. If the stress is long term and unrelieved, the individual may be unable to function well on tasks that are normally easy. Illness may even occur from excess stress. This consequence has led to the development of psychosomatic medicine, where the physical evidence of an illness is present from psychological causation. Some physicians believe, for example, that certain cancers are psychosomatic, along with such illnesses as stomach ulcers and hypertension (high blood pressure). There is even the possibility that much stress over a long period may cause death. Obviously, then, stress is an important concept for those who are in positions where they encounter many stressors, and this certainly applies to dementia patients and caregivers.

The Physical–Psychological Continuum

Stress expresses itself in physical symptoms that are recognizable to the person under stress. These physical symptoms include increased heart rate, increased respiration (breathing), higher blood pressure than normal, faster pulse rate, and a kind of uneasy feeling, usually in the stomach. Such reactions occur in both animals and humans. Although the intensity of any one of these reactions may vary from one individual to another, they are common to all stress-related conditions. If you saw a bear in your yard, for example, it seems reasonable that you would feel fear to some degree. You would note some changes in your body as well.

Your heart would begin to beat faster, you would breathe more rapidly, and you would have a feeling of uneasiness.

Why do these reactions occur? Psychologists and physiologists believe that they prepare us to protect ourselves. In the general sense, we are organizing our bodies to *do something,* and there are two possible things we can do. One is to get away from the bear as quickly as possible. The other is to stand our ground and physically attack the bear if it threatens us. Just which one we do is dependent on a number of circumstances that are both personal and social in nature. If we are unprepared and defenseless, we may well run; if we are hunting bear and have a rifle, we may take careful aim and shoot. The point is that our bodies will be aroused to do something that is consistent with self-protection and purpose.

The "fight-or-flight" idea may not seem very pertinent to the difficulties associated with caregiving of a dementia patient. In the literal sense, it is not. However, the physical expressions of stress are often present to some degree, and, under certain conditions, to a high degree. When a patient leaves the house, for example, unattended and unaware of where he or she is going, the caregiver may experience a stress reaction until the patient is located. If the dementia victim becomes physically abusive and is stronger and healthier than the caregiver, the physical symptomatology of stress would seem a reasonable component of caregiver behavior. We may put less emphasis on this physical dimension of stress but that does not mean it is an unimportant component. If the caregiving act proves too stressful in the physical sense, you may find yourself unable to continue to meet your needs and the patient's. Indeed, *you* may develop physical illness from the many pressures and be unable to continue caregiving.

Being under stress also produces some psychological expressions. Stress that seems to be overwhelming will lead to feelings of insecurity. These feelings will apply not only to the act of caregiving but generalize to other behaviors as well. You may eventually conclude that you can no longer do anything, even though that is not true. As a caregiver, for example, you may find that making ends meet financially is becoming increasingly difficult. Not only are you having trouble paying all the bills each month but you are aware that the fixed income you have to live on is worth less each year. What is going to happen to you and your patient? If there is a medical emergency, how can it be handled? Suppose you have to place the patient in a nursing home? The costs may be prohibitive given your circumstances. Insecurity about your competencies could be a result of such circumstances.

Even if you can feel secure, you may find yourself faced with another of the psychological expressions of stress: feelings of frustration. We experience "frustration" when we cannot reach a desired goal. For example, you may want to continue providing a loving, emotionally secure, happy, and pleasant home for yourself and your patient throughout the rest of your lifetimes. Given the consequences and circumstances of dementia, however, you may find more conflict between yourself and the patient than you want. There may be decreasing loving physical and emotional contact between the two of you. You may find that friends no longer come around and that even your children seem to be deserting you to some degree. If you do not feel frustrated at such outcomes, you are a fortunate and strong individual indeed!

In addition to insecurity and frustration, the caregiving act may lead to overt aggression under certain circumstances. Fortunately, most of us make a special effort to avoid confrontation that will lead to such a consequence, but in some cases it may be unable to avoid. Understanding why an individual becomes aggressive may suggest what can be done when a physical attack occurs. First of all, we must understand that aggression (in either the physical or verbal sense) is the result of frustration—having our needs go unfulfilled or our problems unresolved. If we experience *enough* frustration, aggression is much more likely to occur. How much is enough? The answer to that depends on the individual and the situation. If you are unable to maintain the type of home you would like but you are able to feel secure and worthwhile, the trade-off may be sufficient to keep you from lashing out at the patient or family members. If, however, you are not only frustrated by home conditions but also by the lack of money and the constant demands of the patient, you may have more of a tendency toward some attack. (Hopefully, if that happens it is directed toward an inanimate object rather than a person. Later in this chapter, I will discuss some of the ways we can channel our feelings.) What seems to be the most defensible position is that the more frustration we experience, the more apt we are to be aggressive. Early in the development of dementia, a patient may become difficult to deal with and verbally belabor the caregiver. Although this reaction is undeserved and hurts the feelings of the caregiver, we can understand why it occurred if we examine the frightening and difficult changes that the patient is experiencing. In turn, you may not be happy with some of your own words or actions but you act aggressively because you know of no better way to handle the frustrations. (There are better ways that you can learn and use, as we will see later.)

Finally, a psychological expression of stress may be feelings of conflict. You may feel that it is your duty to care for the dementia patient, but you also wish that you could be out of the situation altogether so that you could lead a fuller life. One of the factors that seems to be involved in early placement of a patient in a nursing home is just this kind of conflict. I know a caregiver who was about 15 years younger than her husband. When he developed behaviors that led to the eventual diagnosis of dementia, she immediately made arrangements for him to go to a nursing home. She was honest: he had already disrupted her life more than she thought defensible. The knowledge that things were only going to get worse was more than she was willing to accept. She could afford the placement and go on with her life. We may not agree with her reasoning, but I maintain that what she did was in the best interest of *both* her and her husband. Had she continued the act of caregiving under such conflict, the misery and discord would have been devastating to both of them.

Although it is likely that any or all of these psychological reactions to stress may occur in caregivers, they need not become overwhelming or destructive of one's personality. If you are willing to recognize and admit to any or all of these expressions, there are actions that can help you handle them more successfully than you might think. If, however, they are not addressed in some fashion, they can be detrimental to you.

Psychological Controls for Stress

Human beings are highly adaptive. The development of the cortex has permitted us to think, plan, and create in ways not possible for other life forms. Essentially, instead of having to conform to the demands of the environment, we can alter the environment to conform to our needs and desires. The result has been civilization, continuing adaptation and change.

Unfortunately, all the change has not been positive. Many of the things done by humans lead to conflict. If I wish to become wealthy, I may have to take advantage of people who have done me no harm. In some way, I need to persuade myself that I am still a "good" and "worthwhile" person. I may defend myself psychologically by explaining and interpreting my actions in some way that resolves the conflict. When I do so, I do not feel the guilt and stress that I would otherwise feel. As an example, the landlord who rents substandard housing may defend his action by saying, "It's all those kinds of people really want or need." Most of us learn early on to use such conflict-resolving mechanisms with facility and skill.

This idea can be extended to some of the actions of both patients and caregivers. For example, if a patient becomes frustrated to the point that he explodes at someone else, the patient may deny that he is in any way responsible. Instead, he may blame the outburst on the other individual. The patient will not consider the various causes for his frustration and the subsequent outburst, largely because they will be things that he feels cannot be dealt with. In the same way, the caregiver may need to resolve conflict. For example, a caretaker may have guilt feelings about wishing to be rid of the caretaking responsibility. At the same time, she feels it is her duty to take care of the patient. These opposing feelings may be handled by refusing to admit to the desire to be rid of the patient. Martyrdom may become the goal in this case.

The "Defense Mechanisms"

Feelings such as those described above, however formed, are most often handled by the use of what psychologists call defense mechanisms. A variety of defense mechanisms have been proposed and described. Although they were developed in psychoanalytic theory (Freudian psychology), they may be given a more behavioral interpretation as well. Some of the more relevant ones for managing problems arising from dementia will be discussed. Although all of them may be used by either patient or caregiver, they are presented here in the situations where they are most often found.

Patient-Oriented Mechanisms

Patients are faced with a world that increasingly presents frightening events that they may neither understand nor know how to deal with. As a result, psychological adjustment will often involve avoidance behaviors. One such psychological device is called *rationalization*, defined as the creation of plausible but untrue reasons for some behavior or thought. Martha Wells "explained" to her husband that the casserole she prepared must have been too salty because of the ingredients. In this way, she did not have to admit to herself (or him) that she could no longer always be trusted to be accurate in her cooking skills. She did not fool her husband but she may have been able to fool herself. By doing so, she preserved her feelings of integrity.

Remember that Martha had spent her adulthood in the tasks of homemaker and felt pride and worth in her efforts. It is not easy to accept the possibility of failure and inability under such circumstances. In fact, it is very probable that rationalization would continue as a part of Martha's behavior pattern so long as she attempts to continue old roles. You and I may say that such little instances of rationalization cannot be all that important. Their "importance" depends on the circumstances and the interpretation. In this case, her husband simply ignored her explanation. In other instances, that may not be so easy to do.

For example, let us suppose that you and a patient are shopping. Since you cannot watch her constantly, you are unaware that she picks up an object that is momentarily attractive and puts it in her pocket. After you have checked out and are leaving the store, the manager stops you and says that shoplifting is prosecuted, and indeed, you find the object from the store in the patient's possession. When you react with some anger, the patient says, "You told me I could take it." The result is a major problem that will require an extensive amount of sorting out. You have been made the agent responsible for the theft! As you see, rationalizations are not always innocent and harmless.

A second defense that patients may use is called *regression*. In regression, the patient uses a means of thinking and behaving that is more consistent with a younger age, even reverting to childhood. There may be a strong display of temper if the patient wants candy, for instance, and the caregiver says that there is none, but some will be purchased the next time they go to the store. The resulting tantrum is more like that of a 3-year-old child than of an adult.

Regression may be displayed in a patient's reactions to requests. For example, a patient may be told that it is time for a bath and not only refuse to bathe but throw a temper tantrum (literally). The tasks of caregiving are magnified under such conditions. The mechanism may be used because it restores the patient to a less stressful, perhaps happier time. It is also a means of avoiding the demands of the present, including responsibility for one's actions. It is a particularly difficult device for caregivers to deal with because of the strength of the denial implied by using the defense.

A third defense mechanism that may be found in patients is

isolation. Here, the patient withdraws from normal contact and may even become reclusive (in effect, a hermit). Isolation may be a reaction to events that the individual feels incompetent to face. With the Alzheimer's patient, this may take the form of refusing to leave the house. The caregiver will find it impossible to take the patient to a doctor, shopping, or any other outside event. A substitute must be found to remain with the patient while the caregiver leaves the house. There is some chance that an isolation reaction is part of the explanation for those patients who refuse to change clothes. The problem may focus on the patient's feeling that he or she can no longer interact effectively with others because there is too much threat of disclosure of one's limitations. In our case study from Chapter 1, Martha may be isolating herself by decreasing contacts with her children and friends. Eventually, Sam may be faced with a spouse who will be unable to carry out any of the duties outside the home that she at present is still functionally capable of doing.

Caregiver-Oriented Mechanisms

As a caregiver, you are increasingly faced with the need to protect two persons: yourself and the patient. To do so, you may have to use *compensation*, that is, substitution of a strength for a weakness. Compensation can be negative if the strength developed is harmful to the self or others. For example, if you compensate for your antagonism toward the patient by becoming a tyrant, the outcome will be greater conflict and discord than before. However, if you compensate for the anger you feel in the situation by concentrating on providing as comfortable and complete care as possible, you may handle the situation much better. In fact, there may be some slow but steady reduction in the antagonism you feel. We *can* modify our attitudes just as we can our behaviors. The technique required is to gradually replace the undesirable attitude in a slow but progressive way, taking it one step at a time. Identify what single element in your attitude may be easiest to change and work on that first. Once you feel secure in the change, go to the next element. You continue, then, until you have successfully changed your manner of thinking.

For the particular feeling of antagonism, let's consider what is involved. First of all, you need to be objective. You must analyze *what* your feelings are and *why* they exist. In an honest assessment you might conclude that you dislike the demands that are placed on you. They seem unfair and they deprive you of any opportunity to do what *you* want to do. We will concentrate on this latter point first: doing what *you* want to do. Specifically, you might ask what it is you would like to do that is possible without leaving the caregiver demands completely. You could even make a list, then examine each item for its plausibility. If your list consists of such items as "get out of the house for awhile," "visit my sister in Chicago," and "spend some time at the lake," a theme is evident. The pressures you feel are real but their solution is not so easily provided.

Certainly, the first item, if it means just a chance to go downtown alone, or sit on a park bench for a while, is the most plausible. Is there someone who can replace you for an hour or so two or three days a week? If so, fine. If not, you may have to be a bit more creative. Call your Alzheimer's Association chapter, or your local Area Agency on Aging, or the Council of Churches. Are there volunteers who will take such a role for you? The chances are good that you *will* find someone. You are also problem solving in a realistic way, and that may reduce your negative feelings somewhat. With success, you can then proceed to make other changes in the situation that would help you feel less burdened. Compensate by using your strengths that are directed toward self-actualization.

The second point in your assessment dealt with unfairness. Of course, the demands of caregiving *are* unfair. You should accept the fact that you are imposed on and that you are justified to feel some anger about that truth. Once that is done, rather than slip into petulance or even depression, remind yourself that you are capable of handling even the burdens that caregiving brings. Recall your strengths and competencies. Take the position that you will cope even under circumstances that are unfair. Reward yourself for efforts you make to control your self-pity. The reinforcer can be a feeling of success or a treat of some kind. As you continue such efforts, positive reactions and actions will become the norm.

Displacement is another defense mechanism that may be used by the caregiver. It is defined as taking out your feelings on something that cannot retaliate rather than the true cause. The old example of "kicking the cat" fits here. If your boss causes you a problem, you may not do anything until you get home. Then you may take it out on an animal that does not know what brought all this on, and cannot do anything about it anyway. In effect, when energy is generated it must be expelled. It can be returned directly or displaced onto an alternate.

Displacement can negatively affect caregiving as well. For example, you may displace your frustration about being ignored by family members by refusing to prepare some dish that the patient particularly likes. In essence, you try to express your anger in a way that will not lead to retaliation but may make you feel a little better. However, there are many positive displacement responses as well. For the same instance (being ignored by family), you may displace your anger by doing something worthwhile. You may have been intending to give the house a good cleaning but have been too tired to do so. Now that you have all this energy, express it by starting your cleaning job. Whatever you get done will improve both the appearance of your house and your personal pique. The point is, whenever you cannot deal directly with the source of the frustration, find some replacement activity that will be positive in its results.

The third kind of defense mechanism that may be used by caregivers is *sublimation*. The use of this device is usually considered a positive effort because some useful or creative product may result. In fact, it is defined as expressing one's unachievable desires in some reasonable and more acceptable form. In that sense, it becomes a means of self-fulfillment. As a caregiver, you may wish to be better educated. Since the demands on your time and energy are so great, you cannot take time to attend classes at a college. This does not mean that you may not reach your goal, however. There are a number of educational sources that offer classes by extension, including by mail. You might enroll in a class of interest, taking it either for credit or audit, receive the textbook and study materials, and take tests as you are ready. There is a cost, of course, and you must find some time to study, but *you* set the schedule.

If money is a problem, you can get books from a local library. Many libraries have bookmobiles so that you don't have to take time every week or so to go to the library. Once you have decided what resources you need, you work as quickly or slowly as you wish.

You may even sublimate by becoming creative. If you have a talent that you want to develop further, pursue it rather than becoming enmeshed only in the caregiving act. You cannot avoid the tasks of everyday life, but you can add some positive factors to your life. With more zest for living, your burdens may not seem so severe.

Defenses Common to Both Parties

In some instances, a defense mechanism may be used by either the patient or caregiver, perhaps even at the same time. In *projection*, individuals deny that a trait or behavior is present in themselves but presume to see it in others. This trait or behavior is normally something that causes shame. The shame is avoided by the projection. We are using projection any time we "see" in others something that we refuse to see in ourselves. I recall many years ago working with a man who professed to be opposed to the more permissive changes in society. As a volunteer, he was the director of a youth program. Whenever several of us were going to a convention, he would always request one colleague to bring his Playboy Club key. Of course, he was not interested in the lurid nature of such places, but it was his responsibility to know what kinds of temptations there were in the world. That way he was better prepared to protect the youth with whom he worked. We suspected that his explanation was more projection than realism.

Either a patient or caregiver may use the mechanism to avoid facing some reaction that would cause anxiety. Thus, there may be some desire to act out a feeling (such as aggression) or an impulsive behavior (such as sexual expression), but to avoid confronting our own guilt or shame we assume the feeling or behavior is present in the other person. Carried to an extreme, the use of projection can lead to paranoid symptoms (described later in this chapter).

Denial is exactly what the word implies: one refuses to admit to a reality no matter how obvious or how definitive the case. We see some denial in almost everyone who has just experienced the death of someone close. In fact, some psychologists consider a period of denial to be a part of the normal grief process. We may also practice denial if some onerous or threatening accusation is made about someone close to us.

Patients frequently deny that they have problems resulting from a developing dementia. This denial is personal (to themselves) as well as public (to the caregiver). Martha Wells (in the case study) denied that she was responsible for irrational behavior when she fixed liver for dinner. In fact, she told her husband that it was his request. Patients also often deny that they have difficulties in ordinary activities. One problem reported by caregivers is patients' denial that they have become too confused to be trusted as the driver of a car. Patients will often protest that they are just as competent as ever.

Caregivers may deny certain objective facts as well—for example, that the burdens of caretaking are causing distress and physical strain. However, caregivers may insist that they are functioning well and can continue without assistance. Or, there may be increasing financial concern; income is just not sufficient to meet all the needs of the two. Yet, if questioned by professionals or even children and family members, the caregiver may say that there is no problem. Denial is not a productive form of defense since it leaves an already vulnerable individual even more vulnerable.

A final defense mechanism is *reaction formation*. Here, we take a position or express an attitude that is really the opposite of what we believe but cannot accept. For example, even if a caregiver dislikes the patient, the caregiver's approach may be an intense effort to appear concerned and involved. Of course, the caregiver believes that this is a true expression rather than a cover-up. If the patient has animosity toward the caregiver, he or she may instead profess how important the caregiver is to him or her. Indeed, there may be expressions of appreciation.

Defense mechanisms are developed by all of us and used in stressful situations. If we are not aware of what our actions really mean, we are apt to assume that our behavior is logical, reasonable, straightforward, and acceptable. Honesty must be exercised, along with objectivity, if we are to control or redirect efforts that are distressing or harmful. It is a good idea for all of us occasionally to examine our own actions and motives with a critical eye. The experience may not be pleasant, but we are capable of change if we are willing to make the effort.

Psychological Disorders and Dementia

There are some conditions that may be found in patients and caregivers that have no known physical cause but that do interfere with the ability to interact successfully with others. These states are called "functional disorders" because they disrupt our ability to function well. When we are under stress, we may not be able to analyze our problems accurately. As a result, we may think *ir*rationally rather than rationally, and our attempts at resolution of the difficulty may be inappropriate. In the patient, such disorders should be viewed separately from the brain disorder. In the caregiver, the potential for functional disorders as a reaction to the stress involved with caregiving should be checked often. Functional disorders are treatable, either with drugs or therapy or both. They should not be neglected, because they can become so severe that the person may suffer a breakdown in behavior that will be expensive and difficult to treat.

There are three functional disorders of concern to individuals who are involved with dementia, whether as patient or caregiver. These are anxiety, depression, and delusional behavior (paranoia). Depression is the most commonly recognized, diagnosed, and discussed. Nevertheless, both anxiety and paranoid symptoms can occur often enough to require some understanding for recognition of symptoms.

Anxiety

All of us will experience anxiety at some times in our lives because we live in a complex and stressful world. In dementia patients and caregivers, however, anxiety can be more intense and disruptive than is true in the rest of us. It is defined as an *intense* feeling of dread that something bad is going to happen. The result is the physical symptoms given for stress reactions: increased heart and respiration rates, high blood pressure, and so on. The feeling of fear that accompanies these physiological reactions can interfere with all normal thinking processes.

Psychologists recognize two expressions of anxiety: reactive (also called panic disorder) and generalized (or free-floating, because it affects much or all of behavior). Reactive anxiety is usually sudden in onset, short lived, and often of known origin. An example is the fear of spiders. Seeing a spider causes some people to react with panic, but they usually do something to remove the fear; the spider may be killed or the person may simply leave the environment. By contrast, generalized anxiety is expressed to so many aspects of life that it is impossible to specify what causes it. This type of anxiety is more common in old age, when there are often many reasons to worry about life's circumstances. Living on a fixed income, physical changes and declines that make one feel helpless, the death of a spouse or close friends, and the like, assume a larger role in the lives of the elderly than in young adults.

It seems reasonable that patients will experience anxiety (or increases in anxiety) as dementia begins to express itself. Seeing evidence that part of your life is out of control, being unable to remember important facts at times, and seeing your skills diminish are ample reasons to be anxious, especially if you are not yet aware that Alzheimer's is the cause of such problems. As the dementia progresses and memory loss and confusion increase, anxiety may subside until it eventually disappears. However, while it is present, it needs identification and treatment to relieve the symptoms.

With caregivers, the sources of anxiety may be few at first. With time, and increasing problem behaviors in the patient, generalized anxiety may become more prominent. Once there is the realization that the difficulties of the patient are only beginning (after diagnosis, in other words), anxiety may well become more intense. Intervention with treatment can assist the caregiver through the years when the patient continues to decline mentally.

Treatment may consist of medication, psychological therapy, or both. The drugs used to treat anxiety are called "anxiolytics" because they help to reduce stress. They are really mild sedatives. Patients will usually not experience side effects although careful monitoring is required. In an aging brain that is experiencing damage to nerve cells, the possibility of some disturbing side effects is increased. Even in caregivers, there may be some undesirable effects, so monitoring is suggested. For both, dosage may be decreased if problems result. Since there are several drugs available, the doctor can change the prescription until a safe drug is found. Overall, treatment with anxiolytics has been successful.

An alternative form of treatment is therapy with a skillful, well-trained, empathic, and competent counselor. In many instances, the most useful form of therapy is short term and insight oriented. Older persons are more likely to accept and benefit from such an approach. This type of therapy focuses on current circumstances in the life of the person rather than on elements in his or her past history. It can be successful with either patient or caregiver when it is instituted at the appropriate time and in a suitable way.

With some persons, biofeedback also helps control the symptoms of anxiety. This procedure requires that a person be trained in ways to control physiological processes (e.g., increases in heart rate). In the training sessions, the individual is hooked up to machines that measure the processes, and is supplied with information about what is happening as control is attempted. There is some dispute over the success of such an intervention and it certainly is not plausible with many caregivers and especially with dementia patients.

If the patient or caregiver has a history of anxiety as an adult, the chances of more severe anxiety reactions and the need for some attempts at intervention are increased. Remember, however, that most older persons experience "losses" that cannot be accommodated or replaced. These almost inevitably are going to cause anxiety even if there has been little or none in the past. Since dementia patients and their caregivers experience intense changes and intrusions in their lives, there is a greater probability that anxiety will be aroused. Patients and caregivers suffer enough without the added burden of a functional disorder. Caregivers should seek diagnosis and help when they notice the symptoms of anxiety, either in themselves or in their patients.

Depression

Widespread across the age groups, depression is a major mental health problem in many parts of the world. When we are depressed, we feel dejected, hopeless, and worthless. For most of us, fortunately, these reactions do not occur often and are mild when they do. Generally, we feel sorry for ourselves but work out of it in a few hours or a day. A mild depression, then, has very little effect on our ability to function. At times, though, the symptoms may be greater and more distressing. When a moderate depression occurs, we will take somewhat longer to recover (say, a few days) but still not incur major debilitating effects on functioning. Even so, both mild and moderate levels of depression must be taken seriously and may require intervention by a professional. It is just as true, however, that *we will come out of the depression after some period of time even without treatment.*

In its most severe form, called major depression by psychologists, we reach a serious level at which we *must* be helped. In a major depression, negative feelings are very strong and will persist for long periods of time unless there is intervention. In addition, a severely depressed individual will lose interest in everything, including the appetites; there will probably be difficulty in sleeping (insomnia) and a feeling of not being rested even when the person does sleep. If you should suffer a major depression, it is very likely that you will feel the situation is hopeless. You will make no effort to help yourself even with encouragement from others. You may even contemplate suicide. This is the major reason that depression is considered so dangerous although the inability to function is also very important.

There are drugs (antidepressants) that can help reduce the symptoms. They have been developed on the theory that depression results from low levels of certain chemicals (the catecholamines) in the brain. Their effect is to increase the level of these chemicals and thereby reduce the intensity of the depression. They do work in many instances, but they also are dangerous in some respects and so they must be used carefully. This warning applies particularly to the elderly, including dementia patients.

As with other functional disorders, various therapies may be used by the psychologist to help the depressed patient recover. Today, there tends to be a preference for cognitive-behavioral approaches with older persons. These place emphasis on the current events in the life of the person in the belief that learning to deal successfully with stressful events will reduce depression. This idea is particularly suited to dementia patients and caregivers since they experience so many events that could lead to depression of some degree from mild to severe.

The therapist will explain that *we* are responsible for creating our own moods. We do so by our thought processes; something causes us to feel gloomy and we can begin to enlarge that feeling until we become more generally depressed. A technique for warding off depression, then, is to interrupt that negative thought process. Better yet, we can learn to recognize it as it begins and stall it by changing our direction of thinking. In other words, as we recognize that we are thinking negatively, we can deliberately reject that notion and move to positive thoughts instead. This approach is based on the model of a psychiatrist named Aaron Beck (one of his works is listed in the Bibliography). A practical application of the procedure and how it works can be found in the book *Feeling Good* by David Burns (also in the Bibliography).

What is important is that *you* can help yourself if you will make the concerted effort to recognize your feelings and interrupt them if they are negative. The caregiving task is filled with opportunities for you to become depressed. Those persons who can meet the demands and burdens of caregiving without at times feeling sorry for themselves are fantastic personalities. Most of us are not so competent. When you begin to feel a little sorry for yourself, STOP! This feeling is the first step to becoming depressed. Force yourself to consider something that is pleasant, and particularly something that was good in the caregiving task recently. For example, if you believe that you simply cannot make ends meet financially and that fact makes you start to feel sad, remind yourself of something that you did well. Perhaps you fixed a dish that your patient has always liked and you were rewarded by an expression of "Oh, how good. I really love it." Even such a minor victory as this can bring feelings of worth: "I can do things that are good, and I do them." Now, the financial problem may not look quite so large and may lose some of its threat. At least you can now look at the problem in a more realistic way.

In the same way, the patient can be helped to be more positive about life. When it seems to you that the patient's mood is one of sadness, you may be able to interrupt that negativity by reminding him or her of some pleasant memories, recent or remote. These memories may help to break and redirect the mood. *After* the patient feels more positive and has returned to his or her usual mood, you might suggest the procedure to the patient and tell how it has helped you to deal with some bad moments. Early on in the dementia process, the patient may well have greater psychological stress than you do. Hard as this is to believe, you must realize that a person who is losing control of his or her mental faculties even though he or she is otherwise healthy is facing an overwhelming strain. It will not be easy to interrupt negative thinking by outside suggestion. Patients are more apt to need professional counseling for their depressions. It is also true, however, that a time will come when the patient has lost enough mental ability that stress is seldom or never present. Negative thinking will not occur under those circumstances, at least in the sense in which it induces depression. *Your* opportunities to become depressed, however, will remain and may even increase as time goes on. Your need to remain as psychologically healthy as possible is all the more necessary. One component of that health is to recognize negative thinking and do something about it.

Although the thinking act is central to warding off depression, other techniques can be used. For example, a depressed patient in therapy will be asked to keep a log of his or her activities during the time between sessions. One portion of this listing will be for positive things that happened and the other for negative things. The therapist will not be surprised when the patient returns for the next session (usually in a week) without such a list. If there is a list, it will almost certainly be full of negative occurrences, perhaps to the exclusion of *anything* that happened of a positive nature. After all, depression is expressed through negativity, and the more depressed the patient, the greater the pessimism. Each item in the list will be discussed and the therapist will try to move the patient in a more positive direction by inquiring about other events before and after discussing the ones listed. In other words, the intent is to help the patient realize that not *everything* in life is bad, it is just that he or she is focusing on the worst elements. You may remember the words from a song by Johnny Mercer that was so popular during the 1940s: "Accentuate the positive, eliminate the negative." Mr. Mercer may not have been trained as a psychologist but he certainly understood one of the crucial elements in cognitive-behavioral therapy.

The discussion so far might leave the impression that cognitive-behavioral therapy is always successful for all persons. That is not true, though the method certainly deserves a try since it can *prevent* a depressive episode which a patient would otherwise have rather than having to receive treatment. You save time, money, and discomfort if the approach works for you. Those elements can be better expended on the realities of the caregiving situation; that is, you are able to invest your efforts in a more positive direction. Both you and the patient benefit in this instance.

For some persons, even with legitimate efforts to use cognitive-behavioral techniques, the method is not suitable and does not work. There are other ways to help those experiencing psychological difficulties. Each is a systematic effort to help alleviate the mental anguish being experienced, and to prevent further difficulties. There are over 100 therapies that are currently being used by professionals. This is not to say that they are all effective; in fact, some may prove harmful to some individuals. For example, one form of therapy advocates that punishment of responses is the best way to help a patient avoid a given response. Usually used with behaviors such as smoking, effort is directed toward punishing the patient each time the negative behavior occurs. The punishment may be verbal or physical. This may work in some circumstances but seems inappropriate for dementia patients or caregivers who are already experiencing considerable punishment.

One of the oldest therapies, and the one most often preferred by psychiatrists, is psychoanalytic theory. Proposed by Sigmund Freud over 100 years ago, it is still used although often with certain modifications in the model and in practice. Freud believed that we have a conscious mind and an unconscious mind. It is in the latter that we store the thoughts and feelings that are unacceptable to us. This process begins in childhood and will exert its greatest pressure as we become adults and face situations that bring conflict. Therapists who use this model favor exploring the unconscious as the means to resolving the psychological disorders we may have. The method takes time, perhaps even several years, and is very expensive. Whether it is suitable for older adults is problematic. Even more so is its suitability for dementia patients and their caregivers.

The point is that you may have so much psychological pain that you cannot handle it. Recognizing the need for professional help is a strength, not a weakness. If you are depressed and cannot seem to shake the sadness and loss of self-esteem that depression brings, you should be mature enough to seek the help you need. In doing so, ask questions that will ensure that you enter an acceptable therapy that will prove helpful to you. All therapists are not alike in their practices, and I am unable to say that any therapist is appropriate. In Chapter 8, there is further discussion of this issue.

Earlier, mention was made of drugs that may be used to lessen the intensity of depression. These antidepressants can only be prescribed by physicians. Since psychologists do not have a medical degree, they cannot give drugs. If you are in therapy and the psychologist believes that you would benefit from one of the antidepressants, he or she will refer you to a physician for a final decision. The therapist's choice of a doctor is not a blind one; he or she will have contacts with certain physicians and, indeed, may be associated as a colleague. Antidepressants may have adverse side effects, sometimes extreme ones, so the decision whether or not to use them is an important one. When should these drugs be prescribed? A major element in the decision is the *degree* of depression being experienced. In all probability, only in severe cases, where the possibility of suicide is great, will such medication be prescribed. Even severely depressed people may recover eventually even without treatment or intervention.

The life-threatening element in major depression, then, is the depressed person's contemplation of suicide. Psychologists are very concerned about this possibility in every case. In fact, they will ask the patient if he or she has thought about suicide. If so, they will inquire about the means contemplated. Finally, they will ask whether the means is already available. When answers to these questions indicate a real danger or if the psychologist feels that the person is suicidal, the decision may be made to seek drug intervention. Most frequently, if the physician agrees, there will be hospitalization while the drug is used. This allows supervision of drug effects as well as avoids the implements contemplated for suicide. Obviously, then, drug therapy for depression is anything but routine.

If you are suffering depression, do not seek some medication or accept suggestions from others about something to take. It can be dangerous to do so. Age brings some alterations to the brain including destruction of neurons. Your body does not absorb and discard medicines as it did when you were younger. Effects from drugs can be more powerful, and interactions between several medications can be even more dangerous. Use appropriate steps: go to your doctor, accept therapy if it is recommended, and know *what* you are taking and *why*. Dementia patients are even more at risk. Their brains have experienced even more changes and cell destruction. More physicians are being cautious in prescribing drugs under such circumstances. Nursing homes voluntarily are moving toward taking residents off as many drugs as possible without threatening their well-being. You should be realistic and use caution to avoid greater problems in the future.

Paranoid Symptoms

Paranoia is a condition in which some personal threat is perceived in the environment. This danger can be either a person or a thing that the individual will try to avoid. The perception is mostly false, the paranoid person having *altered* the nature of reality in some way. Since paranoia is an attempt to deal with some malfunction in life in an adaptive way, it is considered a functional disorder.

The misperception is called a *delusion*. A delusion has some factual basis and is not a total creation of the mind of the individual (that would be considered a hallucination). For example, if a dementia patient complained that you were trying to harm him in some way when you were not, the psychologist would label the complaint as a delusion of persecution. There are various kinds of delusions, including those of grandeur, influence, and reference. In delusions of grandeur, a person feels an unwarranted sense of self-importance or indispensability. In delusions of influence, the person believes that others are trying to control his or her thoughts or actions. A delusion of reference refers to a person's belief that others are talking about or laughing at him or her even though they are not.

Although any of the expressions of paranoia are possible, the most common one in dementia patients is the delusion of persecution. This is understandable since there can be so many factors contributing to a feeling of being abused by others. The patient will interpret reality in ways that are consonant with the delusion, which is usually applied only to certain, restricted parts of his or her life. However, that may be no consolation to the caretaker. In fact, the caretaker may wish that somebody else could share some of the effects!

It is certain that some patients may react to the changes they are experiencing with misinterpretations that may be labeled delusional, and often the theme is paranoid (persecutory). As the patient's delusions begin, there is the possibility for misunderstandings between patient, caregiver, and family members. You need to be aware that paranoid systems may occur so that you will not be misled and hurt by what are undeserved accusations. If you are able to recognize the behavior of paranoia, you can report it to the doctor for referral for help.

At the same time, caretakers are not automatically exempted from some reactions that are paranoid. All of us probably occasionally feel that we are being manipulated or taken advantage of. What you must be willing to do in such instances is to examine the evidence objectively. If, in fact, you decide that your observation of being manipulated is correct, the remedy is to use assertive behavior to reach a resolution with those who are causing you the discomfort. (Assertiveness is discussed in Chapter 9.)

Summary

The demands and burdens of dementia bring enough problems to patients and caregivers that it would seem there should not be other difficulties. However, the very nature of dementia *increases* the probability that there will be ancillary complications. These include certain psychological effects that are recognized by professionals for their adverse effects.

The caregiver and patient are faced with a series of unexpected events and consequences. Mental changes at first may be subtle and so seldom expressed that they will be ignored or explained away. Eventually (from months to years), there will occur an incident so significant that the caregiver must admit that a major problem exists. There will be consultation with a doctor and subsequent diagnosis. If that diagnosis is some cause of dementia such as Alzheimer's disease, the caregiver and patient must move toward accepting the inevitable: progressive and irreversible memory loss, confusion, and disorientation in time and place.

The effects of dementia do not end here, however. There are psychological consequences that affect the personality to some degree. Stress, defined as physical or psychological strain on a person, will affect both patient and caregiver. Stress is shown by changes in heart and respiration rates, increased blood pressure and pulse rate, and other physical signs. These changes are preparation for self-protection. They have been described as equipping the body for "fight or flight." When we are put into a position that threatens our well-being in some way, it has been recognized for many years that we make such physical preparation and then act in some fashion. *How* we act will depend on conditions such as the degree of danger felt, the available resources we have, the need to consider social consequences of our actions, and so on. Since humans live in such a complex and complicated world, a direct action (either to flee or fight) is not often possible. As a result, the stress remains and may be expressed in feelings of insecurity, frustration, aggression, and conflict. Again, what we do about such feelings depends on our history (how we have responded in the past), the social implications, and personal resources.

Part of the attempt to adapt to stress is to use means that will protect us against psychological distress and pain. These efforts are called "defense mechanisms." They are means we have learned through experience to help us cope with problems. There are probably many kinds of defenses available to us, but those that apply most directly to dementia patients and their caregivers are described in this chapter. Many patients will display rationalization (using plausible but untrue reasons for an action or thought), regression (using earlier, perhaps childish, ways of thinking or acting), or isolation (becoming reclusive to avoid facing difficult situations). Among caregivers, typical defense mechanisms are compensation (developing strength in one area to overcome weakness in another), displacement (substituting one action for another that cannot be attained), or sublimation (expressing an unachievable desire in an achievable way). Both patient and caregiver may show instances of projection (seeing in others what we cannot accept in ourselves), denial (refusing to accept reality), and reaction formation (taking a position or attitude that is the opposite of what we really believe).

Functional disorders are psychological efforts to adapt to distressing circumstances when more appropriate coping devices are not available to the individual. Included in these efforts are anxiety, depression, and paranoid symptoms. Each is defined, described, and applied to the caregiving act when dementia is present.

5

Diagnosis of Dementia

Dementia is a medical diagnosis; that is, a physician normally examines a person with complaints that could result from any one of several possible causes. These complaints most often focus on memory disturbance and confusion. Since the doctor will want to be sure that the cause of the complaints is not due to a condition that is treatable, he or she will want tests performed that will identify, as precisely as possible, the true cause. This process is called *differential diagnosis* because it is intended to differentiate between multiple possible causes.

The procedure also helps separate the cause of a disease from its effects. There can be considerable confusion if the two are not distinguished. In the case of dementia, the effects have been described in several ways. The major effect is memory loss, particularly in what is called short-term memory. In addition, there is general consensus that the patient becomes increasingly confused, even in familiar settings, and that orientation in time and space is disrupted. Table 5.1 describes each of these effects and gives examples of them.

There are other effects that may occur. These include physically and/or verbally abusive behavior, emotional fluctuations (from happy to sad, or vice versa, with no good reason for the change), and even personality alterations (such as violence in a person who was once usually calm). Table 5.2 describes several of

Table 5.1
Major Behavioral Effects of Dementia

Effects	Behavioral examples
Memory loss	Early in development of dementia:
	Unable to carry out a few well-practiced tasks
	Unsure of location of familiar places
	Partial finishing of familiar tasks
	Seeming ignoring of instructions or suggestions
	Begins "losing" things
	As dementia progresses:
	Unable to understand many clear instructions and examples
	Cannot perform formerly easy essential tasks in job or home
	Admits "I don't remember" more often
	Needs increasing help from caregiver when questioned about normal affairs
	Avoids answering questions by using well-rehearsed stories
	Gives inaccurate, sometimes childish answers to questions
	Blames caregiver for "lost" items
	Does not recognize familiar persons, perhaps even spouse or children
Confusion	Early in development of dementia:
	Gets order of events or sequences of actions mixed up
	Has difficulty recalling specific facts and may "invent" stories
	Starts for a familiar location on familiar route but gets lost
	Begins having trouble telling what is essential from what is not
	As dementia progresses:
	Cannot find location of familiar places such as kitchen in own home
	Recognizes task but is unable to perform it
	More and more events mixed up
	Thinking process less rational
Disorientation	Early in development of dementia:
	Less able to give date or month
	Unsure of present location if familiar or unfamiliar
	Growing dependence on caregiver to provide support
	Has difficulty understanding and solving some problems

(continued)

Table 5.1
(Continued)

Effects	Behavioral examples
Disorientation (*continued*)	As dementia progresses:
	May not know day of week, month, or year
	May not remember birthday and/or age
	Unable to remember locations and appointments
	Needs caregiver to give answers to questions
	Cannot understand nature of problems, much less solve them
	Is unable to grasp commonly known facts or ideas
	Relies on caregiver for almost total care

these types of changes with examples. Whatever may be included in a description of the expression of dementia (i.e., its effects), it is important to differentiate the cause from the effects. Unfortunately, that process is difficult because the diagnostic labels provided by physicians are varied and unclear.

Diagnostic Labels

Dr. Alois Alzheimer was the first to describe the characteristics that today are associated with the disease named for him. During Dr. Alzheimer's time (late 1800s–early 1900s), it was widely accepted that dementia was a natural consequence of growing old; if you lived long enough, you would become demented. One of his patients showed demented behavior at too early an age, however, so he called her condition *presenile dementia*. This label was chosen to contrast with the normally expected condition of *senile dementia*. Alzheimer assumed that her case was a special instance of vascular dementia—a syndrome that was already identified and accepted. In 1911, Dr. Emil Kraepelin, the most eminent psychiatrist of the time, included Alzheimer's description of the case and the argument to explain it in his medical encyclopedia. Further, Kraepelin suggested that the disease be named *Alzheimer's disease*.

Table 5.2
Effects of Dementia with Variable Occurrence

Effects	Behavioral examples
Verbal abuse	Early in development of dementia:
	As an overreaction to criticism
	If disparity between facts and statement pointed out
	After memory lapse
	If independence threatened
	As dementia progresses:
	At confrontation or correction
	When desires not immediately met
	When demands made (such as bath)
	When dependency needs not met
Emotional outburst	Early in development of dementia:
	As a reaction to criticism or correction
	After memory lapse (usually obvious to caregiver)
	If dependency needs not met
	At confrontation
	When desires not immediately met
	When demands made (such as bath)
	When feeling insecure
	When fearful
	As dementia progresses:
	When dependency needs not met
	When required to take action (such as bath)
	When unhappy
Personality change	Early in development of dementia:
	As insecurity develops
	When deficiencies become obvious
	Under conditions of pressure
	When unsure of competencies
	When challenged or questioned
	As dementia progresses:
	When inhibitions no longer possible
	As wishes are challenged or refused
	When demands are made
	When socially acceptable behaviors not possible
	As reaction to irritation

Since that time, the terms above been maintained and are still used—and several others have been added as descriptors for the same phenomena. A general label that may still be applied to the disease of dementia patients is *organic brain syndrome* (OBS). There are many other conditions than Alzheimer's that are examples of OBS. Physicians who use this label for a patient with the behavioral changes of dementia may do so because they are not sure a specific cause is identifiable, to avoid reactions of patient and family to the dreaded term "Alzheimer's," or for a number of other reasons.

In more recent years, doctors and other professionals have attempted to discriminate various dementias by age at which the symptoms occur. Their intent follows the original concept of Alzheimer; that is dementia that occurs in middle age is atypical and a reflection of early aging in the brain. For convenience, a cutoff age of 65 is used. Thus *after* age 65 there is some increasing risk for dementia whether or not it is considered inevitable. This reflects the concept of senile dementia. The symptoms of dementia occurring *before* age 65 are considered abnormal and indicate that the dementia is Alzheimer's type. However, cases of patients over age 65 are not behaviorally (or histologically) any different from those under age 65! As a result, the label *senile dementia of the Alzheimer's type* (SDAT) has become popular to apply to someone older than 65 who presents the symptoms of a middle-aged patient with Alzheimer's. Since the concept of "senile" has attracted notoriety, increasing reference is being made to *dementia of the Alzheimer's type* (DAT).

If such distinctions seem unnecessarily complicated and indecisive, you are right. It would seem that a single label could be agreed upon and used to mean the same thing by all professionals. Perhaps that day will come eventually but for the present you must expect to encounter any of these terms (and even several others) when you read about dementia. If you are given a diagnosis by a physician, do not hesitate to ask for a complete and understandable description of what the label means. This explanation should include the *cause, expected progression, behavioral involvements,* and *outcomes* insofar as the doctor can determine or suspects.

One of the problems interfering with understanding is the fact that Alzheimer's disease has received so much attention and seems to occur so much more frequently than the other causes of dementia. As a result, the Alzheimer's label may be used even when there is a more appropriate and accurate one. If you are given that diagnosis, ask whether it is being used in the specific sense or a general one. The doctor should be able to tell you why he or she has chosen that label.

Medical Tests for Diagnosis

The procedures followed in medical diagnostics have a history that remains basically unchanged although some procedures have been augmented as diagnostic technology has become more sophisticated. For example, it is now possible to examine the body internally *without* intruding through surgery. An example of this technique is the CAT scan (computerized axial tomography) where X rays of a part of the body are made in a succession of layers. Professionals trained in the technique can then examine and "read" the qualitative features disclosed by the X rays. When used to examine the brain, the physician is able to note the brain's structural integrity as well as features that differ from those expected in the normal brain. (It is true, however, that scientists are not certain what the "elderly normal" brain should look like.) The process may disclose a tumor (operable or inoperable) as the cause of certain behavioral changes. In times past, such a disclosure would not have been possible without going into the brain at the risk of damage to tissue. The scan is relatively expensive but the gains often more than warrant the cost.

In the most basic sense, medical diagnosis still focuses on two assumptions: medicine is concerned with the physical status of the individual, and the cause of a physical disorder is a disease process. Although there are certainly exceptions (e.g., psychia-

trists and advocates of psychosomatic medicine), the large majority of physicians are trained to look for physical causation. When
the patient presents a complaint, it is well to look for the source of
that complaint in a system (or systems) of the body. A "disease" in
the sense used by doctors includes not only germs and viruses but
any other source of disorder as well.

It is not surprising, then, that a complaint of memory loss and
confusion when presented to a doctor will lead to a series of tests
designed to identify malfunction caused by disease. Although
there can be no quarrel with the fact that the problem is a *mental*
one, the physician wants to be sure that the origin of the memory
problem is not something treatable by conventional medical intervention. Should such measures not disclose a cause then other
methods may be tried.

Procedures

The number and types of tests required by the physician
before making a diagnosis will depend upon the complaint. In the
case of dementia, as a general determination, or Alzheimer's as a
specific label, the most common complaint is loss of memory. This
memory alteration frequently affects retrieval of the name for a
common object (though its use may be remembered) or the names
of persons. Further, there may be difficulties in carrying out tasks
that were easily performed in the past. Since memory loss may be
correlated with many things other than dementia, the physician
may question the patient to be sure the memory *has* been affected.
Depression, for example, may mask as dementia; depressed patients often complain of an inability to remember facts. In this
case, the doctor may ask the patient some questions that test an
awareness of reality (such as the day of the week or when the
patient was born). If the patient can answer them correctly, the
chances are greater that the cause of the complaint is something
other than dementia. Depression is treatable and the doctor may
then refer the patient to a psychiatrist or clinical psychologist. In
some instances, the doctor may prescribe a medication or some

other intervention. The point is that the memory complaint may or may not be realistic.

Routine Tests

If the memory loss seems real and if there are other symptoms of dementia such as confusion, the doctor probably will require a series of "routine" laboratory tests. These are intended to disclose if some physical condition is causing the problem. Again, if so, there may be a treatment that will reverse the course of the complaint. There are a variety of lab tests used but the principal ones in the case of dementia are listed and described in Table 5.3. The reason for the ones listed in the table is that, in total, they give a fairly clear clinical picture of the integrity of the patient's status in metabolic and endocrine functions. They will also disclose deficiencies of several types in the body as well as possible sources of infection.

Special Tests

In recent years, the computer sciences have allowed the development of new techniques that can image the interior of the body. These machines are nonintrusive in the sense that it is unnecessary to use surgery to determine the integrity of body organs. This is particularly important for the brain since a biopsy (surgical entry into tissue) may well cause destruction of healthy nerve cells. Since neurons do not regenerate (i.e., once destroyed they are lost permanently), the problems already shown by the patient may intensify after a biopsy is done. In addition, *new* problems may be imposed by the havoc resulting from additional cell injury. Until the hardware became available, diagnoses of causes of dementia were really only educated guesses (as good as those guesses might be). There are still many difficulties in the diagnosis of dementia because the new techniques do not answer all questions. However, the gains are sometimes significant.

Computerized axial tomography (CAT scan) was the first of the

Table 5.3
Medical Tests Used in Diagnosis

Test	Purpose
1. For all patients:	
Complete blood count	In total will reveal many states that are reversible.
Electrolyte measure	
Metabolic screening	Includes metabolic and endocrine deficiencies, and infectious conditions.
Thyroid integrity	
Levels of vitamin B_{12}	Results are considered by physician in combination with patient history and exam.
Immunodeficiency	
Urinalysis	
Electrocardiogram	
Chest X ray	
2. Under some conditions:	
Brain scan (CAT, PET, MRI)	Provides information on integrity of brain. Used when patient history or neurological signs suggest alteration.
Electroencephalogram (EEG)	When seizures occur or where consciousness altered.
Psychiatric assessment	Where depression suspected or evident.
Neurological evaluation	To give evidence of present brain status. To distinguish dementia from depression and delirium.
Speech and language evaluation	To identify language disorders and suggest means of communication.
3. Of limited value:	
Lumbar puncture	Used only when evidence of infection or inflammation of vascular system is present.
Evoked potentials	Insufficient evidence of utility.
Brain biopsy	Presents threat of tissue damage
Genetic analysis	No data presently to assure utility except in limited ways.
Carotid ultrasound	No value except to identify cause of infarcts in limited cases.

Note. Adapted from "Differential Diagnosis of Dementing Diseases" (1987). Available upon request from National Institutes of Health, Washington, D.C. Ask for Consensus Development Conference Statement, vol. 6, no. 11, July 6–8, 1987.

new technologies. The procedure uses computer generation of images with X rays to show detailed features of parts of the body. These X rays are absorbed by the internal body structures, then converted into video images, with or without color. (Color permits highlighting of subtle differences between normal and abnormal tissues.) The result allows an examination and interpretation by the physician that is superior to standard X rays. The CAT scan also is more sensitive to tissue density (thickness) than is the standard X ray. Usually, there will be 12 to 15 independent images in the total scan so that the resultant layers permit a more complete visual. The doctor is in a much better position to make decisions relative to the welfare of the patient than if only a single X ray is used.

In using the CAT scan for diagnosing dementia, the primary gain is an ability to decide if the cause is identifiable and treatable. Thus, if a tumor is causing the problem behavior, the scan will reveal it (at least in the large majority of cases). Not only the placement of the tumor but its size and the tissue on which it is putting pressure will be discernable. The physician can then decide whether or not the tumor is operable. A further, and most impressive, gain is that the occurrence of strokes can be identified. This is particularly helpful in diagnosing multiinfarct dementia, caused by a series of small, silent strokes. The patient may not have been aware of a stroke, but the scan will disclose the damaged tissue that resulted. The number of strokes that were necessary to induce the demented behavior will be clearer to the doctor.

Atrophy (shrinkage) of brain tissue is recognizable to the trained professional when the scan is examined as well. Although there is no concrete evidence of how much atrophy must occur before dementia begins, the extent of shrinkage can be seen. The CAT scan thus is more useful in diagnosing multiinfarct dementia than other causes such as Alzheimer's. Neuronal changes can only be seen under the microscope; the CAT scan is limited to visualizing gross structural changes.

The cost of the CAT scan will vary with geographic region and with demand for such measurement. The start-up expense to a hospital or clinic will be over a million dollars. The charge to a patient for a scan will probably be $600 or more. Although expensive, the greater precision in diagnosis often makes using the procedure a worthwhile investment.

A more recent innovation is *positron emission tomography* (PET). A device of the nuclear age, the PET scan reveals a cross-sectional image of metabolic (energy storage and release for cells) activity in the region that is imaged. The trained observer will find physiological and pharmacological data from the scan. The procedure is particularly useful because it is sensitive to the conscious alertness of the person being examined, reflecting both mental and physical activity. Unfortunately, the cost of the scan is about twice as much (about $1,200) as a CAT scan, restricting the use of this device largely to research facilities.

The most recent technology is *magnetic resonance imaging* (MRI). Like the other devices, it is noninvasive. It has the added potential benefit that it does not expose the body to X rays (as the CAT does) or to radiation (which the PET does). It discriminates between body fluids and tissue and information provided by the other scans is found in MRI as well.

MRI is still a new technique, with much greater potential than has been realized. With the use of MRI, cerebral infarcts, tumors, hemorrhages, and vascular abnormalities can be seen. MRI provides more information on the extent of pathology than the other scans. For example, atrophy of the brain stem and the results of small infarcts can be seen. Still, the specific information needed to make a diagnosis of dementia accurately and directly is lacking. Cost to the patient is similar to the cost for a PET scan but with more definitive findings at the structural level. Somewhere in the future is the technology that will permit imaging at the cellular level. That method will be a dramatic step forward because it will be possible to assess the integrity of individual nerve cells that presently can only be discovered by microscopic view.

Marginal Tests

There are a few other tests that may be done but their usefulness in diagnosing dementia is problematic. Among these are puncture of the spine to obtain cerebrospinal fluid, ultrasound of the carotid artery, and measurement of brain waves following the presentation of a brief stimulus (called evoked potential). These, and other such measures, have not been shown to yield definitive information related to Alzheimer's or other causes of dementia.

Diagnostic Results

Once all tests have been completed, the physician has a responsibility to communicate to the patient and caregiver what the findings were and what they mean. With such sophisticated measures, it is sometimes difficult for the physician to make clear what was done, why it was done, and what was found. This does not, however, relieve the physician of his or her responsibility to explain the test results. At the same time, the patient or caregiver must be willing to let the doctor know when something is not understood. Further, the patient or caregiver should ask for whatever information is missing. Table 5.4 contains a list of questions that should be answered by the physician either voluntarily or as requested. A checklist format has been used; make a copy and carry it to the doctor's office, checking off those things that are satisfactorily answered. The remaining ones can then be asked of the doctor. There should be no reticence in doing so since the fee charged includes the obligation for full disclosure.

Psychological Tests

Since a doctor is consulted for a diagnosis, one might think that a physical cause and its consequences are the only concerns in diagnosing dementia. Although the cause *is* physical (but not always determinable), the consequences are psychological and social. The major complaints of dementia are memory loss, confusion, and disorientation in time and space. In addition, there may be personality changes in the patient. All of these outcomes are within the domain of psychological investigation and measurement. The physician may screen the patient for certain signs of mental incompetence and deficiency.

Psychological diagnosis involves a different kind of testing than does medical diagnosis. Psychologists are concerned with intellect and mind rather than the structure of the brain although they are certainly interested in brain status and integrity as well. Knowing the area of the brain where neuronal damage has occurred may help the psychologist in making decisions about the most appropriate measures to use and potential interventions to try. The evaluation instrument used by psychologists with a person suspected of having a dementia will focus on intelligence, awareness, memory function, and mental status.

One category of tests the psychologist may use is *neuropsychological testing*. These tests have been designed and validated to indicate the specific behavioral problems that are related to brain damage. They will also designate competencies still present to the patient. As a result, recommendations may be made of ways to use the remaining competencies so that the patient remains involved with life. At the same time, the problem areas discovered may be amenable to treatment leading to some improvement in the behavior of the patient. These interventions will not change the course of the dementing condition. Unfortunately, medical treatment to stabilize or reverse such causes as Alzheimer's is still unknown.

A second type of testing done by the psychologist (and often by the doctor as well) evaluates the mental status of the patient. These tests are intended to screen for the ability of the person to remember common and important events, to show familiarity with current conditions and states, to recognize and solve problems, and to communicate with oral or written language in an appropriate and meaningful way. Such tests are not diagnostic in the same way that a medical test is or even as a neurological test may be. They do not indicate cause so much as they show current status. However, the results may be useful for assessing and planning the future for the patient, just as the neuropsychological test data are.

Table 5.4
Checklist of Questions for Physicians

Topic	Appropriate questions
Diagnosis	1. What tests (lab and exam) were used?
	2. What were the results for each test?
	3. What do the results mean?
	4. What seems to be wrong with the patient?
	5. What is the diagnosis?
	6. What does the diagnosis mean?
Cause	7. What may cause the diagnosed condition?
Outcomes	8. What effects may be expected in the short term?
	9. What effects may be expected in the long term?
	10. What is the usual course of this condition?
	11. What is the prognosis?
Treatment for diagnosed condition	12. Is there treatment (drugs or other therapy, surgery, etc.) for this condition?
	13. Does the treatment have side effects? What are they?
	14. What evidence is there for success of this treatment?
	15. Does treatment (1) slow progress of condition? (2) stabilize it? (3) reverse it?
	16. Is cure a possibility?
Associated factors	17. What problems may be associated with but not caused by the condition?[a]
	18. Are there treatments for each? If so, what are they?
	19. Do these treatments have side effects? What are they?
	20. What evidence is there for success of these treatments?
	21. Does treatment (1) slow progress of condition? (2) stabilize it? (3) reverse it?
	22. Is cure a possibility?
Behavioral factors	23. What behavior changes are associated with diagnosed condition?[b]
	24. What behavior changes are associated with other conditions found?
	25. Are there treatments for adverse behavioral changes?
	26. Do these treatments have side effects? What are they?
	27. What evidence is there for success of these treatments?

(continued)

Table 5.4
(Continued)

Topic	Appropriate questions
	28. Does treatment (1) treat symptom completely? (2) partially?
	29. Is cure a possibility?
Overall opinion	30. What should the expectations be for (1) the caregiver? (2) the patient?
	31. What is the expected length of time for patient survival?
	32. What will be the dependency needs of the patient?
	33. Should institutionalization of patient be considered now? If not, when?

[a]For example, depression.
[b]For example, verbal or physical abuse.

Procedures

A psychological examination is conducted to uncover specific details of mental incompetence. The procedure allows, at the same time, an identification of remaining mental competencies. The particular tests chosen for use will be based on the complaints given by the patient. For example, for the frequent lament that one cannot remember as well as formerly, a screening device will be used; to test general ability, an individual intelligence test will be administered; to indicate types and possible locations of brain damage, a psychoneurological exam will be conducted. The costs of these tests vary with the time needed for administration and interpretation as well as the expertness required for their use. Usually, charges will range from $100 to $250 per hour.

Routine Tests

Traditionally, psychologists have avoided speculating about the nature of the mind even though they have accepted that some such entity as "mind" must exist. It is certain that human beings are capable of complex behaviors and that they show talents greater than the structure of the brain might lead one to expect. There must be, as a result, some power emanating from the combinations possible with the billions of neurons in the brain that make us uniquely human. This power may be labeled *mind*. Its form remains a matter of speculation.

One important dimension of the mind is the use of language. Because humans have developed both a spoken and written language, it is possible to share experiences. This allows us to behave in ways that represent shared realities. What each of us considers "real" is a creation of the brain and its capacity to perceive the environment. Since we can communicate through language, we are able to share feelings, desires, experiences, ideas. Such sharing gives us an awareness of our connections with others. Even more, it makes it possible for us to experience our bodies in time or space.

If we are not capable of experiencing time and space, we will not be able to understand and deal with the environment. Each of us may be a unique universe but we share bits of that universe with the universes of others. Each of us knows the personal self as well as our location in time and space. For the dementia patient, however, there has been a destructive change. It is no longer possible to function in the personal world and maintain contact with others as he or she formerly did. Undoubtedly, the patient still has some form of subjective reality but it may not be understood by others. In fact, as the dementia progresses, it appears to others that the patient has lost all contact with reality. The psychologist will need to assess the patient's orientation in time and space to evaluate the ability of the person to understand and deal with reality as the rest of us know it.

To do so requires the use of tests that access the reality awareness of the patient. There are two very popular tests for this purpose. One is called the *Mental Status Questionnaire* (MSQ). This test consists of 10 reality questions. The patient is asked about the date, day of the week, month, and year; about the location where he or she currently is; about his or her date of birth and age; and about the current and past presidents of the United States. Such questions will seem childishly easy to one who is not demented. For the patient, however, the answers may not be recoverable from memory. The further the dementia has progressed the fewer questions can be answered. A patient who had been a successful civil engineer in Chicago, well educated and formerly mentally active, was unable to answer any of the 10 questions. He confessed to me, "It's almost like sticking a pin in me. I know that I know the answers and I know that I ought to be able to tell you, but I just can't get them out." His reality was stunted compared to his predementia state and compared to the rest of us. Yet he was still aware of his deficiencies and knowledgeable that he had the experiences stored in memory. His "reality" was different from ours, but he still experienced reality of a sort. The psychologist tries to determine the texture and limits of that reality with the MSQ.

The other test is called the *Mini-Mental State Examination* (MMSE). It consists of 30 items probing more specific kinds of memories to assess the variety of competencies that may be available to the patient. The MMSE asks for the current time (day and date, for example) and place (current location, for example) as does the MSQ. It goes further, however, by including queries that tap short-term and long-term memory, arithmetic functions, ability to visualize and draw a design, and so on. As a result, the MMSE gives the psychologist a more complete picture of the patient's abilities and losses than the MSQ. I once evaluated an elderly man who had been diagnosed as an Alzheimer's patient. One item on the MMSE requires the examiner to print the following in large block letters on a plain white sheet of paper: CLOSE YOUR EYES. The patient watches as this is done. The examiner then hands the sheet to the patient and says, "Do this for me." In this case, the patient took the paper from me, looked at it, and said, "Close your eyes." I then said, "Yes, do as the paper says." Once again he looked at the sheet and read its contents. We repeated the procedure twice more with the same results. This patient showed that he was still capable of recognizing words and reading them. Yet, there was no encoding of the meaning of those words. Perceptually, he could perform in a way that would persuade most people that he was a functional reader; practically, he had only the mechanical aspects of that task still available. Apparently, there had been cell destruction in the part of the brain where visual stimuli were interpreted (Wernicke's area) even though the optic area was not yet diseased. Interestingly, this man read the newspaper to other residents in the facility where he lived. They could no longer read but they still understood the meaning. He, the reader, could not understand what it was he was reading.

Essentially, both the MSQ and the MMSE measure the same general behaviors. The choice depends on the preference of the psychologist and the level of analysis needed of the functional capabilities of the patient.

Special Tests

Although mental status screening tests may be administered by professionals in various disciplines (and thus are considered routine), there are tests of such a complex nature that special training is required. Rigorous standardization demands that both administration and interpretation of these exams be performed only by competent psychologists. Chief among these are tests designed to measure intelligence, either in children or adults. Also requiring highly skilled and experienced professionals are certain technical tests of memory and neuropsychological measures.

In 1939, David Wechsler, an experimental and clinical psychologist, published the first individually administered test of intelligence designed for and normed with adults. In the years following, the battery proved so useful and successful that it is now in a second revision, called the *Wechsler Adult Intelligence Test-Revised* (WAIS-R). The ability to respond to the environment and its many demands requires that we possess sufficient intellect to recognize and solve problems. Dementia's adverse effect on problem-solving skills makes an estimate of the remaining intellectual competencies of the patient an appropriate part of diagnosis. In many cases the test selected for the purpose will be the WAIS-R.

This test is actually a battery (collection) of subtests. Some of these subtests measure verbal skills and talents while others test the competence to manipulate concrete objects (in a puzzle format, for example). Norms (the range of scores made by a group of persons selected on certain traits) are available to the psychologist for various ages. The performance of the examinee is then compared to and ranked with the scores for his or her age group. Generally, the examinee will be designated as average, above average, or below average, although a more precise designation (such as I.Q.) may be recorded as well.

It would be most helpful if the score obtained from a dementia patient could be compared to the results of tests done *before* dementia began. Usually, however, that comparison is not possible since so few people are tested unless they present behavior problems. The test result obtained, then, is considered in terms of what the caregiver reports to have been the mental competence of the patient in the past along with such evidence as education level attained, types and responsibilities of jobs held, and evidence of success and accomplishment. The discrepancy between present and presumed past test performance will be used to judge the status of the patient and to make a diagnosis.

A second, and more specific, function that will probably be measured is memory, of which there are two kinds. One is called short-term memory, consisting of the ability to maintain information for only seconds to a minute or two. The dementia patient has considerable difficulty with this task. Often, the first complaint has to do with memory loss of this type. Memories are also stored on a long-term basis, usually experiences from the past that may be stored for frequent usage. In dementia, there is often greater loss of short-term than of long-term memories.

Psychologists make a distinction between semantic and episodic memory as well. "Semantic" refers to the substance of symbols—what they mean. It includes the ability to remember the names of objects and people, a problem for most dementia patients. "Episodic" memory refers to important events in the life of the individual. Forgetting occurs here as well although many patients can recite selective events from the past. Memory will be assessed with both verbal and visual (reproduction of a design from memory, for example) materials.

Among the most sophisticated of the neuropsychological examinations are the *Halstead-Reitan Neuropsychological Test* and the *Luria Nebraska Neuropsychological Test Battery*. These tests were designed to determine the amount of brain damage, as well as the kind of damage (i.e., the part of the brain where the damage has occurred). These tests may require several hours to complete, with periods of rest interspersed throughout the test so that the patient will be able to perform as well as possible. Interpretation of the results is done by a psychologist who has studied extensively with experts and who has a solid foundation in brain structure and function. These tests may ask the patient to do things such as connect points distributed in a random fashion, remember and reproduce a pattern tapped out by the examiner, and to exhibit other motor and tactile abilities. Verbal skills are measured also, both with subtests of the Wechsler scale and specially devised tests of reading and arithmetic.

Marginal Tests

In some instances, the psychologist may decide to augment the findings with intensive, focused measures. For example, current status in language function (both in expression and comprehension) may be assessed. When used, such tests are selected because they give more precise information that can help decide both functional level and potential interventions.

Diagnostic Results

Just as the physician will communicate findings to you, so will the psychologist. Even if the findings of the psychologist have been sent to the doctor for reporting to you, you still have a right to meet with the professional who tested the patient to gain as complete an understanding as possible. The physician may know what the scores mean and particularly how they fit into the medical diagnostic picture, but the person who tested the patient may be able to give you some important firsthand information. Again, you are paying for a professional service and opinion and you may expect to have that service fully explained.

Psychometry (the science of measuring psychological characteristics) is a complex, specialized field. The psychologist who selects and administers tests to assist in diagnosing a condition like Alzheimer's is the individual most able to explain *why* the tests were chosen, *what* information they yielded, and *how* the results should be interpreted and applied.

Table 5.5 contains questions to assist you in gaining complete information from the psychologist. Make a copy to take to the psychologist's office and make sure he or she answers all the questions. The results of psychological tests often are useful for identifying not only deficits but remaining strengths as well. The findings can assist you in establishing realistic expectations for the patient, including things that that person *can* and *should* continue doing.

Table 5.5
Checklist of Questions for a Psychologist

Topic	Appropriate questions
Tests	1. What psychological tests were administered?
	2. What does each measure?
	3. What were the results?
	4. What do the results mean?
	5. How do the results relate to symptoms shown by patient?
	6. How are results used as part of the diagnostic procedure?
	7. Are there other tests that might give useful information? What are they?
	8. How would each be useful?

Behavioral Tests

Virtually all measures needed to make a diagnosis of a specific *cause* of dementia or the dementia itself will be included in the medical and psychological evaluation. Still, there are other matters of importance to consider in the determination of interventions for the patient or suggestions for placement of the patient. The principal source for this information is you, either as caregiver or patient.

Functional Level

It is important to know how well the patient is still able to carry on routine activities associated with daily life, called *activities of daily living* (ADL). They include a variety of functions that may have been taken for granted in the past but that can no longer be assumed to be possible for the patient. Generally, there are seven areas that may be included in this functional assessment and all are important to the well-being and peace of mind of both the patient and the caregiver.

A very basic element is the matter of *hygiene*. This will include such behaviors as the ability to brush one's teeth without assistance or supervision, willingness as well as competence to bathe on a regular schedule, and desire to change clothing to maintain neatness and to be sanitary. This area will disclose changes with the progression of the dementia although not in predictable ways. A major concern and complaint of many caregivers is the matter of bathing and changing clothing. Patients may become very resistant to any change in routine (including a change in clothing). Body odor and smelly clothing may not cause embarrassment and disgust to the patient, but they certainly can to the caregiver. The effect on others may also be quite pronounced!

A second area of importance to daily living is the patient's ability and willingness to do some of the tasks that make it easier for the household to run smoothly. This is the region of *chores*. The impact of demands or burdens on the caregiver increases as dementia progresses. It will be very helpful if the patient can do certain tasks, whether or not they were done in the past, such as washing dishes, dusting, or setting an appropriate temperature for air conditioning and heating. Many professionals think it important that the patient be involved meaningfully with life as much and as long as possible. If chores can be and are routinely done by the patient, the double outcome (helping and being involved) will be accomplished.

Other tasks that require the ability to perceive a problem and find a solution (*problem solving*) will be less likely for the patient, and in any event the ability to problem solve will decrease as the dementia progresses. So long as possible, though, the patient should be encouraged to do such things as keep an accurate and complete grocery list, or contact services (e.g., a plumber or electrician). The caregiver must be realistic and this includes a willingness to keep a watchful eye over the patient's tasks but not take them over until absolutely essential.

There is a case to be made for involving the patient as much as possible in *financial affairs*. Again, there may be little likelihood that the patient will be able to tackle these tasks, and the caregiver may need to offer supervision even under the best of circumstances. However, as much involvement as possible in the paying of bills, check writing, balancing the checkbook, and the like, can be rewarding to the patient as well as helpful to the caregiver.

The *social life* of both patient and caregiver will begin to suffer and may eventually end altogether. However, both have much to gain from continuing activity in mutually satisfying pursuits. Shopping, going to church services, visiting with friends, or going to parties need not end until there is no other option. Some patients find larger groups difficult to adjust to but others do not. Even under adverse circumstances, there may be some way to allow respite for the caregiver by having a family member, volunteer, or paid worker (if finances allow) take over for a couple of hours once or twice a week. Humans are social beings. That function should be served by both parties for as long as possible.

The final two activity areas are of dramatic importance to the self. One of these is *interpersonal*. There may be some dramatic personality changes in the patient that lead to discord and discomfort for the caregiver as well as the patient. Other changes may be more subtle but just as devastating. As dementia progresses, for example, the patient may become very self-centered and adopt a less caring attitude. This can be particularly distressing to the caregiver, who is assuming greater responsibility at the same time that the patient is becoming less aware and concerned.

Just as agonizing are the aspects of marriage that add comfort and pleasure to life. As must be expected, the willingness and ability to share sexual gratification often changes with dementia. Some patients become sexually demanding, abusive, and selfish. The caregiver may feel pressure to perform sexually regardless of interest or preparation. There may even be a demand for sexual expressions not experienced in the past and at variance with the moral code of the caregiver. Other patients lose all interest in sexuality and sexual expression. The fabric of life may lose some of its richness when either of these extremes occur.

Finally, there are the changes in the patient that may be labeled *intrapersonal*. As dementia progresses, there will be times that cannot be accounted for, actions that are not remembered, events that cannot be understood. Under such circumstances, it seems reasonable to expect that the patient may be depressed during his or her lucid moments. The depression response is the patient's attempt to deal with these impossible circumstances because a better mode of adaptation is not possible. Depression is treatable and so it should be recognized and dealt with when it occurs.

Another of the intrapersonal changes that may occur is loss of emotional control. The patient may become increasingly negative, demanding, angry, and abusive (verbally or physically), or cry uncontrollably or throw tantrums. Such reactions may be partially due to the patient's inability to understand and deal effectively with the life changes that are occurring. However, these behaviors may also reflect altered brain states brought on by the destruction of nerve cells in certain areas of the brain. Drug treatment is sometimes possible and helpful but in many cases there will be no viable medical intervention. Psychological counseling may help some patients and be nonbeneficial to others.

The importance of the various categories of daily living activities is shown in Table 5.6. This listing is meant to be a kind of "working paper" for the patient and caregiver on which to chart changes as they occur as well as reactions as they appear. Awareness of matters of concern is a first step to implementing control over them. Many of these items will not be mentioned by the physician in the interview or appointment. Yet the physician may be able to offer some advice or assistance if the caregiver brings the difficulty to his or her attention.

Procedures

Since the activities and behaviors of the patient included in Table 5.6 are to be reported by the caregiver and/or patient, the procedure to be used requires objective and systematic analysis. There must be a willingness to document both strengths and weaknesses, and that requires examples of behaviors that demonstrate the category. The procedure requires monitoring behaviors on a regular basis, perhaps even deciding to document for a given period of time. Thus, the caregiver may pay attention to the dimensions listed during morning and afternoon periods of one to two hours. This does not mean that a very remarkable or distressing behavioral occurrence cannot be recorded if it occurs outside the time frame. However, it should be noted as an unusual event.

A systematic record made over several weeks will disclose what are common occurrences in a way that is not possible by a simple reaction of the moment. The procedure leads to more consistency and objectivity because it focuses on the permanent rather than the transitory. With just a little practice, the recorder (caregiver or patient) will find the procedure easier and more meaningful than might appear at first glance.

Table 5.6
Log of Activities of Daily Living

Activity	Selected behaviors	Day/time
1. Carries out normal actions successfully.		
Hygiene	Upon awakening: a. Brushes teeth b. Bathes or showers c. Grooms (shaves or puts on makeup, etc.) d. Dresses appropriately [a]e.	
Chores	At mealtime: a. Helps prepare meal b. Feeds self meal c. Helps clean up table d. Washes and dries dishes [a]e. [a]f.	
Problem solution	During morning or afternoon: a. Helps clean house b. Helps with washing and drying clothing c. Prepares shopping list d. Notes repairs needed e. Fixes items needing repair [a]f. [a]g. [a]h.	
2. Complex behaviors still possible.		
Financial	a. Can keep records accurately b. Can balance checkbook c. Can write checks for bills as delegated by caregiver d. Accounts for money accurately [a]e. [a]f. [a]g. [a]h. [a]i.	

(continued)

Table 5.6
(Continued)

Activity	Selected behaviors	Day/time
Social	a. Courteous and polite to others	
	b. Is comfortable with others in small groups	
	c. Is comfortable with others in large groups	
	d. Can participate in social activities	
	e. Has skills that are acceptable (plays bridge, for example)	
	[a]f.	
	[a]g.	
	[a]h.	
	[a]i.	
	[a]j.	
Personal	a. Controls emotions effectively	
	b. Shows concern and caring attitude for caregiver and others	
	c. Is kind and supportive of caregiver	
	d. Shows mutual respect	
	e. Is unselfish and sympathetic	
	[a]f.	
	[a]g.	
	[a]h.	
	[a]i.	

[a]Space for listing other pertinent behaviors of concern to the caregiver.

Diagnostic Results

In this case, the "diagnosis" is directed toward greater understanding of *what* changes are occurring and in *what ways*. The developing record permits the caregiver or patient to visualize present status, compare it to past status, and speculate upon what may happen in the future. The structure gives a more scientific basis for perception of the demented person. As a result, as new behavioral changes begin, they may not have such frightening effects. Perspective brings the potential for acceptance, adaptation, and adjustment.

Summary

The diagnosis of a condition that may lead to dementia depends on a complex system of data collection from medicine and psychology. When a patient with complaints that are symptomatic of dementia (memory loss, confusion, and disorientation) is brought to a physician, a series of tests will be implemented. The usual array of laboratory and physical examinations will occur first. This is done to find if the cause of the complaints fits within the spectrum of known (and usually treatable) syndromes. If so, appropriate treatment should bring a resolution of the symptoms.

If, however, the tests do not identify a cause and if the complaints continue, more complex (and more expensive) measures may be employed. There may be referral to a neurologist for administration of a brain scan (CAT, PET, or MRI) to disclose the integrity of the brain. Such data can identify atrophy (shrinkage) of the brain tissue, occurrence of tissue damage from strokes (infarcts) and tumors, and other abnormalities. When present and where possible, treatment may be used to correct the problem.

Psychological tests may be administered by a clinical psychologist or neuropsychologist. These tests can yield information on the intellectual status of the patient, and the skills and abilities still present as well as those no longer present. From this array of information, the physician decides whether to diagnose one of the conditions causing dementia.

6

Dementia and the Patient

In the presence of illness, we look for intervention by a physician that will arrest the progress of the disease and, it is hoped, cure the patient. In many instances, this is exactly what happens: doctors find a cause for our symptoms and institute appropriate treatment. There are, of course, some conditions for which there is no way to intervene to prevent the syndrome from doing further damage. Further, the prospects of a cure are even less likely. With dementia, hopes for a cure rest on finding a cause that is treatable and reversible, such as an infection, a nutritional deficiency, or depression. In these cases, medical treatment can be direct and successful most or all of the time.

There remain many causes of dementia for which medical help is as yet unavailable. For one thing, the *cause* of the dementia may be obscure or unknown, even though there may be a diagnostic label to describe it. For example, in a diagnosis of Alzheimer's disease, the assumption is made that a microscopic examination of brain cells would disclose the presence of neurofibrillary tangles and neuritic plaques in the brain. Since there will be no microscopic examination (because a biopsy of brain tissue might cause severe damage), the cause is an educated guess (although it may very well be the correct one).

There is a second reason why medical cure is not possible in many cases. *Dementia* is a word used to imply an adverse change in the behavior capabilities of patients. As a result of an undetermined amount of damage to nerve cells in certain parts of the brain, the patient will become less mentally competent no matter how brilliant and capable he or she may have been before the syndrome began to express its effects.

The essential idea is that dementia is a *mental* expression of disease, not a *physical* one. The cause certainly is physical—destruction of nerve cells in the brain by some process that may or may not be recognized—but there are *no adverse effects on the physical body*. The patient is not sick in the conventional way. The symptoms are behavioral in the sense that they are manifested in the person's actions, thoughts, and understanding. As a result, the kinds of interventions that may be tried are limited at best.

There are literally billions of neurons in the brain; so many, in fact, that we probably use only a small portion of them. No one knows why there are so many cells but it is believed by many psychologists that the great abundance has a purpose. Since a nerve cell once destroyed is irreplaceable, perhaps some of those not already in use can take over the functions that were served by those damaged cells. This argument is based on a belief in what is called "plasticity." If the brain is plastic, then there must be multiple possibilities for the use of cells in helping us adjust to and deal with environmental conditions. Each cell would not serve only a single purpose, but be able to serve multiple purposes. There would also be interactions between cells, permitting almost limitless potential if we put our brains to maximum use. The concept is appealing even though it is theoretical rather than proven.

One of the drawbacks to the plasticity notion, even if it turns out to be true, is that the aged brain is not of the same integrity and quality as the young brain. Cells can be destroyed by accidents, disease, poor nutrition, or any of many other factors. By the time we reach 60 years of age, we may already have damaged significant numbers of neurons without meaning to. The brain will have also experienced a loss of integrity due to changes from the aging process. Being less healthy means that it is also more at risk for effects that earlier in our lives would not have been so detrimental. In old age, the brain is compromised sufficiently that its potential for plasticity is reduced to some degree.

In addition, behavioral scientists have not been able to demonstrate the relation of behaviors, except in the most general sense, to specific kinds of interventions. What can one do when a dementia patient, for example, begins to become confused about the place where he or she lives? What training program is there that will indicate the problem is due to damage to neurons in a certain area? Further, what cells may be trained to take over the functions lost by the patient so that confusion is no longer a problem? Obviously, there are no answers to any of these questions because scientists have only limited and descriptive knowledge of the brain and its many complexities. There are insufficient data to indicate a linkage between certain areas of the brain and certain demented behaviors.

There is, however, some evidence that the brain is capable of plasticity under the right conditions. Years ago, as a young man, I was an administrator of a special school. Although part of the public school system in its educational mission, it was a residential facility where many of the students lived year-round. There were medical services and various special training programs, including physical, occupational, and speech therapies. The "special" part of this school was that all the students had motor difficulties due to brain damage. Most were cerebral-palsied with mild to severe problems in ambulation, use of the hands, and speech. One thing I learned very early in this setting was that such children could be helped. However, the degree of improvement depended not only on the amount of brain damage suffered but on the age at which a training program began. A child of 3 years had better prospects for improvement than a child of 6 with the same degree and kind of brain damage. Still, a child of 6 had more prospects than one of 12, and so on. The programs in this case concentrated on muscle training so that these children might be able to use their hands (and thus be employable), be able to walk without assistance, and be able to communicate in an understandable way. Their potential for learning these things seemed to be directly related to the fact that the brain is capable of plasticity.

It is important to understand, however, that this example does not apply directly to dementia. The point intended is to show how plasticity works, not to imply that the brain can be trained to take over higher cortical functions like thinking by replacing damaged cells with undamaged ones. These children were being trained in skills involving the *motor* cortex, not the association areas. Indeed, many of these children were mentally bright and capable, and they learned well. The analogy might be extended to a hope (and possible belief) that someday we may be able to do for *mental* competencies what is already possible for motor ones.

In addition to the problems involved with an aging and at-risk brain, there is the deterrent that dementia patients show an increasing inability to comprehend; that is, it becomes increasingly difficult for communication to occur even at an elementary level. Understanding is essential before learning can happen. Even with the best of educational programs, the learner has to bring the capacity for comprehending any task and its various elements. Without the necessary skills, yet another level of programming would be needed: instituting the ability to understand, on which other outcomes are dependent. There simply are no techniques to accomplish this task.

In summary, then, there are at least four elements contributing to an inability to "treat" dementia so that reversal and cure will occur. First, there is the medical reality that diagnosis is often an educated guess and the cause is apt to be unknown. This is accompanied by the fact that the presumption of a physical source for the dementia is based more on behavioral consequences than on demonstrated structural changes in the brain. Second, there is the psychological reality that mental competence and incompetence are recognized but are not amenable to intervention by any known procedure. Third, there is the fact that the brain is less plastic and more at risk in the elderly than at any other time in life (at least after infancy). Finally, unless a person can understand the elements of a psychological intervention, the chances for a behavioral change are small indeed. The desired outcome is defeated by the very process that is in need of alteration.

The Progression of Dementia

Some types of development are presumed to show a regular and predictable growth from inception to maturity. For example, it is widely accepted among developmental psychologists that infants progress on a variety of traits as experience occurs. The original state is one of "absence of" an attribute (leading to the necessity for experience) that is replaced by an increasing "presence of" the attribute (both in amount and quality) until maturity is reached. There may be some implicit source of what we call intelligence in every child; its expression and growth, however, depend on opportunity. This increase may be expressed in "stages," meaning that the infant must grow sufficiently in the first stage before movement to stage 2 is possible. Figure 6.1 illustrates this process. In order for each stage to be completed, there must be the opportunity to encounter the right kinds of experiences. Under the proper mix of these conditions, maturity is eventually reached.

Such a model might not seem relevant to disease processes, but the analogy *is* in fact appropriate. For some maladies, there is either an observable and predictable progression or an inference that such a course does actually apply. Consider one of the most feared diseases of the present time as an example. The human immunodeficiency virus (HIV) is the cause of AIDS. The ways in which the virus enters the body are known; that is, the virus is acquired through encounter with certain infected body fluids, such as blood. Once received into the body, the process used by the virus is also known; HIV attacks T-helper lymphocytes, which alert cells in the immune system to manufacture antibodies to defend the body against agents causing illness. Over a period of time (usually several years), the lymphocytes are taken over by the virus, which converts them to its use by incorporating its own

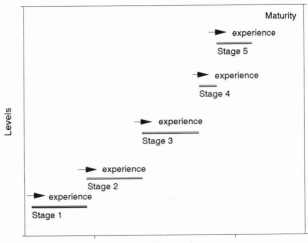

Figure 6.1. Hypothetical stages of development.

DNA into the cells. With so few T-helper cells, the body is less able to maintain immunity against various sources of illness and disease. The result is eventual death from pneumonia or some other disease. The stages and progression are known even if no treatment is yet available.

The question is reasonable to ask, then: Is it possible that dementia and its causes proceed in some predictable fashion? If so, that fact would make it possible for doctors and other professionals to say what the course will be for the diagnosed cause as well as for its consequences. It would also be more likely that professionals could help patients and caregivers plan for succeeding developmental phases and potential interventions. The answer to the question depends on several characteristics of the stage model being met.

1. *A stage must be predictable.* There must be evidence or at least some reasonable basis for assuming that the elements that

make up the stage are present in most (preferably all) members of the target group. In Figure 6.1, you will note that each stage has a dimension that defines the necessary time for the elements of a stage to be experienced and acquired. Though one stage may take longer than another, there is probably no complex behavior where the number of experiences needed to master it is not quite large. Further, all who go through the stage must share similarities in experience.

2. *There must be some necessity for the stage.* Behavioral models must be as parsimonious as possible; that is, they should include only the essentials for the model to work. Every element must be required and there may also be the need for certain experiences to occur at critical times, allowing increasing competence of more complex forms of the behavior. The child who is deprived of the opportunity to experience very basic events may not develop intellectually as completely as if those experiences had been encountered. Head Start is a program begun in the 1960s to provide children from impoverished backgrounds with encounters to prepare them for success in later school tasks. Although one may argue that the program has not succeeded completely, there is evidence that it has been effective in a number of ways. The premise was that children *must* have critical opportunities at ages 2, 3, and 4 or they will probably not be successful in school. Applying this logic to the dementia patient means that there must be certain changes that occur at *specific points* (though not necessarily at the same time for all patients) within stages if the concept of a common expression is to be valid.

3. *The stage must have a predictable completion.* If the model is to have meaning, each stage must include its own (perhaps distinct) elements. These must be acquired in a cumulative form to some point where a new, higher, and different stage begins. There could, of course, be a one-stage model but there could then be no subdivisions. This would mean that the dementing process would be described only as a continuous progression. (In fact, this seems the most reasonable position to take with our present knowledge of dementia.)

In addition to these three necessary postulates, there must occur predictability from one stage to the next and a consequent predictability from the first stage through the last. The acceptance or proof of the first three stages will assure these last two, however, so they need not be described.

As mentioned earlier, the idea of stages seems warranted for a number of diseases, making it possible for a physician to describe expectations of an explicit kind. It may not be possible for the doctor to say *when* each element will appear within a stage, however. An excellent example of this is the process by which HIV enters the body and systematically invades and takes over T-cells. The necessary components are known (e.g., receptor points on individual T-cells where the virus attaches in order to intrude into the cell and change the cell's DNA to its own DNA). The resulting steps (stages) are predictable, although when each stage will occur is not. The eventual outcome of AIDS (the "mature" stage) may or may not occur; that is, some persons may be carriers of the virus without necessarily developing the AIDS symptoms.

Further, as is true in developmental models of any type, *when* "maturity" is completed at a given stage by a given patient may not be evident. Behaviorally, the stage model does not seem realistic; that is, it does not seem plausible to describe stages of dementia except in imprecise ways. Unfortunately, some professionals assume that precision *is* possible and will tell caregivers about the likely occurrence of specific events in a series of stages. In this book, the position is taken that there are no "stages" in the sense described above; indeed, *unpredictability* is more often the case than predictability. The course of dementia, whatever the cause, differs from one patient to another even though there may be common elements of a general type. What follows is a description of this viewpoint.

The Course of Dementia

Dementia, as defined in Chapter 1, is a series of changes in the behavioral capabilities of persons due to deterioration of cells in the brain. It is important to separate the *effect* of the disease from its *cause*, since the latter is a medical condition subject to diagnosis while the former is the observable behavior of the individual. Although knowing the cause is important and may be helpful, the complaints (symptoms) that most concern the patient and the caregiver are the behavioral effects. Most often, they wish to know *why* the behavioral changes are occurring (cause), *what* they mean (for the patient), *whether* there can be treatment and recovery (for both patient and caregiver), and *where* the future may lead (again, for both). As helpful and supportive as precision might be, it is seldom possible to answer any of these questions in more than general terms.

In summary, then, dementia, unless it is due to a treatable cause such as infection or depression, takes a course that is insidious, irreversible, progressive, and untreatable. In some gradual way (months to years), the patient shows decreasing *mental* abilities while physical status is unaffected by the dementia process itself. Of course, there may be some physically destructive syndrome present, but if so, it will not be due to whatever causes the dementia. Some conditions show an irregular but steady decrease in mental competencies while others yield a more linear (straight line) decrease. Whatever the pattern, the outcome is eventual total dependence on others for routine care and supervision.

During the months or years that the dementia process continues, there are three outcomes that are present and that become increasingly prominent. These are so inevitable and so representative of dementia that they may be called *universals*; Every patient shows them to some degree throughout the process. They are memory loss, confusion, and disorientation in time and place. There usually are other consequences for the patient, but they vary both in numbers of patients who show them and in the time they may be present during the course of the dementia. All of these changes will be discussed in some detail.

Memory Loss

The importance of memory to our daily functioning cannot be overemphasized. As we grow and mature, we store our experiences so that by the time we become adults we have a storehouse that can help us to deal with many kinds of demands from the environment. These memories reflect our active involvement with life and its meanings, both good and bad. Since there is no replacement for experience, we have an advantage over youth (and ourselves when we were younger) that can lead to wisdom and understanding. For the dementia patient, one of the most critical losses is the ability to use that storehouse of experiences and information, representing a lifetime of accumulation, in an effective and efficient manner.

The exact way that we acquire, store, and use experience is not known. Perhaps it represents some such sequence as that shown in Table 6.1. To have a memory, we must first have exposure to an event from which we "learn." That exposure permits us to acquire the relevant and essential components of the event so that we comprehend and understand its meaning and use. Once that learning process has occurred, we apparently have a means by which we store it in certain of the neurons (or some portion, such as the axon) of the brain for use at some future time. Once stored, it is then available for reuse through a retrieval process that allows

Table 6.1
A Model of Learning and Retention

Initial input	Retention action	Use
Acquisition of experience (learning)	Storage of experience (memory storage)	Retrieval of experience
Examples:		
1. Operating a word processor	Memorizing key functions	Preparing a document
2. Improving your golf game	Practicing (many times?) how to drive the ball	Participating in a tourney
3. Dealing with emotional outburst by a patient	Reading books and articles; talking to professionals and other caregivers	Using learning the next time patient is emotional

us to apply pertinent past experiences to situations we are currently encountering. This knowledge keeps us from having to repeat previously learned experiences.

Though all three components of retention (Table 6.1) are essential to behavioral accuracy, there is a special importance to memory storage. Psychologists do not know exactly how the process works but there are models to explain remembering that seem reasonable. One of these is outlined in Table 6.2 and detailed below.

There are believed to be several aspects to memory. Each has its own role and is applied to specific purposes for remembering. None is more important than the others in the sense that each serves a use that is responsive to the demands of the environment. The first component in memory function might be called "sensory register" since it reflects the momentary recognition, interpretation, and response to sensory stimulation. It is a process employed for only fractions of a second. Nevertheless, it is important to behavior because it permits us to respond accurately to stimula-

Table 6.2
Types of Memory and Their Expressions

Memory type	Involvement time	Experience involved
Sensory register	Fraction of a second	Very transitory, not affecting behavior beyond the moment; for example, reaction to a stimulus like a traffic light
Short-term	Several seconds to 2 or 3 minutes	Transitory, uses memory storage for immediate use only; for example, remembering a phone number long enough to dial it
Long-term	Several minutes to years	Largely permanent, including data to be used over lifetime; for example, important facts needed to repeat actions like operating a machine

tion that is transitory. Table 6.2 cites the example of approaching an intersection. We are concerned about the traffic light and the possibility of cars on the intersecting street. If the light is red as we approach, we will slow down and stop. If, however, it changes from red to green as we near the intersection, we are apt to hesitate until we are sure that all cars on the cross street are stopped before we enter the intersection. If so, we can proceed without danger. The memory function required us to recognize the color of the traffic light (red or green) and react to that bit of stimulation. For safety purposes, we were also concerned that traffic be cleared through the intersection before we proceeded, so we checked the status of the traffic. Once assured that the light favored us and that no cross traffic was a danger, we drove on through the intersection. If there was no particular reason to remember these details once we continued down the street, we did not deliberately store the incident for permanent use. The memory (called a "trace") was not preserved after the action was completed.

The importance of sensory register cannot be overemphasized even though it seems very limited. It allows us to function in a world where almost instantaneous reaction is common. Not only must we be able to respond accurately and quickly to many situations but we also must be able to release the trace of the experience from the memory store. This particular type of memory has not been well studied in dementia patients, but it appears from evidence and the logic of the model that sensory register may remain relatively intact as the dementia develops. This can be illustrated by the observation that many patients seem to receive the stimulation necessary to this level of memory. For example, a patient may view a television program that has been a favorite of the person in the past. The patient's reaction indicates some involvement with the images even though he or she cannot later report what the plot was. Nevertheless, the individual reports having "enjoyed" the show and certainly appeared to be involved at a rudimentary level. This indicates that an awareness or input of stimuli occurred with little or no trace beyond the momentary experience.

Sensory register is the predecessor of short-term memory, the purpose of which is transitory also. However, "short term" here means from several seconds to a few minutes before the trace is lost. Short-term memory apparently cannot occur unless the brain has the competence for sensory register. Short-term memory is demonstrated (as in Table 6.2) by the temporary memory storage of some details that are used almost immediately. If you wish to call your doctor for an appointment, and you have not stored that number for frequent use, you look it up in the telephone directory, rehearse it while you go to the phone, and dial the number. This action may take several seconds during which you may have said the number to yourself several times, but the chances are good that as soon as you finish dialing, the number will no longer be in your memory. If you get a busy signal you may be a bit frustrated because you are going to have to look up the number again.

This not uncommon experience illustrates the nature of short-term memory. *Why* you do not remember the number when you need it again just seconds after dialing it may be due more to your attitude (since you expect the phone to ring and someone to answer it) than to anything being wrong with your memory. Indeed, one could argue that such forgetfulness is a good example of how competent the memory system is. Why remember something that is done and does not need to be stored and repeated? In most instances, the loss of the trace benefits rather than hinders us. How often do you need to call your doctor? How important is it to remember that number for permanent availability? If such a need arises, you will surely be able to retain the phone number so that you need never look it up again. There is no need, however, to clutter the mind with myriad details that are used only on one or a few occasions. We are well served then by having sensory register and short-term memory.

With dementia patients, short-term memory usually appears to be the earliest and most detrimental loss to occur. Since it involves the necessity to retain some detail for a period of only a minute or two, there has to be the capability to store material long enough to rehearse and use it. A person who is showing the effects of dementia has increasing difficulty in this regard. There may be the very transitory recognition of sensory register, but the memory system cannot move that reaction to the next level— short-term storage. If the caregiver, for example, asks the patient, "Would you like to wear your red dress or the blue today?" there may be an answer that signals understanding. However, the necessary action of dressing may not occur since the patient is no longer capable of storing the idea long enough to act on it.

The third level of memory can be called "long term" because it includes all the experiences of a lifetime. However, it is just as much associated with remembering details of the previous five minutes as it is with the details of 50 years ago. The mechanism that is responsible for such storage is not known; *why* we store some details for years is a personal matter in some regards. All of us have memories that seem spurious or unimportant now, but they remain anyway. Perhaps it is sufficient to say that *most* of what we put in long-term memory is important to remember.

Without short-term memory, long-term memory apparently is impossible. Once stored, we may be able to retrieve a memory, but new experiences that cannot be channeled through short-term memory will not be retained no matter how important. Much of what is stored for reuse is composed of particularly important events in life, skills and talents useful to our work and pleasure, and odds and ends that add texture to life. You may recall some pleasant event of your childhood, such as the birthday when you received a ring you still wear. Of course, unpleasant events, such as the death of a parent, will also be stored and recalled over a lifetime. You may still be employed, using the skills necessary to efficient and quick results. Such details demonstrate the presence and importance of long-term memory.

The dementia patient will recall incidents from the past also. In fact, it seems that memories of long ago are more available than those for recent events, no matter how important or unimportant. Some patients become skillful at reciting the same incidents over and over, almost as though they realized that this may help cover for their inability to deal more successfully with current life. It is not always certain that the things they describe actually happened, or even that they happened as reported, but the repetition *sounds* plausible and is apt to be accepted by those around the patient. Since the present is increasingly unavailable to memory function, the past becomes more the residence of the patient's mind. This brings an increasing dependence for moment-to-moment responses that the caregiver must take care of no matter how much burden is increased for him or her.

To summarize, memory loss is one of the universals of dementia. First affected will be those memories needed for temporary action. Called short-term memory, it is needed for the individual to respond effectively to immediate life circumstances. The loss makes it more difficult for the patient to behave responsibly. Long-term memory seems better preserved, although it may become increasingly spotty in the sense that it is highly selective, more restricted, and increasingly repetitious. Sensory register may remain relatively intact far into the progression of dementia. Why these differences in retention between the three kinds of memory occur may be due to increasing destruction of cells in the hippocampus of the brain. This small, horseshoe-shaped body seems to be the area where memory processing begins. If the hippocampus is intact and healthy, memory retention for brief periods is more likely and the conversion to long-term memory, when needed, more certain. The system is so complex and so little understood, however, that explanations (including the ones offered here) are tentative. Regardless of the eventual facts, memory is the process that allows us to act without having to repeat every event from its beginning.

Apparently, the cortex permits the retention of long-term memories that were not directly experienced; that is, we can learn about and remember things that we have not even encountered. Consider that you can read about the way minerals are mined, understand that process, store it in your memory, and use that memory to explain the details to your child. You do not have to be a miner; you need not even have visited a mine for this outcome to occur. This abstract use of long-term memory is due to the competencies arising from the neurons in the cortex where the so-called higher thinking processes occur. Only as the cells involved become diseased or destroyed does this function cease. Unfortunately, it is just these cells that are affected by dementia-causing processes.

Confusion

Although memory loss must play some part in a person being somewhat bewildered, confusion is an outcome of dementia that must be considered in its own right. The problem focuses on the patient's inability to perform many routine functions and skills, no matter how well done in the past and no matter how important to personal well-being. In its most insidious form, confusion pervades the most familiar of situations and activities. While there is some developmental process involved, confusion begins for some behaviors even before diagnosis and may be the event that precipitates a medical examination.

This latter statement can be illustrated by a case reported to me by a caregiver. She had noticed that her husband, a retired restaurateur, was unable to do some common activities as efficiently as he formerly did. There were no major problems, however, until while out walking one day, he entered a grocery store, saw a box of cigars, and picked up a handful. He was observed by the store manager, who called the police as soon as the man left the store. He was detained until the police arrived and then taken to the station, a procedure that upset and confused him. The police found his home phone number and called his wife. From this incident, she said, she realized that the little problems she had been ignoring could no longer be disregarded. Arrangements were made for him to have a complete physical checkup, and the outcome was a diagnosis of Alzheimer's disease. Fortunately, the police and store manager cooperated with the wife and no charges were filed. Though details may differ, many caregivers can report some such "critical incident" that forces recognition of a severe behavioral problem. In many cases, there is a strong association with a confused state.

As indicated in the above case, there may be some history of events that indicate the difficulties are present and developing. It is not likely that these events will be noted and reported to a professional, however. The older adult may have a history of being able to function well, old age brings minor dilemmas anyway, and, after all, what is gained by making an issue of something that occurs only occasionally. It would certainly be better if such occasions were noted and cataloged but that is not the usual course.

As dementia progresses, there are several areas where confusion begins to display itself. One of these is in carrying out commonly accepted and performed activities of daily living. These were described in Chapter 5, and a form to use in logging such behaviors is found in Table 5.6. Keeping such a log can help disclose some early signs of confusion both in direction of such problems and incidence. These behaviors may interfere only with the home routine and may be dismissed as unimportant. However, they deserve greater attention since they influence the burdens imposed on the caregiver and demonstrate the development of a condition that will become more generalized as time goes by. The case study of Martha Wells in Chapter 1 contains several descriptions of Martha's confused behavior. You will recall that she got "lost" on the way to the grocery store and had to stop for directions. This confusion frightened her by her own admission. She also at times showed confusion when with friends, and several of them had decided to drop contacts because she "gets a little uptight when told that she's mixed up."

Certainly, the confusion produced by the dementing process is most noteworthy when it interferes with the individual's ability to perform on the job. One caregiver reported that her husband had worked for one employer over his entire adult life. He had been successful, working his way up to a supervisory position with important responsibilities and a good salary. However, while still in his late 50s, and long before they had considered retirement, costly mistakes started to occur in his division. The president of the company was understanding at first but soon became concerned as losses mounted. An investigation showed that the woman's husband was overlooking necessary safeguards. He was relieved of his position but kept on in a lesser capacity because of his strong record with the company. Unfortunately, even here, mistakes continued and became more common. Finally, he was retired even though he did not understand why and wished to continue to work. It was only at this point that his wife insisted that he go to a physician. The result was a diagnosis of dementia. As with interruptions and mistakes in home routines, this outcome of confusion is not uncommon in the reports of caregivers.

The range of confused behavior can be great. Confusion can include an inability to locate objects in the home, perhaps even an inability to find rooms (like the kitchen) in a house where the patient has lived many years. There can be a breakdown in performance on highly familiar tasks, ones previously performed with great competence. The homemaker may no longer remember how to do even routine tasks, or carry out part of the job but neglect the remainder of it. The mechanic may become confused about the way to gain access to a part of a car motor he or she needs to work on. All such changes are important because they represent a mind that is eroding without means to stop or reverse the damage.

Disorientation

Finally, there is increasing disability in the patient's awareness of his or her location in time and space. Such problems also may be related to the central problem of memory loss but must be considered as a discrete form of mental degeneration as well.

An essential element of personal reality is an orientation to where we are (space) and the dimension of time. The dementia patient has difficulty with this orientation, illustrated by the patient's responses to questions about time and place. At some point in the development of dementia, the patient will be unable to tell you the day, date, month, even year (time orientation). The patient may no longer know his or her birthdate or how old he or she is. Gradually, even the most familiar of places will go unrecognized. Requests to be taken home will be made even though that is where the individual is. After placement in a nursing home, the patient may say that it is "home" and apparently mean the place where he or she had lived for many years (space orientation).

The major effect of such a loss is on the patient's ability to remain independent. The individual will become increasingly *dependent* on someone else—a caregiver. Without awareness of where one is and what time dimensions are operating, there is no likelihood that one can relate to demands of the environment. Recognizing elements of problems and coming up with solutions will be impossible no matter how effective one was in the past. Decision making must be done by one who *is* in contact with reality. As dementia progresses, the patient will become almost completely dependent, and contact with the caregiver will be increasingly emotional, decreasingly intellectual.

This loss of orientation does not mean that there is no "reality" for the patient. In some ways the patient's reality will coincide with ours, in other ways it may diverge so far as to be unrecognizable. In the former case, there will be a slight alteration. The patient may describe some stimulus in a very personalized way but one that is sensible in its own context. Looking at a picture, the dementia patient may say that it is a scene of his or her childhood and give an explanation of the details that relate to that time period (even though the association is inaccurate). In the more extreme case, the distorted explanation will be nonsensical by our standards. The person may misrepresent facts, for example, and insist on the validity of the interpretation. There may be explanations that are best described as confabulation; that is, the patient may invent things to try to cover inabilities. (You may recall that Martha Wells, in Chapter 1, missed an appointment with her daughter and created an explanation that she came to believe herself.) Because of such outcomes, disorientation interferes with adequate dealing with the environment.

Other Possible Effects

Although loss of memory, the presence of confusion, and alterations in orientation are the pervasive and general results of a dementia, there are other possible outcomes as well. These will be found in some, but not all, cases and often are time limited, occurring for a period of time and then disappearing.

Personality changes may be observed at various times in various patients. Included in these changes will be a difference, sometimes profound, in attitudes. Some patients will remain as they were before the dementia began. Others, however, will vary to the point that they are the opposite of what they were before onset. The mild, placid individual may become dogmatic, demanding, and rejecting. In turn, the forceful person may become increasingly subdued. A rational, objective being may change to one who is irrational and subjective. And a kindly, gentle man or woman may begin to show abusive and demanding behavior. Such extreme outcomes are *not* the norm; most patients who change will do so in less dramatic ways. Why the reversals occur is unknown; the need to be adaptable to the changes requires skills not always anticipated by the caregiver. Such skills will be discussed in relation to specific behaviors in Chapters 8 and 9.

Another change in personality that may occur regards a caring and loving attitude. In many cases, the patient seems to become incapable of expressing appreciation for the caregiver's efforts. The dementia, as it progresses, leads the individual to be less aware of relationships, more dependent on the caregiver, but also increasingly insistent on his or her own needs and more determined about meeting basic creature comforts. There may seem to be no appreciation for the efforts of others or concern about the demands that are made.

This outcome ties in with a potential reduction in the patient's ability to show understanding and support for the caregiver. The roles diverge with time as the caregiver must assume responsibility for greater support. This fact seems almost to be taken for granted by the patient. Probably the mental capabilities involved with recognizing the efforts of others is altered as some part of the general pattern of cell destruction in the cortex. Since we do not know where such relationships are stored or how they may be retrieved, there is no way to explain why such changes occur. As with other personality changes, there are notable exceptions, although many caregivers do find reductions in caring and loving responses as well as understanding of their efforts.

Along with the changes cited above comes the possibility of decreasing sympathy from the patient for others' problems. Some persons are so demanding that they seem to have lost all notions of sympathy for their own plight and its effects on the lives of family members. Regard for others, even if prevalent in the past, now becomes impossible for these individuals. This fact precludes any hope for empathy to be present, the action of being sensitive to and sharing the feelings of others. If empathy is to be found it must be in the caregiver; perhaps a trait of the successful caregiver is the presence of such empathic relations.

Where personality changes of the types described above do occur, it should not be surprising that they will have adverse effects on the patient's interactions with others. Sometimes social skills will remain in place and there will be no noticeable effects on the ability of the patient to relate positively with others. In other instances, however, there may be loss in the accepted behaviors of politeness, regard, and acceptance. The patient may be rude, at least at times, where rudeness is not warranted. There may be times when carping and criticism are directed at others for no visible reason. An elderly patient of my acquaintance is so unpredictable that one is always cautious when encountering her. On some occasions, she is loving and generous; she will embrace you and be very pleasant. At another time, she can demonstrate a vocabulary that would embarrass the devil, and she may even strike out physically without warning. Certainly, she is far from typical for dementia patients. The point is that such dramatic effects can occur. The inconsistency in such cases becomes a source of concern for the caregiver and is perhaps more difficult to accept and deal with than the change itself. When you do not know what to expect, you may end up wanting to avoid social situations altogether.

The patient's character may show systematic transformation in a more general way. Increasing immaturity in actions and thought processes may occur; that is, the patient becomes more childish. On another tack, the patient may exhibit impulsive and insecure reactions whether or not they are deserved. The person may use foul language, perhaps at great variance to his or her former behavior. Given the opportunity the patient may take things belonging to others (although whether the patient is aware he or she is stealing may be debated). In other words, some quite respectful and respectable people become disrespectful and unrespectable under the conditions of dementia.

Morality, in terms of both awareness and actions, may be affected as well. Morals are social decisions and interactions that require general acceptance before they achieve force. The dementia patient will be less able to realize the social contingencies involved, even though many patients do not become "moral problems" to the family and community. Earlier, the case of a man who took cigars without paying was described. In the strict sense, he stole and thus was immoral. In the educated sense, the criteria used to judge him are unrealistic because he was probably unaware that he was acting immorally. Caregivers must accept the more educated point of view before judgment is made, and most of all, help educate those who have not yet learned.

Mutuality becomes less possible for some patients as the condition of dementia continues. As stated earlier, they may become very self-centered, with their energies focused on their own desires and needs to the exclusion of the needs of others. The interaction with people that enriched the lives of both parties may be a thing of the past. Nowhere is this so evident (when it occurs) than in sexuality. Sex drive need not disappear as the mind deteriorates; indeed, in some cases it will become stronger. However, the expression can be so selfish and demanding that the mutual benefits no longer exist. In Chapter 8, this particular behavior will be considered in more detail.

Finally, there may be adverse effects on participatory living skills. Considering the negative behavioral changes already discussed, it is hardly surprising that the patient becomes incapable of assuming responsibility. It is true, though, that not all capabilities are lost, so the caregiver who observes and notes the abilities remaining to the patient will be able to involve that person in certain details and tasks. This will help the caregiver with his or her tasks and at the same time demonstrate to the patient that he or she is still worthwhile and capable. The patient may be able to continue sharing in efforts to maintain the home. Both indoor and outdoor tasks can be rewarding. If the caregiver sees only the losses in competencies, the patient will become an even bigger burden. Many professionals believe that the more the patient is involved and active, the better it is for both parties.

The caregiver must remember that initiative on the part of the patient will be restricted and eventually lost, making it unreasonable to expect a person with dementia to identify problems and provide appropriate solutions to them. Instead, the intent is to identify and use remaining capacities, which may be directed to often routine but necessary tasks of daily living. Some involvement may be possible for a period of months or years even as the patient shows increasing deterioration.

The Illusory Time Line

As stated at the beginning of this chapter, in dementia, sets of behaviors do not occur in a pattern that makes them predictable. The extensive expressions of memory loss, confusion, and disorientation in time and space occur so commonly that they assume the status of "universals," although the variability in their expression among patients prevents stating when and how each may be seen. There simply is no "time line," as helpful as such a representation would be. What *will* happen to virtually all patients and what *may* happen to some patients are possible to describe. The caregiver must be willing to accept such an indefinite statement. Perhaps a successful caregiver is an individual who can adapt to unpredictable changes without losing the balance that maintains stability.

Summary

Dementia is a consequence of changes in brain cells. As a result, dementia is an expression of a "robbing of the mind" without the usual physical signs associated with illness. The brain contains so many cells that there is the possibility that healthy neurons can assume some of the functions of diseased ones (a process called "plasticity"). However, in old age, plasticity is less likely to occur than at younger ages. Even if it does occur, we do not know how to reinstitute lost "thinking processes."

Some professionals describe dementia as proceeding by "stages." A stage is a period in which predictable changes (development) occur. Such discrete descriptions are apt to be in error as often as they are accurate. Instead, it seems more likely that a gradual decline in mental competencies occurs without an assurance of what changes will occur when. The general outcomes of memory loss, confusion, and disorientation are so common that they may be called universals. Even so, there are wide differences in when and how these outcomes express themselves among different patients.

There are other effects that occur in some, but not all, cases. These include personality changes, ineffective interactions with others, and the inability to continue in participatory skills. Each of these is described and demonstrated in this chapter.

Overall, there seems to be no "time line" that allows prediction of the behavioral effects from dementia. At the same time, there are common congruencies and overlapping patterns among patients.

7

Dementia and the Caregiver

Any illness, particularly where the effects are life-threatening to the individual, has consequences for others as well. There is a direct influence on a spouse, with almost as great effects on children. Beyond these immediate relations, there are other family members, friends and neighbors, and colleagues at work who will be affected. From all of these people will come expressions of sympathy and even empathy. However, expressions will vary depending on the degree of relationship. Although in some instances the psychological pain will be as great, or almost as great, for friends as for relatives, usually the greatest impact is on the family.

Most often at the center is the person who becomes the primary caregiver—the spouse or a middle-aged child. Ultimately, the responsibility for the total care of the patient may fall on that individual. As dementia progresses, there will be increasing demands on the caregiver. Potentially, physical illness and massive stress reactions can be the outcome. Even if the demands are handled successfully, problems of a legal and/or financial sort may be experienced. Eventually, a decision must be made about placement in a long-term care facility, most notably when the patient has drained the physical and mental resources of the caregiver.

Other family members, especially children but also close relatives, may become involved with the care of the patient to a greater or lesser degree. Customarily, however, their role is diminished over that of the caregiver so that major decisions and duties remain with him or her. At the same time, these family members may represent a resource because they can support the primary caregiver even when not directly involved with the daily problems. Professionals, especially social workers and gerontologists, have become more aware of the demands imposed by dementia. As a result, they have studied the roles, relationships, interventions, supports, and effects present in the dementia process. This effort has yielded information that is instructive, revealing, enlightening, and helpful to some degree.

The Burdens of Caregiving

The tools of a science are developed to permit the investigation of a problem to find the cause, meaning, and solution of that problem. This scientific method can be used in many situations, including identifying disease processes, handling social problems, or even dealing with everyday difficulties in life. The procedure is not simple and certainly does not always prove to be successful. It does involve systematic and directed effort when it is employed correctly.

Scientific discipline requires a wholesome degree of patient objectivity, and the awareness that leads or hunches may not always produce results. Even with failure, there is some degree of success—there may be a suggestion of what to try next; at worst, some promising lead has been shown to be a dead end. There usually are more failures than successes and finding answers to major problems may take many years before final resolution. Such a deliberate and dispassionate approach is difficult to maintain in the human services arena, where answers are needed *now*. As a result, there may be some attempt to *do something* even if there is no real evidence that the effects of the attempt will be successful. There may not even be an attempt to determine if the intervention that was tried actually had an impact at all! Good intentions are paramount, with the hope that in some way feelings of well-being are sustained or increased for the person in psychological distress.

All this means that there is no tested and verified way to assure that the stresses and burdens accompanying caregiving may be overcome. There is not even assurance that the strain may be eased. Yet there are efforts to help caregivers and patients, and social scientists suggest models that allow testing of procedures. Out of these efforts have come some suggestions; however, there have been many more questions generated than answered.

Defining Burden

It is apparent that demands on caregivers increase as a patient's dementia progresses. Professionals have described the many stressors encountered in the caregiving task, focusing on physical strain, worry, depression, and exhaustion. Subsequently, suggestions are made about the "needs" of caregivers and the solutions for those needs. For example, there are many support groups throughout the country. Meetings are designed to give information or allow caregivers an opportunity to describe problems for discussion by all the group. Other caregivers can then provide examples of what has been done that seems to work with certain behaviors. Such approaches are warranted and surely worthwhile.

However, even when caregivers experience common behaviors among patients, they will not all perceive a problem. Where the behavior *is* seen as a difficulty, all caregivers will not agree on its severity. What constitutes a burden to an individual caregiver, then, is a personal matter. It depends on several factors that may have little or nothing to do with the specific nature of the behavior itself. One reason for this apparent discrepancy is that burden is, after all, a subjective matter. The variables of importance seem to be the following.

Feeling That One Makes a Difference

When a person first assumes the role of caregiving, it might be expected that his or her reaction will be less than enthusiastic. A significant factor in eventual acceptance of the role with its many potential demands will be a feeling that the outcomes are worthwhile. What determines "worthwhile" has its various meanings as well. To some, it means total responsibility and total care for the patient; for others, it means having an influence to bring change in the status of the patient; for still others, it means meeting patient needs but being able to preserve one's own identity. Regardless of the elements important to the caregiver, if personal expectations are not met there is a good chance the caregiver will decide that the effort is not worthwhile. When personal expectations are met, the caregiver can tolerate a number of burdens that to others will appear destructive. As a caregiver you must be honest about your feelings and needs. Denial of self or persevering in caretaking as a duty will not help the patient and may devastate you.

Being Open to Behavior Changes

Caregiving can become a tedious and stifling experience. Most often, the caregiver is not prepared for the requirements of the role. You cannot anticipate an illness that incapacitates a loved one either physically or mentally and so you will not have systematically studied what may be necessary at some point in life. In dementia, the progression may be subtle for months, even years, and will have reached a point of no return, in virtually all cases, by the time a diagnosis is made. There may be not only confusion about what is happening and why, but also some panic about what this state means for the future. Rather than submit to a feeling of helplessness (and eventual hopelessness), you must assume a more dynamic and assertive stance.

Basic to this approach is the willingness to seek out and accept *education*. Instead of trying to protect yourself by avoiding knowledge, an assertive move toward learning more about the disease and its consequences is much more positive. Never assume that you will appear foolish by asking questions of a professional; indeed, this action will normally be expected and accepted. Never hesitate to ask about whatever is concerning you. Request materials from the physician, from social workers, from agencies to increase your understanding. The more informed you are, the fewer surprises there may be. Certainly, what you learn will not cover all contingencies about caregiving but your attitude is more apt to be objective and realistic.

You should also find out about resources available to assist you. Most often called *supports*, some of these may be financial, others social, still others psychological. A primary source for information is the Alzheimer's Association along with its many chapters around the country (even if the diagnosis is something other than Alzheimer's disease). The organization provides educational materials free or at low cost. Local chapters can inform you about the availability of support groups in your area, suggest other sources of respite and relief, and even give you a list of professionals (including doctors) who can conduct screenings and examinations.

Essentially, what you may gain from such contacts is a means of analyzing problems you currently face and developing techniques to solve these problems. No one has complete answers to the burdens related to caregiving, but there are ways of handling stressors that are unknown to most caregivers. Some evidence indicates that the way in which the caregiver interprets events and their influences has a strong effect on competence with the burdens of caregiving. As much as possible, that interpretation should be realistic, objective, focused on relevant details, and designed to yield maximum positive efforts for both patient and caregiver.

As this point, a statement about professionals, their training and education, and their areas of expertness seems warranted. There is a temptation, since the cause of dementia is medically diagnosed, to assume that physicians are the foremost, and perhaps the only, source for information. In fact, most doctors are limited in their knowledge about the details of behavioral problems resulting from dementia. That is the reason that physicians often have caregivers and patients consult with gerontologists, psychologists, social workers, and others, once the diagnosis has been made. These latter professionals have been educated in the behavioral effects that are displayed as patients deteriorate. Through both training and experience, they are also exposed to social and psychological interventions that will help relieve distress, even though the eventual course of the disease remains unaltered. Such resources should be contacted and questioned by the caregiver. Do not expect explicit, detailed, sequential steps to follow. (In fact, if you are given such advice, ignore it and go to some other professional!) Dementia affects persons in various ways at different times. Overall, decline must be expected; the expressions characterizing this decline are too varied to itemize in a set sequence.

This means that you must be flexible, open to sudden and sometimes dramatic changes, willing to function with the demands of the moment, and able to adapt rather quickly. None of us is prepared for such demanding actions. The better informed you are and the more competent at problem solving, the more likely that such situations will not destroy your competencies and strengths. Ignorance is never bliss and it certainly is not an appropriate response to the demands of caregiving.

Research indicates that the mental status of the dementia patient is less likely to interfere with feelings of well-being for the caregiver than is the caregiving situation itself. There also seems to be little relationship between the duration of patient illness and the well-being of the caregiver. Why are some caregivers able to carry on for years without breaking while others become overwhelmed in just a matter of months? The answer seems to be related to such matters as the *perception* of the situation. This interpretation includes having resources available as they are needed, the ability of the caregiver to resolve conflicts between patient declines in competence and unwillingness by the patient to accept such declines, and the realistic nature of demands by the patient. In each instance, then, you as caregiver must be *self-reliant*, even though outside sources are available and used.

The balance needed between supports and burdens is as yet unknown. It might seem that the *more* support provided, the less burdensome the tasks. For some caregivers, this relationship is no doubt accurate. For others, there may be a point beyond which support, from whatever sources, simply increases the burdens felt. Then, for others, the need for support is relatively minor and may become disruptive if too intense. *Availability* and *accessibility* of supports is essential, as is *awareness* of their sources, but the ultimate "best" combination remains an individual matter. Although there has been research by psychologists, sociologists, and social workers on the need for and provision of supports, virtually all of the data are focused on an assumed need for wide provision—the more the better, so to speak. Do not allow yourself to be overwhelmed or short changed. Assess your needs at the moment and seek resources that will assist you at an optimum level. Table 7.1 presents some general circumstances that create burden, what reactions are common, and ways they may be dealt with.

Deciding about Institutionalization

As burdens increase, and even as early as diagnosis is made, the caregiver and others involved must decide whether the patient should remain at home or be placed in an institutional setting. The decision must be based on both patient and caregiver concerns. As noted in Table 7.2, if the patient lives alone and it is not possible to provide someone to supervise and care for him or her, the decision is fairly easy. However, if there is a spouse or child who can provide for the patient, the decision may be more difficult.

The prevailing norm in this society, at least in terms of expectations, is that the patient will remain at home as long as conditions will permit. These "conditions" include a number of

Table 7.1
Burden in Caregiving

Sources of burden	Possible reactions	Ways to handle
1. Roles played by caregiver:		
a. Directly related to giving care	Usually tolerated, though involving some stress	Analyze ability of patient and allow *use*. Survey actual needs for patient's well-being and meet these only. Seek respite when overburdened.
b. Additional roles beyond those related to giving care	Source of greater burden, and more difficult to accept if patient needs high level of assistance	Consider actual need for such role: must it be done; can someone else do it. Delegate to others when possible. Seek respite.
2. Age of caregiver	Younger persons find greater burden	Reduce number of multiple roles. Learn and use problem-solving skills. Do not give up all one's own time. Seek and use respite.

3. Demands from patient:
  a. Disorientation
  b. Asocial behavior
	Burden created by conflict of past behaviors and present ones	Seek education about behavior changes. Use problem-solving techniques. Deal with pertinent behavior. Use respite.

4. Number of negative events during some time period, say a week a. Undesirable nature of such events	Burden greater when perceived as "too many" and "too undesirable"	Examine nature of such events. Determine need for care. Concentrate on essential ones. Determine why some tasks so undesirable. Seek help. Use respite.
5. Sex of caregiver	Females may be more at risk of perceived burden than males	Don't try to do everything for patient. Arrange to get relief every day. Analyze tasks for essential needs of patient. Meet essential needs. Use respite.

Table 7.2
Factors Involved in Institutionalization

Defining characteristics	Needs	Reasons
1. Patient lives alone	High dependency	No one to assist in care
	Low dependency: low risk	Patient still able to meet needs safely
2. Difficult behaviors	Supervision for wandering	Caregiver unable to deal with problem
	Protection against aggression	Caregiver at risk from behaviors
3. Needs not well met by caregiver	Caregiver feelings of well-being low	Caregiver lacks psychological strength
4. Caregiver relationship: Female and younger with outside job	Demands greater than caregiver feels able to meet	Caregiver attempting to play more roles than competency and relationship permit
5. Patient relationship: Older and more incapable	Demands greater than caregiver can meet	Caregiver resources too limited for tasks

contingencies from economic to physical status and well-being of both parties. Thus, in most instances, the patient will remain in the home setting under the care of a primary caregiver, usually the spouse or an older daughter, for a period of years. Even so, should both patient and caregiver survive long enough, institutional placement is expected and accepted by the society. Cost becomes a major element in this decision. (Table 7.3 addresses some factors that should be considered in choosing a facility.)

The decision usually is not an easy one, even when it occurs early in the process. Marriage partners of 40 or more years duration may not have had the happiest of relationships, but there often has developed some kind of dependency that is comfortable. Particularly if the marriage has been a rewarding one for both partners, it takes more than realism and objectivity to allow what appears to be abandonment of one who deserves better from one's

Table 7.3
Factors Influencing Type of Facility

Variable	Major influences
1. Cost	Patient care level offered: basic to complete
	Patient supports: none to complete involvement by staff
	Special resources: none to few to Special Care Unit
2. Location	Access for caregiver
	Reputation of facility
	Perceived skills and patient interest by staff
3. Appearance	Physical qualitites: odors, cleanliness, sufficient para-professionals, registered nurses, etc.
	Rooms decorated for reasonable stimulation
	Halls, dining room, group meeting room attractive and stimulating
4. Patient protection	Ombudsman available at all times
	Trained, skilled personnel
	Administration involved with patients
	Safety features: outside door protection, alarm systems, etc.
	Minimum drug use practiced both day and night
5. Patient freedom	Available protected patio or other outside source
	Freedom allowed in halls and passageways
	Patients encouraged to use remaining competencies (eating, for example)
6. Patient involvement	Activities provided to encouarge patient to remain mentally and physically active
	Reality orientation practiced consistently and accurately
	Patients treated as adults by all staff

partner, if not from life. This is not an issue related to the patient alone. Even in the face of a seemingly irreversible dementing illness, there is the question of what happens when the partner enters the institution. After all, life and its patterns have been well established. One cannot easily go back and begin again, and especially if one is already 70 or 80 years old. What is left to fill the void left by the demented spouse? It should not be surprising that many caregivers, even after placement, spend as much or more time at the facility with the partner as they do in pursuing some remnants of an active and satisfying life.

The conditions that lead to the decision to place a person in a facility are often very difficult ones. Often stated as reasons are such behaviors as aggression (particularly physical) and wandering that cannot be controlled. Seldom is the need for custodial care given as the justification for the placement. Whether or not such explanations are realistic is not so evident. Certainly, one would concede that aggression and wandering introduce severe burden. However, a denial that a primary caregiver can no longer offer the care needed by the patient may represent an inability or unwillingness to admit to the expected caregiving roles.

In some instances, the actual behaviors displayed by the patient (such as wandering) seem less related to institutionalization than to the characteristics of the caregiver. This returns to the ideas expressed above about burden and its origins. Surveys indicate that those who institutionalize are more apt to be female, younger than the patient by several years (even two or more decades), employed, and a child of the patient. This means that a spouse is not as likely to place the patient in a facility as a daughter is. The statement is particularly true if some forms of assistance and support are made available so that feelings of burden are reduced. It is understandable that because children have their own families and, especially today, jobs, there is the danger of "role overload," which leads to greater pressure toward placement.

Essentially, what seems to be a major factor in institutionalizing, then, is what may be labeled *emotional distancing* (Morycz, 1985). The greater the emotional distance between patient and caregiver the more likely is placement to be sought. Complementing this factor are such elements as rapid loss of mental competence, casual rather than close relationships, perceived burden in the role of caregiving, and greater age in the patient. In fact, the relationships among these latter factors may be such that they are highly correlated. Any one alone would be sufficient if the emotional distance is great enough.

There may also be a case made for *social distancing*. Factors such as the patient being widowed or living alone are involved here. The primary element, then, would seem to be *isolation*. There are, of course, many elderly persons who are widowed and living alone, who are in fact isolated, but who neither need nor will accept institutionalization. When the critical factor of dementia is added to the mix, however, the decision can no longer be merely personal preference. Inevitably, of course, the matter of finances must enter the equation as well. Figure 7.1 illustrates these dimensions.

If placement occurs, what does it do for the caregiver? Research indicates that it brings a shift in the type of problems reported rather than relief from problems. Those who keep the patient at home are more apt to report that they have less time for

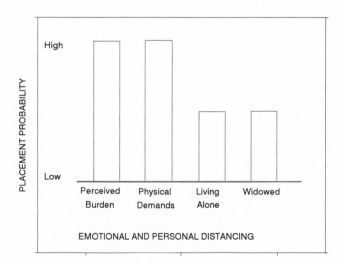

Figure 7.1. Emotional factors in institutionalization.

themselves, more interference with social life and friendships, and less privacy because of the dependency demands of the patient. Those who have placed patients in a nursing home or other facility speak of greater concern about money to pay the costs, along with worry about an ability to continue the care being provided. At the same time, they feel that they are not doing enough for the patient. The "relief" thus becomes a "burden." The catch-22 is apparent: Either way you lose, at least in terms of personal assessment and acceptance of responsibility. If these findings and reports are accurate, it is apparent that caregivers have been poorly informed about self-awareness and realistic expectations.

It seems that placement of a patient in a setting such as a nursing home depends primarily on caregiver characteristics and needs. Whether or not the effort benefits the caregiver is not yet clear. The nursing home industry is predicting significant increases in placements in the twenty-first century. This is predicated on the fact that more and more people are growing older, that the over-85 age group is the fastest growing of any age group, and that dementia is an increasing risk after age 85. There are increasing adjustments to the perceived needs of the patients, including the development of special care units. In these units only dementia patients are housed, and they are self-contained in the sense of staffing, meals, activities, and care. As would be expected, they are also more expensive than other units in the same facility. The predictions of the nursing home industry seem likely to become true, although it is not clear whether the arrangements will be beneficial for the needs of either patients or caregivers.

Coping Strategies

Given our social upbringing and expectations, it is unlikely that anyone anticipates becoming a caregiver to a demented patient. As a result, there is no real way to prepare for such a role. It is true that the increasing elderly population will make many conditions more common than ever before. In addition, more citizens are required to make decisions that did not need to be made by past generations. Perhaps the grandchildren of today's dementia patients will have had more contact and awareness that will benefit them. At the present time, however, it is unlikely that any caregiver has been adequately prepared for the roles that must be played and the burdens that may be encountered.

So, how does a caregiver learn to cope with a situation that becomes increasingly demanding? For some, the approach is one of trial and error; as an incident arises, they do the thing that seems best at that moment. For others, the method is doing as little as possible; when the patient presents a problem, they try to mollify or agree with the patient or whatever it takes to keep things calm. For still others, there may be an attempt to impose control; they try to take command and be stronger and firmer than the patient. And for some others, there may be an attempt at problem solution; they try to see what the problem is and what it means so that it can be handled in a way to bring resolution and growth rather than conflict.

As with many other practical matters about dementia, the behavioral scientists have not been able to present a systematic set of guides and assists. There is some evidence that a problem-solving approach is the most likely to avoid stress. The technique, however, must reflect the fact that the caregiver is a competent problem solver with confidence in his or her ability in this area. There is also evidence that the more passively the caregiver behaves in the confrontational process the less likely will any successful resolution occur. Figure 7.2 demonstrates this continuum and Table 7.4 gives examples of each.

There are skills and techniques that are helpful in problem solution. They are also developed through training. Such programs often are available in some senior centers at low or no cost. One of these skills is *assertiveness*. This term is used in a specific sense when applied to interaction between two or more people. Some persons create problems for themselves (including a loss of feelings of self-esteem) because they cannot or do not make their feelings and desires clear to others. Such people often feel that

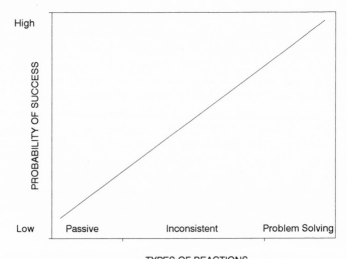

TYPES OF REACTIONS

Figure 7.2. Caregiver attitudes and results.

they are used or taken advantage of by others. Although they resent this outcome, they do not know how to change circumstances as much as they might like to do so. Their lives become a series of losing encounters that leave them frustrated and unhappy. Training in assertiveness is intended to supplant the incapable behaviors with more fulfilling and capable ones, but without creating new difficulties in relationships.

There are some behaviors to avoid. For example, the purpose in assertiveness is not to become abusive and aggressive since that will simply increase conflict and complications. Sarcasm and threats must be avoided; they are apt to be challenged, and, even if you carry out the threat, you will not have solved any problems in relationships. Apologies are acceptable when they are warranted but do not overdo it. If you apologize almost every time you express your feelings about circumstances, you will soon be seen as a wimp who does not deserve equal treatment from others.

Table 7.4
Effects of Caregiver Attitudes

Caregiver reaction	Message to patient	Effects	Probable success
Passive	Lack of interest by caregiver Lack of caring by caregiver	Decreasing competence in patient	Very low
Inconsistent	Sometimes active acts by caregiver: "cares for me" Sometimes inactive: "does not care for me"	Confusion in patient	Low at times, moderate at others
Problem solution	Strong interest by caregiver Strong caring by caregiver	Stimulates involvement with caregiver and with life Utilizes competencies as available Feelings of self-worth by patient and caregiver	Often high

On the other hand, the assertive personality is able to accept criticism without becoming emotional. If your position is criticized justly, accept the responsibility for it and make amends as needed. When your faults are pointed out to you, accept the comment and resist becoming offensive or rude. Above all, you must be aware of your feelings, honest about their presence and meanings, and willing to defend them in a calm and positive manner. Table 7.5 contains a description of incidents that may occur between caregiver and patient, and ways the assertive person would handle them. If you need help in developing assertive techniques, seek the appropriate resources. Find out where assertiveness training is being offered, and become involved. Your Area Agency on Aging, local Council of Churches, Alzheimer's Association chapter, and similar agencies can be very helpful in your quest.

Table 7.5
Caregiver Assertiveness Examples

Patient behavior	Assertive procedure
	Calmly but firmly say:
1. Refuses to eat, bathe, or change clothes	"We agreed to do this at this time so that we will be able to (*give specific activity or reward*)"
2. Says she/he wants to go home	"I know you miss some of the places we used to be. This is our home now and together we are safe and happy here."
3. Demands immediate gratification	"It's not possible to have everything we want. As soon as I've finished (*describe your task or actions*), we can discuss other things we want to do."
4. Accuses caregiver of taking possessions	"We both enjoy our own things. I'll help you look for (*specific item missing*) so you can enjoy it just as soon as I have finished (*describe specific task or action*)."
5. Is angry and/or rebellious	"I like to be treated fairly just as you do. Let's discuss what's bothering you so we can go back to our usual good relationship."

Circumstances requiring coping behaviors involve negative choices, often where all the alternatives seem undesirable. The process contains personal strategies that are applied to problem solution. However the individual may accomplish the task, there must be some conscious examination of the nature and extent of the dilemma first. Through self-reflection, strategic means of assuring survival emerge and are applied. Initially there will be uncertainty about what to do. The very unpredictability inherent in the condition magnifies the problem to some degree. Persistence and practice gradually bring more fruitful and satisfactory methods of problem solution—a growth in ability to realize, face, and resolve difficulties.

One of the factors involved in success or failure is called *self-efficacy*. Proposed by a psychologist named Albert Bandura, the concept states the effects that our perceptions and beliefs about our *own* competencies have on our actions. The function is task specific in the sense that we may have greater feelings of efficacy about one problem but lower feelings of efficacy about another. The idea is individual also since a problem yielding low self-efficacy to one person may be the type of problem that generates feelings of high self-efficacy in another. This means that your *belief* that you can or cannot succeed—that you can or cannot achieve certain goals—influences what you do and how well you do it. The perception may lead you to attempt a task or to avoid it. Further, your perception of self-efficacy will affect the effort you will make and the persistence of that effort.

There are four sources of information that we use as wellsprings on which to base our perceptions of efficacy (Table 7.6 details these and gives some examples of how they work). First is the personal history of our actions and successes with such problems in the past. If we have not had personal contact with such a difficulty before, we will compare it with a similar *type* of dilemma. If we have been successful with this kind of thing in the past, we will have an expectation for success again; success, in this case, helps breed success. Our second source of information is based on observations of others and how they deal with problems. Called "modeling," it is an observational technique where we store the behavior observed and use it at some future time. Since modeling is based on past observations, if you have never observed anyone who has faced and resolved problems with a dementia patient, this source may not offer you any cues about how to behave.

The third information source comes from verbal assurances from others about our past problem-solving skills. This source is a relatively weak one, however, and may be particularly ineffective with the severe problems accompanying dementia. Finally, a means of knowledge is our emotional control. If we are emotionally involved, and particularly if the emotional feeling is charged with negative attitudes, there will be a strong likelihood of *in*efficacy. After all, the emotional reaction may most often indicate to us that we are *not* successful. Unfortunately, failure

Table 7.6
Sources Influencing Self-Efficacy Feelings

Source	Effects	Examples with dementia
Past success in problem solving	Positive effect on attitudes about competence and outcomes	Patient demands are anticipated and met with success Patient competencies assessed and used where appropriate Emphasis placed on things done well, not on difficult tasks or failure
Observations of problem solution by others	Some positive effect, in terms of future situations and actions, on attitudes about competence and outcomes	Listen to others describe how they managed similar problems Note caregiver actions that were successful and problems you may encounter in future
Feedback from others about successful problem solution	Positive, but low, effects on attitudes about competence and outcomes	Others point out ways you have dealt with problems in past Other caregivers tell you that your history of successes forecasts success even with difficult problems
Emotional reactions toward problem solution	Often negative effects on attitudes about competence and effect	Demands seem overwhelming and insoluble Feelings you *must* do something for patient Feelings you *must* do better with demands than so far Feelings it is your *duty* to take care of patient Feelings that only *you* can handle tasks of caregiving

never tells us what a better response would be. As you are emotional in your reactions, you provide yourself with strong evidence of your own ineptitude.

Of these four instances from our experience, two are positive in their effects. One of these is performance based: We prove to ourselves that we can accomplish difficult tasks. This, fortunately, is the most influential on our feelings of self-efficacy. The second positive force is the observation of successful problem solution by others. The other two, unfortunately, are less positive in their influence and may even lead to reduced self-efficacy. These include the feedback provided by others that we have done things well in the past. At best, this seems to be a weak support. If it conflicts with our own perception of our performance, it may even serve negative purposes. Emotional reaction (the other negative source), particularly in the form of anxiety or fear or similar strong feelings, may be quite detrimental to our self-assessment and reduce our belief that we can succeed at a task.

Bandura's idea indicates that our belief and our expectation about success in a specific event may express themselves separately. Thus, I may *believe* that I have the competency and I may *expect* to succeed at whatever task demands I have at the moment. In another setting, however, or at a different time, I may *not believe* that I have the competency and I may *not expect* to succeed. Between these two extremes are two intermediate possibilities. I may *believe* that I have the ability but I may *not expect* to succeed, for whatever reasons. By contrast, I may *not believe* that I am capable but I may *expect* to succeed anyway, again for whatever reasons. Table 7.7 illustrates these possibilities.

If you perceive your own efficacy in terms of the two positive elements (category 1 in Table 7.7), you will show positive, assured, and probably successful effort. This will add to the mental fund of your belief in yourself. This, of course, is the ultimate goal we should all like to achieve although no one will be able to maintain it consistently. More likely, we experience more positive instances than negative ones, so that, on balance, we feel self-efficacious. In contrast, you may encounter settings where the two forces are negative (category 2 in the figure). Whenever this occurs, you are most apt to feel apathetic and resigned to failure. You may give in and refuse to face the "problem" that is a part of this event.

The intermediate stages will also occur on occasion. Where you feel adequate but do not expect to succeed (category 3), you

Table 7.7
The Self-Efficacy Hierarchy

Relationships	Effects on personality
Category 1: Positive effect	
a. I *can* perform (+)	Bringing positive, probably successful effort
and	
b. I *will* succeed (+)	
Category 2: Negative effect	
a. I *can't* perform (−)	Bringing lack of interest and surrender to defeat
and	
b. I *won't* succeed (−)	
Cateogry 3: Mixed effects	
a. I *can* perform (+)	Bringing remonstrance and complaint
but	
b. I *won't* succeed (−)	
or	
a. I *can't* perform (−)	Bringing dejection and personal devaluation
but	
b. I *will* succeed (+)	

From Edwards (1993). Reprinted by permission of Plenum Press.

may express some protest against others and grievance against policies of government and agencies. You may become an activist in the social sense. Instead of facing and resolving your problems, you will express a type of aggression against society and against yourself. The other combination in category 3 may lead to self-devaluation and despondency. Even where success is achieved, it will be discounted because of a lack of belief in your own competencies. The result was not achieved *because* of self but *in spite of* self. There will be little or no increase in feelings of self-efficacy in this case.

If your feelings of competence become too negative, you may draw the conclusion that you cannot succeed at a task and, worse, make no effort to do so. There may result some anxiety that will interfere with normal functioning as well.

For caregivers, there needs to be some concern for maintaining feelings of effectiveness and competence. Each event in the caregiving day must be considered for its meanings and effects. Temporary disasters must be accepted as just that—temporary. Where conditions are handled well, that should be recognized and used to bolster feelings that "I *can* succeed because I *do* succeed." The demands can become overwhelming unless an attitude of positive self-regard is more common than an attitude of self-rejection.

One of the means to help maintain feelings of positive self-regard is to find and use sources of *respite*. This is a term used to indicate receiving relief from the varied and demanding tasks of caregiving. Those providers who manage to become involved in some activities outside the caregiving setting will be better able to contend with demands than those who find themselves isolated in the tasks of caregiving.

How respite is provided depends on circumstances. For example, family members may relieve the primary caregiver for a period of time, from hours to days. Volunteers may take over the supervision of the patient, usually for a short period of time. Professionals may be employed to attend to the patient if economic conditions permit. Whatever the means used, the object is to reduce the burden felt by the caregiver, to give a chance for that person to experience other aspects of life. Caregivers report that just an hour or two a week when they can sit in the park, visit a friend, or go window shopping can help relieve some of the pressures felt. In a course in aging that I taught, a requirement was that students spend two hours a week in visiting with an elderly person. This experience gave them an opportunity to see the "real life" aspects that lectures and books cannot supply completely. One semester, at the request of a caregiver who was feeling overwhelmed with the demands of her husband who had Alzheimer's, one of our students went to their home for an hour twice a week. The caregiver told me that the student had helped in a way that could never be measured and could not possibly be repaid. The caregiver used the hour to walk, sit, listen to birds sing, things that might not seem very important but that were immeasurable in the positive effects they had on her. As a result, she felt more competent to deal with the demands of all those other hours in the week.

Some caregivers would not wish to be away from the patient for long periods of time. Some cannot release themselves from the task of caregiving even for an hour. Respite, then, is for the majority that do not experience these extremes. One of the problems for those who wish respite is to find a substitute caregiver. Sometimes there is no family member available, or not one who will agree to provide the relief. Outside sources may be limited and expensive. Volunteers may be few and far between. Fortunately, the Alzheimer's Association has made provision of respite a major focus, including setting principles to be used by policymakers and by urging funding to assist caregivers in achieving respite.

To some degree, successful caregivers find ways to provide their own respite. It is no accident that such successful persons find a sense of humor even in a forest of gloom, so that incidents can be seen not only as problems but as sources of laughter as well. Such people can recount incidents that show they will not be overwhelmed by the continual demands. For example, one caregiver told of the problem he was having in getting his wife to bathe. The physical struggle was exhausting and he was beginning to lose the battle. One day he decided to try a different approach. In the bathroom with his wife, he undressed and told her that he was going to take a shower. He asked her if she would like to join him. Apparently she was sufficiently intrigued because she also undressed and climbed in the shower with him. There was the bonus, of course, that his concern over hygiene was resolved; the pleasure he took in relating the incident made the outcome all the more positive. Caregivers learn to be resourceful if they are successful, and an ability to see humor and relish it can be a great relief.

The upshot of the factors discussed in this chapter yields two points to consider. First, no caregiver is really prepared for the experiences that will come as a patient becomes increasingly mentally incompetent. Second, since there are so many adverse incidents, one would expect that there are resources to help meet the burdens. In actual practice, the most useful resource is *you*. Ultimately, it is your competencies that will meet the tasks of caregiving. If you are open to education, willing to learn and to try techniques, modify and expand them as needed, and take responsibility, the burdens will be less overwhelming and may even be solved. If your personality does not include assertive behaviors, develop them. If you do not feel self-efficacious, retool your thinking and efforts. If you need respite, find it. You are more likely to control your destiny, for better or worse, than any professional possibly can.

Summary

Dementia is a condition that may continue over several years before the patient's death. In fact, average length of life after diagnosis is estimated at eight years, and some patients live 15 years or more. During this time, mental competence gradually decreases with a consequent increasing need for caregiving. There are many who become involved—spouse, children, relatives, friends—to some degree; however, the major impact is on the primary caregiver.

Caregiving brings increasing burdens—perceptions of success and failure in efforts, feelings of imposition and demand, insecurity about the future. *Which* elements are most burdensome depend on the perceptions of the caregiver. Very similar demands are not viewed equally by caretakers. Elements involved in the subjective state of burden include whether one feels that one's efforts are worthwhile along with being open to personal change.

At some point, it is likely that a decision will be made to institutionalize the patient. This usually happens when the demands of caregiving are greater than the strengths remaining to the caregiver. The result of institutionalization is not relief so much as it is a shifting in perceived burdens. Major factors in the decision are emotional and social distancing.

Those caregivers who experience the least burden tend to be those who develop coping strategies. Skills included are assertiveness, feelings of positive self-efficacy, and the ability to find and accept respite.

8

Facing Problem Behaviors

There are so many different ways in which dementia expresses itself among patients that any attempt to describe and discuss them all would take volumes. There are, however, certain behaviors that are more often cited by caregivers as causing distress and burden. The nature of a "problem" is personal, with its intensity depending on the perspective of the caregiver. For some, a given behavior will be experienced as extremely burdensome while for others it does not cause a problem. Some problem behaviors will be handled effectively by some caregivers but produce only ineffectual efforts by others. This means that no definitive listing either of behaviors or techniques to handle them can be proposed. It is possible, however, to describe clusters of difficulties and demonstrate their natures, effects, and handling. From these, caregivers may be able to extrapolate or generalize to other problems as they experience them.

How often and when a "problem behavior" (i.e., one that produces a severe burden for the caregiver) occurs is unknown. There are some behaviors that are more often mentioned and described than others, but such data usually come from support groups or surveys, which means that the sample of individuals used for the cataloging may not be representative of the majority of caregivers. It may be that those caregivers who are not sampled experience different kinds of problems altogether. It is possible, even, that the unsampled group has developed better coping skills and thus experiences less burden. The most probable case, though, is that the kinds of dilemmas included in this chapter are a fair representation of the most demanding actions encountered on a day-to-day basis.

Many times the frustration and helplessness felt by the caregiver is due to the fact that the patient does things that are incomprehensible when compared with past behavior. What caregivers may not know, or under the pressure of the moment do not remember, is that the brain of the patient is not competent in the same sense that it was before the disease process began. What was well rehearsed and accurate responding in the past is no longer available to the patient because the basic unit of the brain, the neuron, is now dysfunctional. Because they are diseased, large numbers of neurons in specific parts of the brain no longer allow the person to function adequately. One caregiver, for example, reported that one of the most maddening things her mother (who had been diagnosed as having Alzheimer's) did was to ignore instructions. She had given her mother some medication that the doctor had prescribed and told her that there was water in the blue cup on the table. There were also some pieces of china, silverware, a flower vase, and so on, on the same table. What her mother did was to pick up successively every item but the blue cup! This was interpreted by the daughter to be a deliberate and perverse behavior to irritate her. If so, the mother was successful. There is the alternative possibility, however, that diseased cells that would have functioned efficiently in the past were now destroyed. Another pattern or pathway now had to be used. In some unexplainable fashion, the cells now involved *excluded* the correct response and "ordered" every other possible response instead.

Another example says something about the generalization of damage influencing actions and behaviors that may still be technically healthy. Many caregivers report that the patient now loves sweets and sometimes will refuse to eat anything else, or will eat the other parts of the meal only if given dessert first. In addition, the patient does not gain weight even though he or she may eat large quantities of sweets. This may mean that the metabolism of the dementia patient differs from that of the rest of us. Does cell destruction interfere effectively with metabolic processes in dementia? It would seem that this may very well be the case.

Ultimately, no matter what the behavior and reactions to it, caregivers wish to know why such bizarre actions occur. Our knowledge of the brain, the cells that allow us to remember and stay oriented, is incomplete. There can be no sensible explanation with our present knowledge. This is yet another reason why research efforts are vital and why funding must be increased to meet the need. In the meantime, the destructive tendencies of dementia continue and must be faced as effectively as possible by the caregiver.

Major Problem Behaviors in Dementia

The dementia patient, in a few cases, may remain much as he or she was before except for the fact that memory loss and dependence increase. In most cases, however, there can be one or more changes in the behavior of the individual. Some of these changes may be marked and represent a difference that is difficult for the caregiver to understand and accept. Others may be less severe yet contribute to an increasing burden on the caregiver. The effects experienced are as much a matter of perception and coping by the caregiver as they are inherent in the behaviors themselves.

A discussion of "major behavior problems" must be based not only on number of occurrences but on how they are perceived and reacted to by the caregiver. There are at least three principal divisions or types of behavior that may become severe burdens to the caregiver. One of these includes actions that express some attempt by the patient to maintain independence but that require additional effort on the part of the caregiver. A second area revolves around activities that are a routine part of daily life under normal circumstances. Since "normality" becomes less likely in the patient's behavior, these too may come to represent disruptive

and stressful events to the caregiver. The third classification includes a variety of behaviors that reflect the incompetence of the
patient to function in a socially acceptable manner. Examples of
each of these three areas compose the remainder of this chapter.

Independence Behaviors

Some of the most often reported sources of frustration and
anger in caregivers focus on behaviors that seem to indicate the
patient is trying to continue to be independent. Unfortunately, the
patient does not have the cognitive control or awareness that is
expected in the normally functioning adult. The patient's actions,
as a result, create conflict because they may be dangerous or
impossible to deal with. The caregiver must try to maintain some
order and sensibility under a set of circumstances where the
patient no longer understands and communication is difficult and
sometimes impossible.

Wandering

The focus of this behavior is movement; wanderers are persons who walk whether or not there is a destination to be reached.
In its most acceptable form, the patient will move around in a
contained and safe area for some period of time from minutes to
hours. Since exercise is healthy, such movement should be allowed, perhaps even joined for our own physical well-being. If it
is necessary to have the patient do something else, and he or she
will not attend to requests, a tour or two with him or her may then
be diverted to the kitchen for a meal or the bathroom for a shower,
or wherever needed. Though it may not work out as you wish, it is
worth the effort. Should the patient persist in walking, delay any
action that is not essential until later. There are some attitudes and
actions that you must be willing to practice: stay calm, be objective, maintain a sense of humor, be realistic.

There are instances where more concern must be present. A
patient who cannot remember where he or she lives, who will

ignore traffic to go where he or she wishes, or who will become lost must be protected. For those who leave the house, it may be necessary to remove door handles, or replace them with locks that the patient cannot open. Slide bolts may be a solution to prevent the person from leaving the house. If you need to constrain the patient to certain areas, put warning devices on doors of rooms you do not want entered. A bell that rings when it is struck by an opening door can alert you to a potential danger in an inexpensive but practical way. You can even have different-sized bells on different doors so that the sound alerts you to a particular area of the house. Since you cannot always be present when a patient wanders, make sure that dangerous objects and toxic substances are out of sight and reach.

Outside, if there is a fenced yard with a gate that has a foolproof lock, the patient can be left unattended to move about as he or she wishes. Be certain that when the patient is outdoors he or she has proper identification. A bracelet or sign sewn onto clothing containing name and address, phone number, and other informative details can help others notify you in case the patient escapes and becomes lost. Let the police and neighbors know that the patient has a severe memory problem. If and when they see the patient, they will know better how to react and return him or her safely rather than cause confusion and distress in the patient.

If the patient wanders during the night, it is best to have the house well lighted so that he or she does not feel insecure or does not blunder into things. If you have a multistory home, it may be necessary to place safety gates at stairways, both top and bottom. Provide labels on doors so that the patient can recognize the function served there. If the person can still read and comprehend, words will be sufficient. Thus, "bathroom" in block letters can help signal the patient that this is where he or she goes for elimination. If reading is a lost skill, prepare a sign with pictures: a commode and lavatory, for example. This can be done with pictures cut from magazines and pasted on a piece of cardboard or wood that can be attached to the door in a semipermanent manner. It may not be beautiful decor but it can help your sanity. After all, psychiatrists are expensive!

Wanderers apparently have an abundance of energy without effective ways to work it off. Involving them in household chores and tasks may help to reduce the need to walk. Probably this will have to include shared duties so that you can supervise. This also gives you an opportunity, however, to talk and to reassure the patient that he or she is someone who is still important, helpful, and dependable. In the same way, for a patient who walks for longer periods, take a stroll in the park or through the neighborhood with him or her if that does not lead to other kinds of difficulties. Whatever arrangements you make, be alert to the physical welfare of the patient. Severe weight loss can result if inadequate nutrition is present. Adequate food and fluids are essential to well-being. Though the patient may say that he or she is not hungry or thirsty, a calm and deliberate attitude from you along with *shared* food or water may lead to participation. If the patient takes too little and starts moving again, after a few minutes repeat your efforts. The patient is not apt to remember what happened just minutes before anyway.

There is one other possibility if you have exhausted every effort and cannot succeed in caring adequately for the wandering patient: physical restraints. However, restraints should only be *a last resort* and they may be the least successful. To restrain a person can lead to resistance, physical and mental distress, loss of cooperation in other phases of life, even accelerated decline. If you do decide to use restraint, do so as little as possible. Only when it is essential to the welfare of both the patient and you should it be employed.

Why do so many patients wander? No one knows exactly though there has been speculation by many professionals. Perhaps it serves a need that is not easy for us to recognize, such as the working off of restlessness and agitation. Perhaps it is a reversion to old habits. Maybe it is a reaction to a medication the patient is taking. There may be too little stimulation in the life of the patient and this action provides some. The changes occurring in brain cells may be in an area that is associated with a need for movement. Whatever the reason, wandering must be recognized and it must be provided for. Your ability to be creative in the presence of a distressing behavior can help you to cope more effectively.

"I Want to Go Home!"

One of the most distressing statements that a caregiver can hear is "I want to go home," particularly if the patient has been placed in a nursing home. It is apt to be interpreted in the most literal sense no matter where the patient may be. What the patient actually is trying to communicate is not so clear as the caregiver may believe. In fact, there have been active efforts to return the patient to the home from which he or she was removed without reducing the request. Where the demented person is still at home, there have been attempts to return the individual to a former home, even to the home of his or her childhood when it still exists. None of these work very often to reduce the request.

When the patient repeatedly asks to go home, it is best to analyze the dynamics of the situation. In the nursing home, for example, it may be well to consider how recently the move was made, how well the patient has adapted to the new setting, and how stimulating (or overstimulating) the facility may be. If still at home, there may be a need to consider conditions of stress and isolation. The statement may be a cry to overcome insecurity or stress. Boredom may be a factor as well, so an attempt at distraction may offer relief.

As with all other behaviors, the caregiver must remain calm. For example, when the patient says, "I want to go home," the caregiver may offer reassurance and support by saying, "You don't need to be concerned. You and I will be able to get along fine here." Then follow this with a distractor: "Let's have some coffee and talk about what we will do tomorrow." If these attempts do not work, take the patient for a walk or a car ride—not to find "home" but as a distraction. By the time you return, the issue may no longer be present.

Keep the setting where the patient resides as familiar and comfortable as possible. Changes are apt to be upsetting, so it is better to keep things as they have been than to redecorate or remodel, as much as that might be needed. In the home, keep reminders of past homes as muted and out of sight as possible. This does not mean that all memorabilia should be removed, or that there may not be times when it will be worthwhile to review the past. For the patient who keeps asking to go home, however, the fewer things that stimulate that response the better.

There are some drugs that can be prescribed by the doctor that will relax the patient when he or she is under stress. The use of medications should be carefully controlled, however, since many have adverse side effects. Remember that the brain of any older person has already suffered some effects of damage to nerve cells. This is even more true in dementia patients. A damaged or diseased brain will react more intensely to drug therapy than a healthy one. Further, the aging body does not metabolize as efficiently and effectively as it did at younger ages. Drugs have been shown to be more potent in the elderly than in younger adults. With the demented person this potency is even greater. Tranquilizer use can actually increase the problems experienced by the patient. There is even greater danger in using a sedative with a dementia patient. If used, careful monitoring is mandatory and any sign of adverse effects must be reported immediately to the physician who prescribed the drug.

Why do some dementia patients repeatedly ask to go home? As noted in the first paragraph of this section, no one really knows. In part, that is because you cannot be sure, with a person in a demented state, whether the statement represents a conscious and deliberate mental process or not. Since many patients who have been taken back to past homes still ask the question, it seems reasonable that they do not mean the request in the literal sense in which it might be interpreted. The brain may be malfunctioning so that a previously well-rehearsed connection is triggered even without awareness or intent. This would mean that the expression has no real meaning; it is a residual of some past times and events.

One could argue just as strongly, however, that the request occurs because there is too little in the environment to assure the patient that he or she is at home. This would imply that more reminders of the past should be present. Just as plausible would be the assumption that the phrase is meaningless in any real sense. It is a kind of routinized "noise" or chant that is not intended to lead to a response by the caregiver.

Whatever the true meaning, the same cautions must be observed by the caregiver: objectivity, support, humor, realism, and rationality.

Agitation

Agitation is a state that may occur in concert with other behaviors, such as wandering. However, it may be present without expression through other actions and so must be considered in its own right. An agitated individual is one who is apt to be upset, argumentative when challenged, rebellious, abusive, and irrational. It is often impossible to use a rational argument with a person who is agitated. There may be anger, even rage. The reaction is more likely to occur early in the process of developing dementia as the patient recognizes that he or she is losing control over his or her personal life. However, some individuals express agitation at any point in the process. An agitated state may bode danger to others, so caregivers must be prepared to encounter physical abuse and know how and when to protect themselves.

If there is an attempt at physical attack by the patient, the caregiver must act so as to prevent being hurt (or causing hurt to the patient). So long as the caregiver is stronger (and willing to use the necessary strength), it may be possible to overwhelm and control the patient. Where the caregiver is hesitant to use physical prowess or is not physically strong, self-protection must include escape, at least for the moment. There must be resources that can be summoned to help control the patient. These may include other family members or neighbors—but they must be immediately available and accessible. It may even be necessary to call the police, but this should be done cautiously since it brings in a legal element that may lead to misinterpretation of the patient's actions and your responses.

Once agitation has been expressed and is seen as a problem by the caregiver, a physician may be consulted. Examination may disclose some physical condition that is treatable. If not, the doctor may prescribe a drug (such as a tranquilizer) but side effects must be recognized. An analysis of the situation in which the agitation occurred may help identify a particular incident or stimulus that generated the episode. If so, the environment can be controlled to reduce, even exclude, the possibility of a reoccurrence.

Involving the patient in interesting activities that require expenditure of energy may also help reduce the occurrence of agitation. Keep the environment as calm and secure as possible with stimulation at a minimal level. Consistency is often reassuring to dementia patients and increases their feelings of security. Respond to expressed needs as quickly as possible, and in a calm and controlled manner. Never leave tools that can be harmful to the patient or caregiver within reach. As agitation begins, distract the patient with some favorite activity or reward.

The causes of agitation are no better known than the causes of other behaviors already discussed. It seems likely that strain and unexpected change can be one factor in its onset. Personal events that may contribute to agitation include physical problems, loss of control over life as dementia expresses itself, drug side effects, sensory loss (such as vision or hearing), even stress and fatigue. Environmental factors include change in surroundings, unexpected and unreasonable demands, loss of control by the caregiver (no matter how deserved), and either under- or overstimulation from the setting. The caregiver may have particular difficulty in pinpointing the reasons for agitated states, so preparation must include willingness and ability to remain calm, objective, and supportive, anticipating when to respond and when to distract.

Restlessness

A behavior that often accompanies wandering and states of agitation is restlessness. However, the behavior may occur on its own. Restlessness is characterized by a relatively persistent nervousness, movement—perhaps accompanied by vocal sounds that are not directed at anything in particular—picking at clothing or objects, an appearance of insecurity, and an inability to attend (listen) to instructions or conversations. In fact, it may be impossible to get the patient involved with an activity no matter how interesting. Mealtimes may be difficult since the person concentrates so little on what is immediately at hand. Having the restless patient take responsibility for tasks (either physical or mental) he or she is still able to do requires constant supervision and reminders. For this reason, caregivers may find it simpler to do these tasks for the individual than to go to the trouble required to get the patient to do them.

Restlessness may be a way in which the patient fills time that has no real meaning. Disorientation is strongly implicated in the behavior, particularly when there are no other accompanying symptoms such as agitation. The person is "lost" in a time and space vacuum that is filled with purposeless behaviors. These behaviors are well coordinated at the same time that they are meaningless. As a result, we are faced with an individual who may have more competence available than seems apparent. The problem becomes one of attempting to tap that competence. With our present knowledge and skills, the chances that actions can be better directed are very small. There should be efforts to engage the patient in conversation on past events that had significance. Try to get the person to walk or participate in other forms of exercise. Any engagement will represent a gain, and may offer a clue of more ways to involve the individual with life.

Since disorientation in time and space is one of the universals of dementia, it would help if we knew why it occurs. In part, disorientation results from memory losses that are predominant in the condition but it has its own aspects as well. Each of us operates in the dimensions of time and space, creating our personal realities. When we share portions of our reality with the reality perceived by others, we can communicate and relate. If our version of reality differs markedly from that of those around us, there is less basis for contact and relating. The problem for the restless patient may come from altered and malfunctioning brain cells, but there is no evidence that some specific part (or parts) of the brain is directly involved in disorientation. It seems more plausible that the function of awareness in time and space has evolved as a part of our intellectual competencies. As humans, we have developed skills that permit us to use both spoken and written language as tools for communication and we intellectually deal with verbal symbols to increase our notion of reality. With the restless person, one who seems largely or totally abstracted, this behavior with verbal symbols may be altered or lost. The reason why is not known but the effect is obvious. The interventions suggested above, then, are based on self-awareness and contact with others. The effect may be less than desired but, as mentioned, any breakthrough can be a step toward reestablishment of reality by the patient.

Abusiveness

One of the most frightening of the behaviors allied with attempts at maintaining independence is abuse, either verbal or physical. This expression is not necessarily related to past behaviors. Persons who have been gentle may become terrors as the dementia progresses. (Conversely, some who have been abusive in the past may become subdued during the progression of the dementia.) Though abusive behavior may occur at any time during the course of dementia, it is most likely to occur in the earlier developmental period. Early appearance suggests that it may reflect the frustration, anger, and fear of the patient as he or she becomes aware that changes are occurring that cannot be controlled. There is a consequent lashing out, perhaps at the environment in general but more probably at one who is and has been close—the primary caregiver. Under these conditions, it seems that the abusiveness is a kind of cry for help from a person who cannot conceive of any ways to help himself or herself. This explanation does not make the effects any easier or more acceptable for the caregiver but it does provide some rationale for why the actions occur. After all, the two parties have probably supported and assisted each other over many years. Why, then, when things seem so terrifying does the other not reply, do something, reverse this terrible thing that is happening?

The abusive events are usually unexpected because they are not provoked by the caregiver. In the mind of the patient, distortions seem to be occurring that demand some control. The patient's intellectual functions are dissipating but at the same time lucid and conscious periods still remain. The effect is a channeling of energy that must be expelled and a focus on some object that merits the role of responsibility. Unfortunately, the patient is not apt to express the pent-up energy on some suitable target, something inanimate that can absorb the blows without damage. Where the patient still can and will participate in situations that provide such an opportunity, they should be used as often as possible. For example, if golf has been a favored pastime, continue the activity as much and as often as possible. Engaging the patient in strong physical activity expends energy and may reduce the occurrence of abusive attacks. Rug beating, spading in the garden, whatever will engage the individual in exertion should be attempted.

If the abusive behavior continues as the dementia progresses, there is less likelihood that such distractors will work. When abusive behavior occurs, the caregiver must make sure to protect himself or herself. Do not remain in a dangerous situation. Have resources such as family or neighbors alerted to answer a call immediately. Talk to your doctor about some means to keep the patient as calm as possible, perhaps with a tranquilizer. As a last resort, call the police but remember that this may involve the legal community in a way that is difficult to control.

The direct cause of abusive behavior is unknown. Because it is more often found earlier in the dementing process, it may be a more conscious behavior than some of the other conditions discussed in this chapter. However, since it can occur at any time, it is just as likely that it is a lashing out by the patient that is not really understood, under conditions where he or she feels a loss of control. The danger involved makes physical abuse, particularly, an outcome for which the caregiver must exercise care and self-protection.

Daily Life Behaviors

Though perhaps less dangerous than some of the independence behaviors discussed above, there are changes influencing normal and routine activities that may also become major problems. When they occur, they provoke frustration and, sometimes, anger. They interfere with the flow of daily life and make consistent demands on the caregiver. Because such matters seem so simple and reasonable, many caregivers find them almost impossible to accept calmly and rationally.

Bathing

We are a nation that believes in hygiene. Compared to many other modern and advanced countries, we appear to be fanatical about the need to bathe daily. The old adage Cleanliness Is Next to Godliness is more than a catch phrase to most of us. We are so concerned about body odor that we put on lotions and preparations—most containing scents that are pleasant—even after we have bathed ourselves! No wonder other people find us a bit strange and gauge our behavior as too focused on being disinfected. In fact, we probably do carry cleanliness to a greater degree than is required or necessary.

In any event, we pander to the need to be clean. It is no surprise, then, that caregivers who deal with a patient who refuses to keep immaculate find the consequences almost overwhelming. Some persons with dementia not only refuse to bathe daily, they refuse to bathe at all. Their odor becomes disgusting to everyone but themselves. Caregivers find themselves in an almost constant battle to get the individual to take a bath. How to handle the situation becomes an issue that may be resolved only with the greatest ingenuity. As with other behaviors, calmness and objectivity, combined with humor and preparation, are important tools to use. For some patients, for example, having a tub of water drawn and then informing the person that his or her bath is ready may be all that is necessary—at least sometimes. Or the individual may be offered a choice: "Do you want a bath or shower today?" Perhaps sharing a shower or tub may bring acquiescence that otherwise would be denied. Do not try to present elaborate arguments as to why a bath is necessary. Certainly avoid a shouting match, since the patient will respond to an emotional state with emotionality, not rationality. There is even the suggestion that a bath every day simply is not necessary, especially when the patient is not active. You may even want to combine the bath with a favorite reinforcer—for example, candy, as a reward may stimulate agreement. If the problem becomes too great, ask your doctor about the use of a medication (say, a tranquilizer). Remember, though, that if one is used, there must be careful monitoring for side effects. There is no sense in adding a second, and perhaps even greater, problem to the offensive odor.

Older persons react more to both hot and cold. Be sure that the water used for the shower or bath is warm but not excessively hot or cold. The patient may not realize what is wrong and be unable to tell you there is a problem. Just because you like a hot bath does not mean that everyone does. Nor is the traditional cold shower the effective answer to sexual arousal or any other sign of unacceptable behavior, even for those who are not suffering a dementia.

The usual disclaimer about a reason for refusing to bathe applies here as well. No one knows why this change occurs. Perhaps the brain damage that affects memory so adversely causes the person to feel threatened about getting into water.

Perhaps some individuals are hesitant about exposing themselves before others, even a partner, whom they no longer recognize. Even the momentary change in a routine that is comfortable may present itself as a kind of threat to be avoided. One likely possibility is the fact that the sense of smell is less acute in older persons. When a young person enters the house of an elder person, for example, he or she may be offended by the odor and wonder why the house smells. In fact, the odor may not be noticed by the owner. In dementia patients, this loss of sense of smell may be even greater. Whatever the reason, when you do get the person to take a bath, make it a thorough one. Be sure that the parts of the body that are susceptible to odor and that are often covered most or all of the time are cleaned and dried completely. The armpits, genital area, and anus are critical areas. As to the use of deodorants or perfumes, use them or not according to the patient's reactions. With creativity, humor, and calmness, the problem of bathing may be considerably reduced.

Dressing

Problems with getting a patient to change clothes frequently are associated with bathing problems. Caregivers report examples where the person insists on wearing the same clothing for days at a time even when clean clothes are available. Indeed, insistence and argument may simply intensify the difficulty. There are other instances, however, when the patient does not dress because he or she is unsure of what to wear or the order in which clothing should be put on.

The latter problem is simpler to deal with, and so let us consider it first. When a person is unsure of appropriate clothing, preparation can be a valuable assist. Give the patient some options by showing the right kind of clothes and then permitting him or her to choose what to wear. If the choice is for the next day, put the clothes out in a place where they can be seen easily. Always use the same location. If the order is a problem (i.e., what goes on first and what last), place the clothing in such a way that the underwear is always on top, followed by succeeding pieces. Should the patient still be capable of choosing clothing correctly, but unsure of the place where his or her clothing is kept, label dresser drawers, cabinets, and closets. The patient must be able to comprehend the labels (whether words or pictures) for this technique to work. Make sure you always check, as completely but unobservedly as possible, that the patient is dressed appropriately. Such arrangements will take little added time but will save embarrassment to both you and the patient.

A much more difficult matter to deal with is the patient's refusal to change clothing regularly. As with bathing, it may not be necessary to change clothes each day. After several days, however, even inactive persons need a clothing change. Follow the advice mentioned before: be calm, objective, realistic, creative, and maintain a sense of humor. Rational arguments are not going to be understood, in all probability, and irrational arguments may likely bring irrational behavior. Where a particular article of clothing is worn over and over, purchase another just like it or as nearly like it as possible. Even if the patient refuses to take off the clothes at any time, you can show him or her the articles and say something like, "Look, here is a gift. It's just like what you have on. Wouldn't you like to try it on to see that it fits okay?"

The reasons for refusal to change clothing are no better known than the reasons for not bathing. Possibly, the decrease in the sense of smell is important. Perhaps there is some sense of control in wearing the same clothes; it allows the individual to feel secure in a state that may be full of insecurity. On the other hand, the patient's brain may have suffered neuronal damage in an area causing distortion in understanding and perspective about this kind of issue. Whatever the explanation may be, your efforts must be controlled and consistent.

Eating

Appetite can be difficult to judge. Some dementia patients continue to eat and enjoy foods while others must be coerced to take just a bite or two at a time. Although elderly persons in general show changes in metabolic rate (the way in which energy sources are used by the body's cells), there seem to be somewhat more exaggerated changes in dementia patients. Some caregivers report, for example, that the patient will eat only sweets yet not gain weight. Whether or not weight gain occurs, sweets do seem to be a common preference. Caregivers sometimes have problems in assuring themselves that the patient is receiving a healthy diet.

You should maintain regular meals and mealtimes. Serve nutritious food, and serve the meal in a place that is traditional for the two of you to eat. Keep the setting as uncluttered with distractions as possible unless the patient still reacts positively to such things as flowers and candles. Do not offer too many choices; usually having one- or two-course meals will be more successful. If the patient demands some food that is normally not served with the meal, do not get involved in an argument. For example, if the person wants cake first, serve it and then move on to the other dishes. If the patient will not eat the meal after the cake, have cake *with* the meal (at least for the patient) next time. Use what the patient will eat in order to get him or her to eat what an adequate diet demands.

A quiet, relaxed meal will more probably be eaten than one that is too "busy." If the patient wants to eat with a spoon, allow it. Do not insist on dainty table manners at the expense of nutrition. In this respect, finger foods may work well and should be tried at least occasionally. When the patient has difficulty using a utensil, provide one the patient can use. An example might be a spoon with a wooden attachment that makes it easier to hold. Such items are for sale in many medical stores, but if you cannot afford the prices, get some assistance from a family member or a neighbor who does woodwork. It does not have to be pretty if it is effective. Never serve too much; a full bowl of soup can become a disaster that disrupts and even ends the meal. Nor should food be too hot or too cold.

The cause of extreme loss of appetite can be due to any of

several factors. Since the brain interprets signals from the body about discomfort of any sort, it seems possible that due to nerve-cell damage the signals from the stomach that cells need nutrition are not being received or interpreted. Loss of sense of smell may reduce the stimulation the rest of us get from smelling foods as they are being prepared. The consequent effects on the digestive system are no longer present. How often have you said, for example, "My, that smells good. My mouth is watering." Smell is even more important than taste to our enjoyment of food. The taste buds on the tongue (sweet, sour, salty, and bitter) show deterioration in the elderly, and consequently food may not taste as good as it once did. Sometimes we see older people adding salt to dishes that are already salty enough. That is because they are getting less stimulation from salt taste than they did when they were younger, and particularly where they have overused salt anyway.

Eating is also related to habit. As memory fades, well-rehearsed behaviors are forgotten, at least partially. As a result, the patient forgets to eat or avoids eating. Even after a bite or two is taken, there may be a tendency on the part of the patient to stop and go on to something more stimulating. Do not give up; in a few moments, bring the person back to the table and start over. Even if it takes many attempts and much longer than you would like, the goal of a complete meal can be achieved.

Hoarding

Some patients will hide objects that may or may not have value. *Why* they do may be based on a need for security or to maintain as one's own something that is personal. In some cases, the word "hide" is really not appropriate. With such poor memory, it may be a matter of misplacement or losing rather than hiding. Whichever is the best explanation, the behavior causes concern for caregivers and sometimes leads to conflict with the patient. For example, if the person has misplaced some valued item, he or she may accuse the caregiver of taking it and demand its immediate return. When you are investing so much effort in making the patient comfortable and secure, the accusation can be distressing.

When hoarding behavior occurs over a period of time, it is possible that the same place will be used for the hoarding practice. It is a bit like the squirrel who puts nuts in the same tree cavity every fall. By being observant you may discover this favorite place. When the patient complains of some object being taken, you can retrieve it quietly and quickly. If you do not know the hiding place, try suggesting that the two of you look for the object. For example, you might say, "I know that it's one of your favorite things. Let's see if we can't find it by looking together." Although you may not have any luck, the search will give you an opportunity to distract the patient in another direction.

Forgetting may well be the best explanation for "lost" objects. The more extreme examples of hoarding may also involve the need to possess something of one's own. This provides a sense of security and control over life. As with other frustrating behaviors, as a caregiver you must remain calm, objective, good humored, creative. I may be sounding like a broken record by now, but it is still the best advice. Ultimately you are the most responsible and responsive agent for the patient.

Functional Behaviors

There are a variety of behaviors that reflect actions or functions that do not fit the independence or daily activities categories. Sometimes they are clearly a part of life processes, like sleeping and sexuality, yet some are also unusual manifestations of normal processes, like incontinence. The discussion that follows describes a number of these types of behaviors.

Sleep Disturbances

Sleep is recognized as a necessary action that allows restoration of the body through rest and dreaming. However, there are many myths about sleep and its expressions, particularly among elderly persons. Most older people subscribe to the belief that each of us requires eight hours of sleep during the night in order to be healthy. This sleep must also be "deep" in its texture so that we feel rested and reinvigorated when we awaken. These ideas, though they may be popular, are not quite accurate.

The amount of sleep needed to restore the body depends on several factors. Babies and teenagers, for example, are growing and may well need more than eight hours of sleep. Adults who are involved in strenuous work and exercise may also require more than eight hours sleep. Those who work in jobs that require little physical energy do not necessarily need as much sleep. As we grow older, we may become more sedentary (unless we exercise and use the body's muscles regularly) so we will not need as much sleep as we did earlier in life. This means that some people may require only six hours of sleep while others may need ten hours or more. Further, whatever amount is needed for restoration of the body is during a 24-hour period, and not just at night. If an older person naps for an hour or two after lunch and goes to bed at ten o'clock, he or she might expect to awaken around three o'clock in the morning and not feel sleepy. This is not unhealthy, and sleep during different parts of the 24-hour period is sleep nonetheless. Night sleep is not better for you than daytime sleep.

There is also the matter of deep sleep. Physiologists who study the sleep phenomenon have found that *no one* goes to sleep and stays in deep sleep the entire period. In fact, there are usually five cycles that occur in a normal sleep period. Figure 8.1 illustrates both the stages and cycles of sleep. Note that early in the pattern, there are longer periods of deep sleep (though not continuous) than in the later cycles. In addition, in stages 2 and 3, there occurs what is called "rapid eye movement" (REM) sleep. It is during REM sleep that we do most of our dreaming. REM sleep occurs in short periods initially but increases in time as we approach awakening. Though there is incomplete agreement, it seems that dreaming is both natural and necessary, whether or not we remember the dream content.

This pattern of sleep stages and cycles is based on the study of

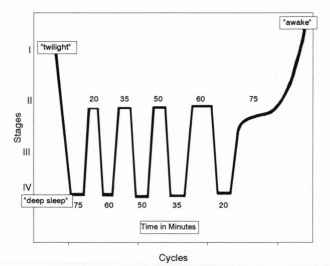

Figure 8.1. Idealized sleep pattern of adult during complete cycle.

healthy young adults and so may not be typical of the elderly. Generally, we not only need less sleep as we age but we also spend less time in deep sleep and more time in stages 2 and 3. This does not mean that older persons do not get enough sleep or that their sleep is less healthy.

The patient with dementia may show changes in sleep pattern, but there may be additional factors that mean problems. Some caregivers report that the patient will sleep very little at night, get up often, demand breakfast, want to go out, and generally cause a loss of sleep for an already exhausted attendant. A first step if you have such a problem is to chart the sleep time and activities of the patient. Note whether or not the person is napping during the day, when and how long the naps are, and what the total hours slept are in a 24-hour period. Table 8.1 has been prepared for such a notation. Keep the record for a week, at least, in order to assure stability in the results. If you find that the

Table 8.1
Charting Patient Sleep Patterns

Time	Asleep?	Activity before sleep	Activity after sleep
Midnight to 3 AM			
3 AM to 6 AM			
6 AM to 9 AM			
9 AM to noon			
Noon to 3 PM			
3 PM to 6 PM			
6 PM to 9 PM			
9 PM to midnight			
Note unusual events and variations:			

patient does sleep during the day, you can do one of two things. The easiest is to nap at the same time, but that may not always be convenient. The other is to engage the patient in activity at the time the nap is normally taken. There may then be less likelihood that only brief periods of sleep occur at night.

Stimulants should be avoided in late afternoon or evening. Do not serve coffee with the evening meal, for example. Alcohol with the evening meal, in small quantities and if not contrary to medical recommendations, may be relaxing and help the patient to sleep better. Do not give the patient more than four ounces of wine or a one-ounce cocktail, however, or the effect may be more detrimental than helpful. Ask your doctor about the effects of any medications that the patient is taking. If a medication is contributing to the problem, it may be possible that dosage can be adjusted, time of day when it is taken can be changed, or a different and less stimulating drug can be prescribed.

The bedroom should be a restful place. Do not use "busy" bedcovers, for example. If the walls are brightly colored, change the wallpaper or repaint in more restful tones. You want the patient stimulated during waking hours, not during sleeping hours. Make sure that a glass of water is available at bedside, if needed during the night, and that the bathroom is lighted sufficiently for the patient to locate it without trouble. Sleeping powders or liquids must be used carefully if at all. Sedatives very often produce side effects even in the healthy brain. A doctor should approve any such medication if it is going to be used.

The causes of sleeplessness at night have already been partly described. A tired and sleepy patient will sleep better than one who is well rested. Even with the best efforts, however, there will be times when the person does not sleep for very long at night. The damage to brain cells may account for such behavior since stimuli cannot be interpreted accurately or may not be sensed at all. Let's rehearse the same litany as for other problems: stay calm, be objective, prepare as well as you can, maintain a sense of humor, and be creative in your efforts. If your house is safe (in the sense that the patient cannot get out and there are no dangerous objects easily available), you may even allow the patient to get up and move about the house freely while you rest.

Verbal Noises

A patient may call out, make noises that are not understood, or use words over and over. Sometimes moaning occurs that sounds as though the person is in pain or psychological distress. In other cases, words like "help me" will be said over and over although it is not clear what the request means. Usually, these kinds of noises begin to occur only after the dementia has progressed to the point where communication is very difficult.

It may be that the sounds do imply some discomfort that the patient can no longer identify or express directly. Check him or her to be sure that clothing is not chafing or binding, that there are no lesions or sores that need treatment, or that he or she has not been incontinent. In most cases, there will be no such problem, or any other identifiable cause of verbal noise. It is possible, of course, that the noises do not have meaning; they may be a repetitive pattern that is generated from the brain even though there is no stimulating event present. We do know that, even in individuals without dementia, some responses can be elicited without stimulation, principally in highly practiced actions. For example, my heart and respiration rates may increase if I think of a frightening event even though there is no physical threat present.

It may help to reassure the patient by speaking gently and softly. Say his or her name, and talk about some pleasant event from the past. Touch the patient's hand to provide a contact that may help establish reality. Keep the environment calm and peaceful for less stimulating effect. If the noises are so loud or continuous that they become disturbing, ask your doctor about a possible drug to use. Remember, however, that drugs can introduce more problems than they may be able to help. The more you can deal with difficulties on the behavioral level the better.

Repetition

Though this topic is certainly related to the one above, it has its singular effects also. For one, repetition of verbal messages from a patient may begin much earlier than the less specific verbal noises. Caregivers often report that the patient will ask the same question over and over, always accepting the answer, but soon thereafter repeating the question. After a meal is over, and even when the patient has eaten well and cannot be hungry, there may come the query: "When are we going to eat?" The caregiver may say, "We just ate a few minutes ago. You had some meat and vegetable and salad, remember?" The answer may come back, "Oh, sure, that's right." There may be quiet for a while, even conversation on other topics, but eventually comes the question about eating again. Indeed, the repetitions may be so frequent that they become the source of an angry outburst by the caregiver. Of course, the patient does not understand why, and the caregiver may feel guilty.

The source of such questioning over and over is in the fading memory. The problem is related to short-term retention. When there is some stimulus for memory from the environment, the stimulus must be encoded by the brain and stored. As the damage to nerve cells accumulates in the hippocampus (a portion of the brain where memory functions begin), there is less possibility for healthy cells to carry out the processes of reception, encoding, and passing the message to other centers for storage. In other words, the message is never really perceived. Since the idea of eating and being satiated (satisfied) has occurred over and over again in the life of the person, a reminder by the caregiver may momentarily lead to recognition of the relationship. That recognition, however, is only for the moment. Whatever stimulates the question itself is not monitored by the brain and the question will reoccur.

As much as possible, the question should be answered directly and calmly. It may be possible to ignore the patient at times though that will not necessarily lead to the end of questioning. Be as supportive and reassuring as possible. Use some humor as a means of changing the structure of the situation. Say, for example, when asked about eating, "Goodness, if we eat every time you ask, I'll get too fat to be able to fix a meal." This may distract the patient enough to change direction. Other means of distraction may also engage the patient and avoid the dreaded repetition. It is best to use such distractors *before* the question is asked, not just after. "Shall we take a walk?" may appeal to the individual who otherwise will keep repeating the same message.

Incontinence

We assume that when an individual loses control of the bladder or bowel that there is a physical cause. Thus, a dementia patient with such a problem should have a complete medical checkup to find a cause and suggest a treatment. In many cases, though, the loss of bladder or bowel control in dementia is related to a dysfunctional brain.

When the bladder is full or the bowel needs to be evacuated, you feel a distention and discomfort that you, via your brain, have learned to associate with elimination. In the case of dementia, however, the message may not have been received by healthy brain cells. There can be no accurate interpretations as a result. The patient may urinate or defecate in his or her clothing, wherever he or she is. This may be as embarrassing to the patient as it is to the caregiver. It is not done to cause a problem or to irritate anyone. It is a manifestation of a brain that no longer functions effectively.

To avoid such problem behavior, make a chart of the times when the patient eliminates. This chart must be plotted over several days, perhaps even a week or two, to assure that a consistent pattern is established. Once plotted, the caregiver can anticipate when there is likely to be a need to go to the bathroom. It is also a good technique to avoid liquids before going out or in the evening before going to bed. Indeed, establish a schedule when liquids and food will be consumed. This will fit the pattern as well. Underclothing is available that will absorb liquids and save embarrassment. Its use may be well worth the cost.

Cleaning a patient after an incontinent episode is an unpleasant task. This makes it imperative that you understand the dynamics involved in the patient's behavior, anticipate needs, and calmly and gently handle the situation.

Sundowner Syndrome

For some unknown reason, many dementia patients become restless and agitated during the late afternoon and early evening.

They may become more active than at any other time of day and want to walk or move about. The term "sundowner" was chosen for this behavior because of the time of day when the occurrence is most frequent. Attempts at dealing with the behavior often focus on distractions. Involving the patient in some activity that requires action may reduce the evident tension, direct the energy in some more productive direction, and lead to greater calmness.

The time of day the agitation occurs suggests that the period when day turns to night makes the person insecure. Insulate the person from the stimulus of decreasing light by closing curtains and turning on bright lights. Be reassuring and calm in your own reactions. Talk in a soothing tone. Keep the patient in an environment that induces relaxation. If necessary, consult with your doctor about medications, but remember the problems that may result from use of drugs with a brain that is already dysfunctional.

Sexuality

Perhaps the strongest drive affecting human behavior is that for sexual gratification. Although it is true that we must have fluids, nutrition, and air in order to live, we do not need sexual relief to survive. However, the drive to perpetuate the species is extremely strong. There is the added factor that sexual expression is a highly pleasurable state. The act of orgasm is so intense that it will be induced as often as possible by most persons. Human beings can achieve sexual arousal and satisfaction at any time. It is not necessary for the female to be receptive; there is no period when the woman is "in heat" as is true in many other animal species. In fact, it is not even necessary to have a partner of the opposite sex. Indeed, one does not need a partner at all in order to reach an orgasm. Yet human societies throughout history have put constraints on sexual expression by designating when, where, with whom, and how sex is "appropriate." Such strictures have not prevented achieving pleasure although they may have reduced the frequency of occurrence. Certainly the taboos have invited the presence of guilt and denial, leading to the possibility of psychological maladjustment.

In dementia, the formerly held attitudes that acted as inhibitors of sexual expression are no longer present in many cases. This applies to both men *and* women. Since the socially determined suppressors are no longer active, the patient may react solely on the basis of a pleasure principle. The demand may be made on a spouse when the urge is present regardless of whether or not the partner is willing or interested. There is a good chance that foreplay will be bypassed completely in the seeking of immediate sexual gratification. The patient may even accost an unrelated person, or a stranger, because there is no longer the mental control that once was present.

In some cases, maybe more often in men than women, masturbation may be practiced—wherever the patient is, with no regard for other persons. It is possible also, of course, that the patient will be secretive in the practice. There is even the chance that sexual desire will no longer exist for the patient. All these conditions make the life of the caregiver more difficult. Marriage often is enriched by the mutual achievement of orgasm. Though drive may slow down in older age, desire frequently does not. Studies tell us that sexually active older men and women remain competent to practice sex in a satisfying manner. If the normal sex drive cannot be satisfied in a manner acceptable to the individual, life can lose some of its value.

Sex is not a subject that is openly discussed by older persons in our society. Gathering data on sexual preferences and practices has, as a result, been difficult. It seems reasonable, however, that as a person ages, as long as sexual pleasure is desired, some means to accomplish it will be found. There may even be more practice of masturbation in older persons because of reservations about finding a partner or having homosexual contacts. Heterosexual contact no doubt is the most preferable but it may not be possible. Among those over age 65, for example, there are many more women than men. If a spouse dies, finding another may be difficult. Even if one is willing to practice sex outside marriage, the available choices are limited.

Why the dementia patient loses awareness of the social reasons for private sex with a proper partner may well be due to neural destruction in the frontal lobe of the brain where higher thinking processes are located. The *drive* is no different, really, than that found in lower animals. Yet humans are capable of understanding relationships and consequences in a way that lower animals cannot. This is due to the development of the cortex, the top part of the brain. Conditions, such as Alzheimer's, which cause dementia, primarily affect the neurons in the cortex. The rational qualities learned and practiced over a lifetime may be lost as a result. Meanwhile, the parts of the brain involved in sexual arousal and action are undisturbed. In one sense, then, the patient responds more like an animal than a human so far as sex is concerned.

Control of inappropriate sexual behavior will require ingenuity. The usual procedure of being calm and objective will have little effect on such a strong state. Distractors will have equally little effect; the sexually aroused patient may have little interest in anything else. Some caregivers seemingly simply give in to the demand and accept a one-sided act. Others resist, although this may lead to physical abuse. Still others apparently encourage the patient to satisfy himself or herself. Perhaps there are those fortunate people who also enjoy sex on any terms so that satisfaction is achieved by both parties. There is a great need for systematic study, which will occur only as caregivers are willing to disclose intimate, sometimes embarrassing, facts. It is hoped that future generations will escape many of the distressing feelings found in older caregivers today since sexuality is more openly discussed and accepted.

Summary

Behavior changes that evolve with dementia occur in great variety and with different intensities and meanings to caregivers. The dementia process that destroys the brain cells brings these alterations in behavior without consistency or order. The diversity makes it impossible to tell caregivers what to anticipate and when to expect it.

There are three behavioral areas that provide the opportunity for major problems to develop. One of these involves an attempt by the patient to maintain the independence expected in and by adults. This area includes behaviors such as wandering, expression of wanting to "go home," agitation and restlessness, and both verbal and physical abuse.

A second area encompasses daily life behaviors. Included here are problems of bathing, dressing, eating, and hoarding. Finally, there are behaviors involved in functioning in a normal environment. They include sleep disturbances, verbal "noises" and repetition, incontinence, the "sundowner syndrome," and sexual expression.

In this chapter each problem is described, examples given, potential interventions suggested, and possible causes discussed.

9

Helping the Caregivers

Whenever we are faced with major upheavals, we must be concerned with protecting our well-being and feelings of self-worth. Certainly, the process of caregiving can become extremely exhausting physically and psychologically. Stressors may become so intense and diversified that the concept of "major upheaval" is justified.

It is important for a caregiver to believe that he or she is a worthwhile individual, capable of mastering problems and dealing with consequences no matter how disturbing. Knowing *how* to maintain such beliefs is difficult in the face of anxiety and stress that disrupt the abilities to attend to what is happening and to deal effectively with the multiple changes. In this chapter, we consider some basic coping devices that assist in this task.

Maintaining Self-Worth

In defining self-worth (or self-esteem, as it is also known), we need to remember that the term applies to both long-term and short-term beliefs about ourselves and our efforts. When speaking of the long term, we refer to *general* beliefs about ourselves over a period of years perhaps. On the short-term basis, we mean literally moment-to-moment feelings based on immediate circumstances in life. Caregivers may experience reasonably high self-esteem in the general sense because most of life may have yielded evidence that they are worthwhile and capable. However, the contingencies of caregiving bring increasing emphasis on stressful day-to-day and moment-to-moment events. Evidence indicates that it is easier to affect (in either a positive or negative way) short-term feelings about oneself than long-term ones, which means that the increasing burdens of caregiving will make it easier for the caregiver to feel decreasingly worthwhile as the experience continues.

To reduce the negative effects on feelings of self-worth, there must be some understanding of the dynamics of the caregiving relationship. Several principles are involved.

1. *Caregiving, in its immediate status and impact, is a task with lessened, perhaps even low, opportunity to be successful.* It is tempting to think that you should feel good about caring for another who is less capable of caring for himself or herself. The problem is that, with dementia, there can be no realistic hope for cure (as can happen with many physical illnesses, for example). Indeed, there is no tangible evidence as to when the condition will reach its maximum and eventuate in death. The dementia patient may live for a number of years after diagnosis, becoming less and less concerned about seemingly anything but personal comforts. Our society supports the idea that caregiving is a rewarding behavior, and each of us tends to accept that view uncritically. Placed in a situation where the belief is thwarted, we have difficulty accepting the discrepancy.

You must be willing to accept the reality that the caregiving act is not a "win" situation. If you cannot agree to this fact, you should admit your inability to do so and remove yourself from the role. To preserve feelings of self-worth is impossible when you hope to have a positive influence that does not happen. These words may seem overly harsh and critical but they must be considered in terms of the goal of having self-esteem. If the primary caregiver is acting on the basis that he or she is essentially ineffective but perseveres because caretaking is a duty, interactions with the patient will reflect this attitude. You may feel used and bitter about a fate that others have obviously escaped. There will be few, if any, attempts to encourage the patient to use whatever competencies remain. Indeed, you will become so engaged in sacrificing yourself that life is tedium and punishment. Undoubtedly, there are caregivers who are trapped in this mode of operation. What it gains for either patient or caregiver would be hard to justify or defend.

2. *If a sensing of failure and perceptions of worthlessness begin, you must reorient.* You must first concentrate on situations that are not so heavily loaded with emotion—things that do not seem so critical, efforts that do not dispose you so much to self-deprecation. Instead, there must be some selection of situations and actions that appear easier and more attainable. It is then a matter of analysis: What did I as caregiver do? What worked? Why did it work in this case? Is there information I can apply to more difficult situations? This problem-solving process reinforces feelings of self-esteem, directs effort toward positive outcomes, and provides cues as to capabilities that may apply more broadly.

3. *As successes are appreciated, as you feel psychologically stronger and worthier, move to the next level of problems.* Identify those behaviors where you know you can succeed, even though they are minor. Remember, success breeds success. Never start with the most difficult and seemingly impossible situations in the caregiving task. Move toward them only gradually and, even then, only as you feel increasing competence and strength. Obviously, major difficulties cannot be ignored. Do *not* invest all your energy in them, however. Make sure you have positive instances during every day to reward your efforts. What you cannot yet handle will be easier to face.

4. *Reward Yourself!* Any gain you make is worthwhile and should be reinforced. Caregiving is no time for modesty—just as it is no time for assuming only failure. On a bad day, or at a bad time, stop and ask yourself: What are some of the things that I have done well recently? Keep a log of your efforts with an

objective evaluation if you wish. Then when the bad times happen, you do not have to try to reconstruct good ones. You have a written record that permits easy and immediate access to renewing feelings of self-esteem.

5. *Set objectives at an achievable level.* It is unrealistic to expect complete reversals in the demands of the patient. This is in part because Alzheimer's is untreatable. After all, if a physician cannot reverse the cause of the behavior problems you encounter, how can *you* expect to do so? The dementia process brings increasing mental incompetence in the patient, which you must accept and adjust to.

6. *You must be able to change yourself; you can never expect the kind of change in the patient that reflects awareness and adaptation.* Become more self-protective; provide as well as possible for the patient but maintain the advantage of protecting your own well-being. The expectations and demands you place on yourself must be adjusted to the moment-to-moment demands from the patient. Do what you *can* but do not try to do every possible thing for the sake of the patient while your own needs are neglected to a secondary status.

Table 9.1 provides an example of a log that you can use to document what you are doing and what succeeds. Make a log using this format so you can keep a running record for yourself.

Dealing with Patients

Despite the fact that an Alzheimer's patient will often seem aware and capable, there will be evidence that some mental functions are decreasing. Memory loss disrupts the ability to use past experience in an effective manner and, increasingly, makes it more difficult for the patient to react capably to current happenings. Essentially, then, there is a growing problem of communication between caregiver and patient. As the condition worsens, there are some basic steps that caregivers should follow to help

Table 9.1
Log of Interventions by Caregiver

Behavioral examples	Meaning	Action taken	Outcome
Refuses to bathe[a]	Maintenance of independence	Asked whether tub or shower wanted	Chose tub and then bathed
Used bad language[a]	Insecurity and fear	Ignored words used. Distracted with candy	No further bad language at this time
Said I hid jewels[a]	Maintenance of independence	Calmly told I'd help find	Became angry and cried

[a]Given to show how entries are made.

achieve better understanding between themselves and their patients. The Alzheimer's Association (1988) has published a booklet that discusses some of the basic techniques that are helpful in working with Alzheimer's patients. (This document is listed in the Bibliography at the back of this book.) Their recommendations form the basis for the descriptions below. Table 9.2 lists the techniques with examples of patient behaviors and both appropriate and inappropriate caregiver responses.

Caregivers should practice each of the suggestions below as it is needed and pertinent. Make a copy of the suggestions and post it in a prominent place. Rehearse yourself so that they become as automatic as possible in situations that require them.

1. *Be consistent.* Though we may seek out some variety and stimulation to make life more meaningful and invigorating, at least part of the time we want stability, peace, and tranquility. There is

Table 9.2
Techniques to Use with a Dementia Patient

Technique	Patient behavior	Caregiver response
1. Consistency	a. Reacts adversely to stimulation	Reduces or removes source
	b. Eats only a bite or two	Allows patient to stop but brings back to table after a few minutes
	c. Reacts poorly to change in routine	Maintains regular schedule for as many activities as possible
	d. Unsure of time or place	Practices reality orientation
2. Calmness	a. Questions many statements	Repeats quietly and firmly
	b. Reacts with anger to some request	Keeps voice low and calm. Is rational but understanding
	c. Seems unsure and insecure	Talks in warm and encouraging manner
3. Reassuring gesture	a. Patient seems insecure and at a loss	Touches patient, holding hand or arm around shoulder; Talks gently and calmly; smiles; is relaxed
4. Keeping eye contact	a. Patient is disoriented	Looks directly into patient's eyes as caregiver talks; smiles to offer feelings of security
5. Use of voice	a. Needs understanding and communication	Uses normal voice tone; Is not condescending; Talks in quiet place without distraction; Shows respect and acceptance

(*continued*)

Table 9.2
(*Continued*)

Technique	Patient behavior	Caregiver response
6. Keeping message simple	a. Patient does not understand	Uses reality method with orienting information first Speaks naturally without hurrying
	b. Patient to be given instructions of some kind	Uses sentences with only one idea Checks understanding before proceeding
	c. Involvement to assure understanding	Has patient explain ideas to you; presented in a way that you need help for understanding
7. Active listening	a. Patient is agitated, wants to express feelings or needs	Does not interrupt Signals acceptance of message by nods, smiles when apt Repeats what patient has said when message completed
8. Using distractors	a. Patient is demanding, unhappy, perhaps abusive	Listens and accepts message, but offers some activity or distractor when message completed
	b. Patient is bored, restless, overly dependent	Offers some favored activity or option; if necessary, tries several
	c. Refuses to eat, or eats only sweets	Offers reward of sweets as meal is eaten, or with meal as option
	d. Refuses to bathe	Offers option of tub or shower; sets routine time for bath with reward to follow

(*continued*)

Table 9.2

(Continued)

Technique	Patient behavior	Caregiver response
9. Being punctual	a. Patient will not delay or wait	Keeps routine in consistent manner
	b. Patient left alone for period of time	Arranges for someone to keep contact
	c. Unfamiliar place, such as an office	Keeps waiting time to a minimum. Has contact during wait

Note. Based on *Special Care for Alzheimer's Patients* (1988). Alzheimer's Association.

something reassuring in knowing that many things are relatively fixed and predictable. With the Alzheimer's patient, this principle is very important. Remember that this person has problems remembering even some simple things (such as the name for an object) at times. In addition, there is a certain amount of confusion about well-rehearsed events and places. Added to these is disorientation about time and place, which leads to a feeling of lack of control and contact.

These facts emphasize the need for an environment that is stable and predictable. Even minor changes in routine can be overwhelming to the patient, and may evoke verbal or physical reactions. Obviously, you cannot always ensure that everything will remain constant. (Indeed, for your sake, they should not always be.) Continue to go shopping, to church, or to visit a fried, and take the patient with you. *Plan* for such events carefully, be *certain* the patient is calm before you leave, *rehearse* with him or her a number of times what the two of you will be doing while you are away from home, be *alert* to signs that this is not the time for the planned excursion, and *inform* whomever you will be visiting that last-second changes in plans may be necessary. Although these precautions will not ensure that all will go well, you may reduce the chances that an unpleasant situation will develop at the same time that you are alerted and aware that the patient's responses can change suddenly and plans may go awry. Be Prepared is a good motto for more than just Boy Scouts.

In the same way, you must maintain a home environment that is consistent. Schedules are necessary and should be shared to the limit of the patient's understanding. Keep routines orderly and stable to reassure the patient. Ask family and friends to alert you if they plan to visit. You can set an appropriate time and help the patient better understand what is happening. Just as important, if you are having a particularly difficult time with your charge, you can call off the expected visit if you wish.

2. *Be calm.* A loss in mental competence means that the patient cannot think in the rational, logical, and orderly way that he or she once did. As a result, he or she may become more alert to emotional contexts than formerly. (Of course, it is just as likely that there is no real change in emotional awareness, just that it plays a more prominent role as thinking abilities diminish.) Whatever the reason, patients become increasingly dependent on caregivers and more sensitive to the moods and attitudes that the caregiver expresses. You cannot (and should not) become an automaton, an emotionless robot. Instead, you must understand your own feelings and moods, and maintain a calmness that will help the patient feel that things are under control and secure. There will be times when you need to cry and that expression can help you to cope better with overwhelming difficulties. Do so, but arrange, if at all possible, to have someone else watch the patient while you relieve your emotional burden. The more you are calm (and consistent) the less difficulty you will experience in caregiving.

Part of this appearance of calmness is shown in communicating. Whenever talking to the patient, keep your voice low and express whatever you say in a calm and direct fashion. Be easygoing in these situations, with a feeling of warmth in what you have to say. As much as possible, encourage the patient; do not lecture. If you feel yourself losing control and becoming emotional, Stop! Take a deep breath, remind yourself that you must be in charge but calm, and try again. If it is impossible to carry on, give up the effort for the time being. Remember that the patient may not recall what the discussion was about and will react more to your emotion than to the reality of the situation.

3. *Use reassuring gestures.* As we become excited, we tend to use flamboyant gestures. When calm, we appear relaxed and self-assured. This attitude projects reassurance to others and helps achieve a feeling of well-being. Actions can speak louder than words because nonverbal communication is a powerful determiner of the reactions of others.

There are some rules to follow here as well. First, do not get too close or too far from the patient when you are trying to communicate. When someone is too close, that may be interpreted as a threat. When too far, a lack of interest may be communicated. Although we do not know that patients interpret distance in these ways, it seems reasonable that a distance of about 18 to 24 inches is best to help ensure a feeling that what is being said is important and that the listener should attend closely. Second, stand or sit directly facing the patient. Maintain direct eye contact since this also conveys the idea that both the message and the listener are important. Finally, do not hesitate to touch the patient, say on the hand or shoulder. This conveys affection. A smile when appropriate is a powerful reinforcer under most circumstances.

4. *Use a pleasant setting.* Though this aspect has already been mentioned, it is worthwhile to emphasize it in other ways. When you wish to communicate with the patient, do so in a place that is quiet and does not have distractions. It should be a place that carries feelings of warmth and caring, perhaps even with a history of being the place where the two of you discussed important matters in the past. For example, it may be that you have talked about many things over the years at the kitchen table over a cup of coffee, or in the living room in your favorite chairs. Such settings will establish the atmosphere that is helpful to the communication process even if it is not possible to overcome all the interferences.

Control yourself; try not to express anger or hostility. To do so will only make the other person fearful and may even produce a strong emotional reaction. Always use your normal tone of voice. Avoid being condescending. No adult wants to be treated like a child and this applies just as much to an Alzheimer's patient as it does to you and me. Respect what the patient has been and may still be in some regards, and that will generate respect in turn.

5. *Keep communication simple.* Even if the patient seems to be following your remarks with understanding, be careful that you do not overload and overtax his or her remaining abilities. Without making the patient seem a child, make sure that understanding *is* taking place. You may first have to take some time to remind the patient of the reasons for your talk, even having the patient remind *you* of what has been said after you have explained the purpose. This action is a form of rehearsal by the patient and an assurance to you that you have been understood. As often as possible, make it appear that you are the one being helped by this initiative. For example, instead of saying, "Now what did I just tell you?" try something like, "I'm not sure I said that right. Please help me by reminding me what I just said." For someone who feels a lack of control and power, such a device can be stimulating and rewarding. Most important, it is a sign that the communication process has a chance to be successful.

Keep the communication simple and direct. Use common words and short sentences with a single idea, repeat as often as necessary, and have the patient explain what he or she has understood from your remarks.

It is best to plan in advance what *must* be understood and make that the primary, perhaps only, goal. Put down on paper for your own use what you want to communicate, then outline the elements involved. Take a single element at a time when you start the process and do not go on until it is understood. What you wish to come out with is a compilation that reaches the goal, and that process will be additive, bit by bit. Table 9.3 illustrates some major ideas that need to be communicated, the elements that make them up, and ways to proceed. Use it as a guide for your own efforts.

Do not expect miracles! Remain calm, and be satisfied with whatever you accomplish even if it is not everything you hoped for. As much as possible, use the competencies remaining to the patient. In your initial planning, then, detail what the patient is

Table 9.3
Caregiver–Patient Communication

Idea to be understood	Elements involved	Possible procedures
1. Appointment with a doctor or lawyer	a. Leaving home today b. Visiting strange place	(1) "I have to see the _____ today. I'd like you to come along." (With agreement by patient): (2) "The office is a place where there'll be lots of other people. You'll need to keep me close to you so I'll feel safer." (Rehearse other cases where the two of you have been in a group of strangers. Emphasize positive actions of the patient.) (With agreement by patient):
	c. Some waiting	(3) "We'll have to wait awhile before we see the _____. Shall we take your (favorite book or picture album, or similar item)?" (With agreement by patient):
	d. Seeing a stranger	(4) "The _____ will be a stranger to both of us. I'll need your support while we're visiting." (Rehearse instances where both have been with a professional, emphasizing things that went well.) (Repeat any procedures necessary until time to leave.)

2. Going grocery shopping

a. Leaving home today
b. Visit strange place

c. Many people; perhaps noise

d. Time needed to select groceries

e. Checkout may be slow

(1) "We'll need to go to the grocery. We're about out of food. You can be helpful to me."
(With agreement by patient):

(2) "There'll probably be lots of people there, and sometimes it's noisy. But you always make me feel secure so stay close to me, please."
(Rehearse times where crowds and noise have been encountered before. Remind patient how well she/he handled it, and how reassuring it was to you.)
(With agreement by patient):

(3) "It takes a while to shop. You can help by reaching for the canned goods and other things I can't get to so well anymore. I don't know what I'd do without you."
(With acceptance by patient):

(4) "It will take a little while to check out with the groceries. You can help by taking the things out of the basket so the checker can get them sacked."
(Repeat procedures as needed before leaving. Emphasize skills and help the patient gives.)

able to do that is congruent (even if it is not a perfect match) with what you are trying to accomplish. Don't rush: The processing of information by a patient will be quite slow in many instances and faster in others, depending on what abilities remain.

6. *Listen actively.* You not only must talk, you must also listen. Give the patient the opportunity to show that he or she understands what you have attempted to communicate. This also provides an opportunity for you to find out what has not been understood. Do not feel that you are the only responsible adult in the setting. By showing respect and genuinely trying to involve your charge in achieving understanding, you may well encourage the patient to show competencies that otherwise might be suppressed or overlooked.

7. *Use distractors.* As Alzheimer's disease progresses, the patient will show decreasing retention (memory) and attention span. This will allow you to distract the patient with something else almost immediately after some event causes a problem. Eventually the incident may need to be faced but if the patient is disturbed or upset, do not make a point of it at that time. Control your own feelings and move to something that is less threatening. More times than not you will be successful. Like other things, practice makes you more proficient at using distractors in a satisfactory manner.

The use of such aids as the ones described above depends as much on your ingenuity and willingness to try options as it does on their demonstrated value. Unfortunately, there is no assured time or manner when you will be able to employ a particular one of these suggestions. As mentioned earlier, *you* must be open to recognizing and reacting to situations at the same time that you must be self-protective. When you are overwhelmed, you are more apt to respond in an emotional rather than a logical and rational manner. The emotions can be helpful and are certainly deserved in the circumstances of caregiving. However, they must be appropriate and controlled or they will interfere with successful action.

Supports Available for Caregivers

There are various sorts of supports for caregivers in the community. A certain support will be needed and useful for some persons, while it may not be for others. Awareness of the kinds of resources that may be found is a first step to knowing what to seek when the need is present. You should remember that agencies such as the Alzheimer's Association can supply you with lists of professionals and services, even though they cannot (and should not) recommend any one over others.

Support Groups

In this country, support groups have proven to be a popular means of helping those in psychological distress to find some relief. There are meetings for patients and families dealing with cancer, divorce, children on drugs, alcohol abuse, suicide, or any other disruptive and destructive influence. Dementia is no less a reason for support to be offered, principally for caregivers though sometimes for patients as well.

Support groups may serve one or more of several purposes. To some, the support group is a social gathering and, as a result, an avenue to maintain contacts with others experiencing similar problems with life. Frequently, the group may have the opportunity to receive education about a topic of concern to the group, presented by a professional who is well prepared and authoritative on the subject. In other instances, members of the group will have an opportunity to express their feelings and describe major problems they are experiencing in an atmosphere of acceptance, empathy, and concern. For some attendants, the meeting is a form of respite, an escape from the intensive demands that otherwise would be overpowering. In some instances, the support group may provide all of these functions in a single meeting, or each in turn in different meetings.

Since the group may have such diverse functions, it must be

expected that meetings may have different appeal to different persons at different times. A few persons will attend every meeting, no matter what the topic or direction. Others will be more selective, showing up only when and if there is something of highly personal interest being presented. Still others may attend a single meeting and decide that there is little or nothing worthwhile for them in such affairs. There is some correlation between the attendance at support groups and the patient's increasing dementia. Just after a diagnosis of a condition leading to dementia, and explanation of prognosis, many caregivers are not ready psychologically to benefit from support group functions. Later they may well be, since experience with the patient will help to clarify needs of the type that can be addressed by support groups.

Since the group can participate in any of several kinds of activities, the number of attendants may vary widely also. Although there may be a loyal core of several persons who attend each time, there may also be meetings when only two or three are present. At other meetings, there may be a dozen persons or more. The ideal size of the group is no easier to describe than the average attendance. For an educational topic presented by a professional, the number could be 25 or so since there will be limited participation by attendants even if there is a question-and-answer period. For a sharing of feelings and experiences, a group of six or so is more defensible. In this case, all will have an opportunity to talk, if they wish, and the small size allows a more intimate setting.

How often a support group meets is still another variable. Some will meet weekly, others every two weeks, and still others only once a month. The "best" arrangement is a matter of need and convenience. Leadership may be professional, volunteer, or none at all. Generally, support groups will have a trained and experienced convener, not to control what happens or direct the meeting so much as to assure that all who need to talk get a chance to do so. This type of leader, then, will observe and intervene only if it is apparent that someone is dominating the meeting, more or less to the exasperation of the others, or if someone needs to talk but hesitates to interrupt or volunteer. In either of these cases, the leader may join in and say, "Some good points have been made but I think we'd all benefit by hearing some other points of view. You seem to have a point you'd like to make." This statement would be made to a person in the group who can then have an opportunity to participate. As a particularly important idea or suggestion is made, the leader may also say, "Did you all hear what was just said? Why don't you tell us again so that we can all benefit?"

Obviously, "support group" can have many meanings and effects, some of which would benefit you and others of which might not. Sponsoring agencies (like the Alzheimer's chapter, or a hospital, or a church) can supply you with information on meeting times and places as well as leadership. If the agency cannot give you answers to your questions about meeting procedures and content, call the leader and ask your questions. You will be able to screen for the most likely groups to meet your needs using this procedure. Once you have decided on one or more group meetings to attend, you should look for answers to other questions.

1. What does this group accomplish? Does there seem to be some reasonable chance that your needs can be met, at least at times and in part?
2. What are the goals of the group? Is it clear what the attendants and leader are trying to achieve? Do these goals coincide with your goals? Does the group, in fact, assess in any way the objectives they have established either formally or informally?
3. Is there some evidence that those who attend are better off or changed in some positive way by participating in this group? This question cannot be answered in a single meeting; it will take several meetings to get a feel for this outcome.

Certainly, if the answers to questions 1 and 2 are negative, you will probably never get around to question 3 anyway.

Support group functions seem better defined than do their effects. That support groups improve the lives of caregivers (or patients, at least indirectly) by providing the opportunity to participate in regular sessions has not been proved or disproved. The surest thing that can be said at present is that caregivers who attend support group meetings, even if irregularly, usually state that the sessions are "helpful." This statement probably does not mean that caregivers are better able to deal with problems at home with the patient. What seems to be meant, instead, is that caregivers experience solidarity as they find that others also have severe problems; "I am not alone, everyone seems to be struggling much as I am; I have some place where I can vent my discouragement, anger, and frustration." Perhaps this is sufficient evidence that support groups are meeting a need.

Reality Orientation

The caregiver can use a procedure at home that may assist the patient to continue functioning with less confusion and disorientation. The procedure is called reality orientation. First described about 30 years ago, it was developed on the assumption that certain portions of the brain remain intact even as dementia progresses. These unimpaired areas may be retrained or reeducated to take over some of the functions of the damaged or destroyed areas. Included in this rationale is the notion that a patient will function much better if orientation within the environment is maintained. Thus, the strategy focuses on providing stimulation to the patient that will increase the possibility of adequate orientation.

The caregiver must supply the sources of stimulation and also provide reinforcement and support. The attitude must be supportive and friendly. As the patient is able to perform more competently, he or she may experience renewed feelings of self-worth and an awareness that someone cares and wishes to help with some of his or her problems. Progress will be slow but there are no major strains or demands on either party.

Consistency is a key word. If you decide to use reality orientation, you must dedicate some time and effort to the positive actions that will allow the procedure to work. When the patient is confused, you must provide information needed to help relieve the confusion. To do so, you tell the patient where he or she is, what is happening currently, why this is going on, and so on. In addition, you can create a "reality board" where the day, date, month, year, and other information will be posted. This can be a reference point that helps reassure the patient. You can even post upcoming events such as what the next meal is. Several of these boards can be placed throughout the house. The bedroom, for example, should have a reality board as well as labels printed and attached to drawers of chests stating what they contain or other such needed information. Whatever kinds of information need to be available to the patient to increase reality orientation should be posted.

There must always be a positive air about the provision of information as well. One does not correct error, one supplies fact. If the patient is confused about what color socks to wear, for example, he or she should be addressed in a supportive way. You might say something like, "Well, the pair you have there is attractive, but you like this color too, don't you? I believe that I prefer them." Never say, "That color won't match your slacks. I don't know why you insist on picking out things that don't go together." A positive atmosphere, then, is just as important as the accuracy of facts.

Reality orientation has been a popular procedure in many settings. If you have visited a nursing home, you undoubtedly saw the reality boards posted at various places around the facility. The staff may attempt to use reality orientation so that residents will feel less isolated and more involved with life. Success is hard to verify although a problem in nursing home settings frequently is inconsistency in administration of the principles. In the home, of course, the caregiver can provide the consistency needed to maximize its effects. In this context, there is some evidence that carefully controlled and prescribed procedures, administered with consistency by all who have contact with the patient, can bring about behavioral change for the better. For the changes to continue, the implementations must be maintained and intensified.

The validity of reality orientation seems to be limited to very particular circumstances and content. The effects are transitory, because of the effects of dementia, but reality orientation can help to improve the quality of life of the patient and reduce some of the strain on caregivers.

Decisions about support group participation and the use of reality orientation in the home are within the capabilities of caregivers and are best left to their discretion. There are other kinds of assists in the community that require professional evaluation and administration. Two of these are group therapy and individual psychotherapy. Here, of course, the caregiver decides whether or not to seek out help but must depend on the skills of others for effective outcomes.

Group Therapy

Therapy should be provided only by highly trained, competent psychologists who have gone through both formal training and an internship under professional supervision. This requires five or more years beyond the college level. Group therapy is distinct in that it is offered to several individuals at one time. This allows a common experience to be shared and the influences and changes needed by at least one member can be worked out by all members of the group together. The therapist will have had training in counseling or clinical psychology and have demonstrated the skills required for certification by the state in which he or she practices.

If you decide that you would like to investigate the possibility of group therapy, you should contact the state office on licensing, division of psychology or of counseling and therapy. (Different states categorize services in different ways so that you will need to know just what office to contact.) Such an agency can provide you with a list of certified personnel within the state, including the locality where you live. Do *not* go for any form of therapy to an individual who has not been properly certified! Although the certification process does not assure that you will receive the treatment you need, you will be dealing with an individual who has subscribed to an ethical and legal code that makes him or her responsible for all actions and outcomes. Indeed, such persons will tell you if they feel their methods are inappropriate for you. They may even recommend someone they feel more suitable.

If you decide to participate in group sessions, you will have to adhere to the requirements established by the therapist. Before beginning the sessions, ask the therapist about the methods he or she uses in the therapeutic setting. Some therapists are more cognitive and behavioral in their preferences, which means they will emphasize ways of analyzing and dealing with current problems. Others may prefer a more humanistic approach and thereby try to help the patient become more self-sufficient and self-directive (called self-actualization). A few even believe that an aversive method is the best to use. This approach employs negative responses, perhaps even derogatory and accusatory statements about caregiver behaviors.

The clients who make up the group must be considered as well. The kind of balance sought by the therapist for the group is an issue here. In some instances, the therapist will attempt to have as much group cohesion as possible by combining those with similar problems, background, skills, and the like. Other therapists may establish a group where differences exist between the members in order to maximize the directions growth may take.

Since there can be such wide differences between therapists and the consequent groupings, the better informed you are from the beginning the more likely you are to receive the help you need. No doubt it is apparent that Bob Newhart will not lead any of the groups you might consider.

Psychotherapy

This form of therapy is practiced in a one-to-one setting. You as client have the full attention and care of the therapist during each session. Psychiatrists (all of whom are medical doctors with highly specialized training) and clinical psychologists are licensed by the state in which they practice. They have to meet and maintain rigorous standards before they receive their licenses.

As with group therapists, there are individual preferences about treatment that you should determine before entering therapy. Many psychiatrists, for example, may employ a psychoanalytic technique. This may be in the form advocated by Sigmund Freud or one of the derivatives of that model. Such practitioners are apt to use hypnosis to relax you and permit inhibitions to be more easily released. Often, also, psychoanalysts assume that the relationships of childhood (particularly between child and parents) are crucial elements in the adjustment problems of adulthood. Under hypnosis, then, they will encourage thoughts that emerge from the unconscious about such relationships (called anamnesis).

Other clinicians will be cognitive and behavioral in their method, particularly clinical psychologists. The cost of therapy is substantial and it should be used only by those with major adjustment problems. Unless you are experiencing severe depression, perhaps with suicidal thoughts, or some other functional disorder such as delusions, psychotherapy is probably uncalled for. It is available in most communities and should be used where appropriate.

Professionals and Dementia

There are a number of professionals who deal with dementia patients and caregivers. Several of them are in disciplines that will seem obvious, yet they should be mentioned in any list that attempts to be comprehensive. Most of them serve the needs of more persons than those with dementia, which means that their training may not be directed solely, or even closely, to dementia itself. At the same time, their education and experience may vary concerning the nature of aging, the needs and problems of the elderly, the meanings of cohort (age) experiences, the abilities and limitations that accompany the aging process, and even the effects of conditions more commonly based on studies of young adults. This means that having a certain degree or a particular title does not ensure that a given professional is going to be well informed or competent. The discussion below is written to explain the general characteristics of individuals in a certain profession. Determining the specific abilities of that person for your needs and purposes must be determined on a case-by-case basis.

Physicians

Doctors are an obvious professional group involved with any patient. A physician is the individual who can make a diagnosis and suggest the meaning and outcome from that diagnosis. Further, if there is some medical intervention (particularly a drug for some complaint), doctors are the only ones who are permitted to prescribe a medication. There is only one drug available as yet that has been approved in this country for symptoms of dementia (described in Chapter 10). It is true that several other drugs have been or are being tried on an experimental basis, but to date none of them has proven to be beneficial for their purposes. The medicines that a doctor may prescribe for a dementia patient, then, are usually to treat other symptoms, not dementia. Some of these may be helpful but there is always a danger of side effects. There has already been considerable damage to the brain of a dementia patient so it is more at risk than that of the normal adult. Drug treatment is thus a difficult issue for the demented. If medications are used, they must be monitored carefully for side effects. Where problems are noted, they should be reported to the doctor immediately.

In making a diagnosis, the physician uses data from various tests and complaints reported by the patient. *Which* tests and *what* complaints depend in part on the training and specialization of the doctor. If you consult a *family physician*, standard laboratory tests will be used and there will probably be extensive questioning by the doctor about the problems being experienced. There may or may not be referral for additional tests—to a neurologist, psychiatrist, or neuropsychologist. If the family physician is well informed about dementia, its causes, and its consequences, the chances are better that such a referral may be made before a final diagnosis is given. If the physician who is consulted is certified in *internal medicine*, a battery of laboratory tests will be required and there will be at least some emphasis on complaints. Referral for neurological testing is somewhat more likely if, in the opinion of the doctor, this appears to be a case of Alzheimer's or other cause of dementia. The most probable request would be for a brain scan and reading. There may also be involvement by a neuropsychologist, who will gather information on capabilities that depend on intact portions of the brain.

The *neurologist* or *psychiatrist*, upon referral, will decide upon the appropriate neurological test or tests for the purpose. Most often, the tests will include CAT or PET scans or MRI. These instruments permit an examination of the brain without an intrusion that would destroy tissue. The integrity of the brain can be examined for atrophy (shrinkage), infarcts (damaged tissue due to strokes), tumors or lesions, and other gross physical signs that might explain the complaints voiced by the patient and caregiver. The tests are not competent to disclose the status of nerve cells (neurons). Because disease processes such as Alzheimer's have their adverse effects on the neurons, an absolute diagnosis of the presence of the disease cannot be made on the basis of the scan results. What is gained is the elimination (if no evidence is found) of potentially treatable and correctable conditions. In other words, where the scans are negative, the deduction must be made that the problem is probably at the cell level. The report to the internist will include such a possibility, and a corresponding diagnosis will be given in all likelihood.

It is important to know if there is a treatable cause, and results of the lab tests and scans will help to determine this. In this sense, then, the more tests the better. However, physicians will explain to the caregiver what is involved and what may result since such procedures are expensive. Scans, for example, cost from $600 to $1,200, and in cases where dementia is caused by a neuronal disease, scans offer no information that allows a definitive diagnosis by the doctor. Ultimately, the decision for such testing must reside with the patient and caregiver.

Neuropsychologists, who are not medical doctors but often associated with them, bring particular skills to the diagnostic procedure. They are trained in the administration and interpretation of tests designed to indicate possible damage in particular parts of the brain. Further, they can gather information on discrete behavior deficiencies that are correlated with brain structure and function. Again, the costs of whatever tests are used, analysis of the results, and interpretation for the doctor will be added to the overall cost of the diagnostic procedure.

Once the patient and caregiver have decided to consult with a doctor and the process is begun, there may be a period of several weeks before a final decision is made. In some instances, the news will be good because a condition is found that can be treated, leading to a reversal of the complaints. In most cases, however, no evidence of a reversible syndrome will be found. What is left is the probability that an untreatable cause must be presumed. In this case, treatment and reversibility are not possible. When this is the state of affairs, other professionals become the focus of education and preparation for action.

Social Workers

Social work professionals help persons who need services and assistance provided in the public sector. Social workers are educated in ways to communicate, understand, and encourage their clients to identify their specific needs. The social worker will then assist in linking their clients to appropriate services for which clients are qualified. They must know regulations for both federal and state programs and be acquainted with private or benevolent sources that will benefit clients. They probably will not have extensive training and education in the aging process or in dementia.

Some clinical social workers are also available in communities. These individuals have had graduate (advanced) training and education and have passed examinations that demonstrate their knowledge. In some instances, they will have had some training in counseling techniques, but social workers usually are not clinically qualified as psychologists. Often, social workers are associated with agencies, clinics, home health centers, hospitals, and other programs that offer social services to citizens. As professionals, they are often a link between the physician and opportunities for assistance to patients and caregivers. Whether or not the clinical social worker has received education and experience with older and/or demented persons depends on the components of the degree program.

Nurses

In addition to assisting physicians, nurses can often provide information to clarify the decision about diagnosis and its meanings. They may be able to suggest resources and to help in finding explanations. They cannot go beyond the doctor's findings or suggest alternatives to a diagnosis. They can and will answer questions that will give you better understanding. They may suggest ways to handle difficulties, although they are more likely to propose that you contact a suitable source (and may be able to tell you of some).

Nurses are trained in the healing arts and may serve in a variety of situations. Your initial contact will most probably be with the nurse in the doctor's office. Eventually, however, you may use a home health care service, or a nursing home, or the visiting nurse association. In any of these settings, you should accept the professional education and experience nurses bring. Do not hesitate to ask candid questions about the patient and about yourself. You will find that more often than not you will get an honest and complete answer. If you ask something that is not relevant to the discipline or that might violate their accepted roles, they will be honest with you.

Psychologists

There are two kinds of psychologists, either of whom you may be referred to or decide to consult after dementia is identified. One of these, and the more commonly found, is the clinical psychologist. These professionals normally will hold the doctor of philosophy degree (Ph.D.), although there are an increasing number who have specialized and received the doctor of psychology degree (Psy.D.). Whichever status they hold, they will in addition have spent a minimum of one year in a supervised internship in a facility or location of their specialty (e.g., older persons or children). They will be certified by the state in which they practice, and many will belong to one or more professional organizations that set very high standards in practice. Although all clinical psychologists have been well trained and educated, they differ widely in the kinds of problems and age groups with whom they practice therapy.

The clinical psychologist will work with patients who present major maladjustments requiring expert intervention. This includes such disorders as severe depression, which can occur in older persons in general and in both patients and caregivers in particular. The treatment method will vary according to the preference of the clinician, but a cognitive behavioral approach is frequently used by those who work with older persons, meaning that primary emphasis is put on defining current conditions in the life of the client and helping to identify skills that will assist in handling problems more positively.

With the depressed older person, for example, the psychologist may emphasize the fact that we can "think" ourselves into a state of depression. When things are not going very well in life, we may begin to feel sorry for ourselves and start a cycle that leads deeper and deeper into depression. The result can be feelings of great sadness, loss of interest in any source of pleasure, assumptions that one is worthless, and even a decision that life is no longer worth living. As treatment, the therapist will encourage the client to identify positive elements in life (through what are called "homework" assignments) and alert the client to the beginnings of the negative thought patterns that induce the depressive episode.

There are other cognitive treatment modes, and even other kinds of treatment, that may be selected as the psychologist feels they are appropriate. Currently, there are some drugs which act as *anti*depressants. If the psychologist feels one of these might be warranted, there will be a referral to a physician for possible prescription. Generally, the research indicates that a combination of therapy and drugs most often yields the best results.

The other kind of psychologist who may be recommended is called a geropsychologist. This individual may be a clinician but need not necessarily be. The geropsychologist has studied the elderly and specializes in the problems of older persons. This emphasis is reassuring because you will know that the literature and models that influence the geropsychologist's interventions for older clients are pertinent to that group. As an example, the geropsychologist will more likely believe that older persons can change, that they are not rigid, that they are not senile simply because of age, and that they are individuals who can benefit from psychological help and deserve the chance to do so. Other psychologists may not make such assumptions, particularly if they specialize in young adults who have a lifetime ahead of them that the old person does not have. As with other professions, then, all psychologists are not alike no matter how capable each may be for some groups of patients.

Gerontologists

In recent years, academic programs have been developed by colleges and universities for education and training in gerontology. These programs are available at either the undergraduate or graduate levels. Gerontology is the study of aging, making these professionals particularly well trained in the aging process. Most often, their education is multidisciplinary, meaning that they take courses in several departments (e.g., psychology, biology, nutrition, economics, sociology, and so on). The courses have been developed with emphasis on aged and aging persons. Thus, a course in the psychology of aging will explore the literature about such factors as stress, mental changes and abilities in adulthood, personality stability and change, and so on. The research and theories about these topics as they are expressed in old age will be the content of the course. Often, the gerontologist will have spent some time (up to a full semester) in a supervised practicum as the final element in the program.

A gerontologist, then, is a person who will have wider knowledge and understanding of the aged than any other professional. Whether or not the gerontologist is knowledgeable about dementia depends on the elective course work and/or the practicum. As you encounter such persons, they can be a useful and informative source about what happens during aging, what is usual and unusual, what leads to behavioral change, and how to deal with specific events.

Other Professionals

With time, and particularly if you decide on placement in a nursing home, you will meet other kinds of professionals. Often, these persons lack the extensive training and certification requirements of those categories described above. They will include activity directors, program evaluators, directors of special care units, in-home care workers, paraprofessionals of several sorts, and the like. Most often these individuals are important *because they will have more contact with the patient than anyone else.* You will want to become well acquainted with them and support them, but be observant that they are doing what is in the best interest of the demented patient. If there are problems, report them to the ombudsman (a person who acts as an advocate for nursing home residents) or to the supervisor in charge of that service. In nearly all cases, these are dedicated and competent persons; this warning is not a signal for you to anticipate trouble.

Professionals, of whatever type, have the responsibility to give you the tools you need to understand and cope with the difficulties of caregiving. Their task is to ensure that the right advice and best interventions are done for you and the patient for whom you care. For this reason, no one professional is more important than the other; all are important when they are present and ready at the time they are needed.

Summary

No one is so competent that he or she can deal easily and effectively with the tasks of caregiving all the time. Although some persons seem to experience less difficulty than others, many caregivers find the burden almost overwhelming at times. To deal with these stressors requires both internal and external supports.

The major resource that can benefit the caregiver is the personal one. It is essential that feelings of self-worth be maintained. The dynamics of caregiving require awareness that the act simply is not a "win" situation, that one must emphasize the successes and not be destroyed by the failures. It is necessary to reward yourself when you do something well, no matter how small. You should set reasonable and attainable objectives, and accept their importance as you attain them.

In dealing with the patient, it is necessary to be consistent, calm, diligent in communicating, and able to recognize when and how to use distractors. Some aids are cited to assist in this task.

In the external environment, there are many resources. Support groups are popular and meet a need for many caregivers. Reality orientation can be employed at home, just as it is in institutions, and may help keep the patient engaged with reality and functioning better. If maladjustment becomes a problem, you should consider the possibility of professional help. This most often will mean therapeutic intervention by a psychologist or psychiatrist.

Among the many professionals in the community with whom you will have contact are physicians, social workers, nurses, gerontologists, and psychologists. All of these professionals have special training and education that can assist you in coping better if you recognize the need and seek out their help.

10

Dementia Today and in the Future

In reading this book, you may have concluded that dementia must be a major concern for our society. In fact, it is a worldwide problem since the causes of dementia do not respect any group and especially not the elderly. What causes dementia can be any of a large number of conditions. Some of these (such as depression or infections or toxins) can be treated if properly recognized. Any dementia resulting from them may be arrested or reversed as a consequence. Other conditions, however, are not amenable to treatment. These conditions usually have unknown causation, and their effects on brain cells are at present untreatable.

The foremost of these dementia-causing conditions is Alzheimer's disease, first described by a German physician in the early 1900s and today considered to be the principal cause of dementia. The nature of Alzheimer's is unknown, but its behavioral effects (the dementia) have been recognized for centuries. Specifically, the disease process alters neurons (nerve cells in the brain that control our actions and thought processes) by producing neurofibrillary tangles and neuritic plaques. The tangles are fibers that invade the nerve-cell body and increase in number over time until they interfere with normal cell action. The plaques are the result of cell death and are believed to be due to production of a protein called beta amyloid. As brain cells die, they collapse and form clusters that are called plaques. The effect of Alzheimer's disease is not some physical change in a person that can be recognized as an illness but a mental change that reduces competence without adverse physical effects. Alzheimer's is diagnosed most often after age 65 and becomes an increasing threat with advanced age. Patients may live for 15 years or more after the onset of the symptoms.

Although Alzheimer's is the principal diagnostic cause of dementia, there are a variety of other conditions that may lead to irreversible and untreatable dementia. These occur rarely, though they must be a source of concern for a society that is concerned for the well-being and functioning of its citizens. Among the syndromes identified diagnostically are Pick's disease, of unknown origin and untreatable, usually occurring in middle age and bringing death within eight years or so. Another untreatable cause of dementia is Creutzfeldt-Jakob disease, which is caused by a virus that remains unidentified. This disease process also occurs most often in middle age with a short period of survival after onset.

Multiinfarct disease is the result of small strokes that destroy a limited number of cells at a time. These strokes are also labeled "silent" since their effects are so mild that they may not be recognized by the patient and leave no evident effects. (By contrast, a major stroke is apt to produce pronounced effects on muscle groups of the body.) Multiinfarct dementia expresses itself most often during middle age (especially in one's fifties) and the patient usually will die within 10 years or so. The "good news" about multiinfarct dementia is that it seems preventable if we are willing to follow reasonable practices in our lives. A diet low in fats and cholesterol, regular aerobic exercise, reduced salt intake, and control of stressors will reduce the chances of arteriosclerosis, the disease that seems to be the major contributor to multiinfarct dementia.

The available evidence indicates that, in some cases where

both Huntington's and Parkinson's diseases are present, dementia may result. Some scientists believe that the condition called normal-pressure hydrocephalus, characterized by shrinkage of brain tissue in later life leading to increased cerebrospinal fluid, may lead to dementia.

Regardless of cause, and whether treatable and reversible or not, the resulting effects of any of these conditions are devastating to the afflicted. As adults, we are expected to be capable of identifying and solving problems, thinking rationally and capably, maintaining responsibility for our actions, and providing for our own needs. Unfortunately, dementia increasingly prevents us from meeting any of these goals because of its three major effects. First is memory loss. This begins with little errors and forgetfulness that normally would not occur. The individual begins to forget commitments and even loses abilities of long standing. With time, such incidents become more obvious and occur more commonly. Eventually, it is evident that this person is not functioning mentally in the expected way. Over time, losses in memories of past events of importance will occur. It is even possible that the patient will no longer recognize spouse and family members. The alterations are slow in their development, and the course is not predictable, but the outcome is certain if the patient lives long enough.

Accompanying memory loss is increasing confusion in well-known places. A person suffering dementia may become "lost" in the home where he or she has lived for many years. The meaning and use of common objects may be reduced. Thus, the location of the bathroom may be forgotten; even if the patient finds the bathroom, the proper receptacle to use for elimination is no longer recognized.

Another common effect of dementia is disorientation. The patient is no longer aware of time and space dimensions. This results in an inability to give the day of the week or the year. The patient may be unable to tell you where he or she is, and particularly if taken to some relatively strange location and even if told a number of times what that place is. The serious effect of this outcome is to make the patient increasingly dependent on others, particularly a caregiver. Reality, in the sense expected of an adult, is no longer experienced. Combined with memory loss and confusion, disorientation reduces a competent human to a largely helpless being over a period of some years.

Meantime, other effects of the dementia may be expressed also. The personality of the patient may be altered in some ways. Placid, controlled persons may become demanding, or vice versa. Kindness may be replaced by abuse, restraint by tantrum, loving and caring by disregard and disrespect. Such changes do not always occur and tend to be muted in most cases. There is the possibility, nevertheless, that these changes will impact the caregiver.

As a result of these changes, caregivers will experience increasing demands and may eventually give up personal needs and desires for those of the patient. The cost to both parties is too great to allow, and particularly when there are increasing numbers of persons being so adversely affected. It is currently estimated that some 4 million individuals have Alzheimer's disease, and this number is expected to increase to 17 million in the future. For all causes of dementia combined, there are about 5 million cases now. Because we are an aging society, with the largest percentage growth in the population over age 85, it is predicted that the number will rise to 20 million in the next 40 years. The longer we live the more at risk we are, not just for some decline in abilities but for contracting terminal illness and a condition that may produce dementia. The problem for the society is already severe and will become worse *unless* something is done.

Such dire events and consequences require that we evaluate their meanings. An appraisal is necessary of what we know at present and what we will need to know in the future. This "knowledge" must include an examination of medical and scientific efforts, the provision of supports for both patients and caregivers, and policy to ensure that positive and productive outcomes are achieved.

Dementia and the Present

There is much to be said for the progress that has been made in knowledge about dementia and its causes—most of it occurring in the past three decades. Indeed, both awareness and understanding among professionals have accelerated in the 1980s and early 1990s. At the same time, there are gaps that need filling and further efforts that must be made.

The Status of Medical Training and Education

Physicians in the United States receive intensive and extensive medical education. They are prepared to deal with the many physical conditions that affect individuals of all ages. Although a doctor may specialize, there is evidence of an attempt on the part of most of them to be conversant with medical matters outside the specialization, at least so that proper referral will occur if necessary. There is one group that has not been well served in medical schools, however: the elderly. As a result, geriatric medicine is not always covered except in a cursory way, and specialization in this area is only recent and in sparse numbers.

One reason for this benign neglect is the fact that what is "normal" development in old age has been largely disregarded. The awareness of an aging population is a recent phenomenon. In the past, few persons lived to be 80, 90, or 100 years old, whereas now the numbers are significant and increasing. There has also been the bias that older persons are expected to be infirm and incompetent. The emphasis has been on those with life ahead of them. As a result, birth, infancy, and childhood have attracted major interest, with adolescence and young adulthood close behind. Even the middle aged have not been systematically studied. Given these attitudes, it is not surprising that the norms (normal characteristics of groups) for the elderly are more presumptive than empirical—few facts (empiricism) but lots of opinion (presumption).

As an example, we might ask what are the normal characteristics of the body systems of a 60-, 70-, 80-, 90- and 100-year-old. Actual data that would answer this question are limited, although increased effort will bring an answer. By contrast, norms on infants and children are much more complete. Consider, for example, that at birth a child will be tested for certain reactions to ensure that the brain is properly developed for subsequent growth demands. The Babinsky reflex (where the toes curl up when the baby's foot is stroked) is an example of an assurance that the brain is capable of receiving stimulation, interpreting it, and responding accurately. With growth, it has been found that most children can support the head at 12 weeks and sit alone at six months. These are only averages, so it should not be seen as a danger sign if the behavior is not yet present.

In recent years, some measures called neuropsychological tests have been developed to help specify the area of the brain where damage has occurred. These tests are based on normal functions of parts of the brain as they are related to behaviors. For example, we should be able to draw lines connecting points that make up a pattern if the areas of the brain permitting the perception are intact and if the motor cortex is adequate. When a patient is having difficulties with certain tasks, performance on such a test (and others that are pertinent) can yield information about the integrity of those parts of the brain. In addition, psychological measures of orientation in time and space have been developed to indicate brain malfunction, though these tests have not been correlated with specific brain defects.

Beyond such relationships, gross as they are, there is little knowledge about appropriate expectations in older adults. Medical schools thus have little knowledge to teach and, combined with the emphasis on care of the young, have not developed courses on the characteristics of the aged. Indeed, there is apt to be the assumption that a well-trained doctor can deal with the medical problems of any age group. This reflects the attitude that old people are like the young so far as medical problems and causes are concerned. Such an assumption is increasingly rejected as physicians encounter more and more older patients in their practices. Already, there are efforts to establish a specialty in geriatric medicine, with criteria specified and means to qualify enacted. The thrust is deserved and will produce needed specialists in the future.

The Status of Medical Diagnosis

A separate issue concerns the decision to be made about the *cause* of behavioral problems that reflect the presence of dementia. Diagnosis is a major step in informing patients and caregivers since it not only specifies *what is* but also *what will be* (prognosis). It is not possible to examine brain cells except by biopsy and the use of a microscope. This limitation requires that physicians use the procedure of differential diagnosis. Every possible cause of behavior changes must be considered until the culprit is identified or only plausible alternatives remain. With dementia, in cases which are untreatable and irreversible, there are only the "plausible alternatives." Since Alzheimer's disease is the most common occurrence, that will often be the diagnosis simply because it is the most probable. However, that does not mean that this kind of diagnostic procedure is filled with error. From autopsies done on patients who had been diagnosed with Alzheimer's disease, the evidence of neurofibrillary tangles and neuritic plaques has been significant in about 90 percent of cases. This speaks well for the accuracy of differential diagnosis.

The diagnosis of multiinfarct dementia is as accurate, and perhaps more so, since there is usually a medical history of hypertension and other reflections of arteriosclerosis. In addition, the use of a brain scan will disclose the presence of infarcts even if there is no demonstrated history of strokes. The combination of the two ensures a high probability of accuracy. For other causes (Pick's and Creutzfeldt-Jakob, for example), there is insufficient evidence to evaluate the correctness of diagnosis.

Knowledge of Alzheimer's

Crucial to the diagnostic procedure is understanding of what Alzheimer's disease is, how it expresses itself (symptoms), and how the process progresses from inception to completion. These facts are important because the symptoms of dementia (memory loss, confusion, and disorientation) can be caused by *many* conditions. Depression, for example, usually leads to complaints about memory along with an apathy about matters of life that may be mistaken for confusion. It is essential that the doctor be alert to the distinction so that a treatable condition (the depression) will not be overlooked. In the past, misdiagnosis of this kind happened often enough to cause concern among professionals in general and physicians in particular. Today, the chances of misdiagnosis are less but the mistake may still occur if the attitude is that *all* old people are apt to develop dementia and, as a result, no effort is made to make certain that the diagnosis is correct. This factor alone is a good reason to seek a second opinion once the diagnosis of Alzheimer's has been made.

The physician must have knowledge of the behavior patterns that are more characteristic of Alzheimer's patients than they are of other conditions that mimic the disease. One of the things that will be done routinely by the concerned doctor is to test the patient with some reality questions. Items such as day of the week, the year, where the patient lives, the year born, and so on, will be included in the interview. Usually, reality questioning will be casual and not a formal test. Such information is useful because depressed patients still answer correctly, while the dementia patient will make some (and perhaps many) errors.

The doctor may use short-term memory items, like repeating a series of numbers presented in a random order. Usually, the task will begin with a series of two or three numbers, then go to the next level, and so on until the patient is unable to repeat them accurately. Psychological research has shown that most of us can retain seven digits long enough to repeat the series accurately. (Have you ever wondered why telephone numbers have seven digits?) Being able to remember five or more randomly presented digits is considered normal. If the patient has difficulty retaining and repeating only three or four digits, it is possible that the brain cells in the hippocampus—the seat of memory function—have been altered. Alzheimer's seems to affect short-term memory function first and most adversely. The doctor, by using such a seemingly simple device, can get some clues to assist in the diagnosis.

There are other matters that the doctor may inquire about from you as caregiver. For example, you may be asked about the awareness level of the patient. Is the patient still alert to the meanings of actions and their effects? The fact that the patient seems increasingly less concerned about what must be done for him or her and unaware of the burdens being caused to you may be helpful diagnostically. Alzheimer's patients show such unconcern more than do persons developing dementia from other causes. They also have greater difficulty in learning. If you show an Alzheimer's patient how to do a certain task, and are careful to keep it explicit and simple, you are not apt to be very successful. By contrast, a multiinfarct patient may be able to learn such a task and perform it until the dementia progresses to a new level.

Such distinctions, and others that might be cited, are not so definitive that they assure an accurate diagnosis of Alzheimer's disease. They can assist the doctor in feeling more certain that the cause of the patient's problems is Alzheimer's and not something else. To be used, however, the physician must have the ongoing training that permits exposure to such findings. It is not rude or unkind of you to ask your doctor about the medical training sessions on Alzheimer's that he or she has attended in the last two years or so. If there are at least one or two reported, you can feel more confident that this physician is very apt to be abreast of what is currently known.

Knowledge is important because it signifies openness to more possibilities. Few doctors any longer are adamant in their attitudes about the negative meanings of old age. Remember that age as such indicates only that time has passed. What has occurred during that passage can range from little or no significant changes in the person to variable and significant changes. Knowledge also encourages the attitude of exploration for as many important facts as possible before making a decision. When a diagnosis of Alzheimer's is made, the implicit meaning is that this person suffers an irreversible condition that has no treatment. Doctors, just as caregivers and patients, have no desire to consign an individual to such a future without strong assurance that it is the most likely diagnosis.

Labeling and Diagnosis

The result of all the medical tests and procedures is the label that the physician decides is most appropriate. As just mentioned, this diagnosis is filled with significance because it can affect the attitudes of all who come in contact with the patient. This is particularly true of professionals (social workers, gerontologists, nurses, and the like) since a label carries an implicit message of what is wrong and what may be done about it.

Medical diagnosis at present is based primarily on the results of tests designed for identifying known diseases and conditions producing physical problems. This means that doctors are usually at their best when faced with the complaint of chest pain (which suggests heart disease), muscle aches, gastric disorder, vision difficulties, and so on. Mental problems and psychological disorders are the proper practice for neurologists and psychiatrists and are less understood by other disciplines. Referral is the common step taken when a physician you are consulting feels that the problems presented are more properly (at least in part) in the area of a specialist. A more precise and accurate analysis may be obtained through referral before a final decision is made by your doctor.

In the current procedure of diagnosis of a cause for dementia, referral to a neurologist may be made when your doctor can find no reasonable explanation for the complaint presented by you and the patient. The neurologist can conduct examination of the functioning of the brain that is not possible otherwise. In addition, there are a number of scans now available that can be helpful in eliminating possible causes for behavior changes. These scans use techniques (expensive and very sophisticated) to examine the structure of body organs and systems (including the brain) for integrity.

The use of one of these devices can disclose possible causes of dementia that routine medical examination would not find. If such a cause is not found, the chances are increased that the behavioral symptoms are due to a reduction in the quality of brain cells. Unfortunately, there are no devices or tests that will give an indication of the health status of a neuron. Only microscopic examination will accomplish that, and there may *still* be some doubt about the cause of alterations that may be found. Diagnosis today often requires the cooperation of several doctors just to eliminate various possibilities and not to ensure that a diagnosis of Alzheimer's is correct.

This rather disappointing position is still much better than what was true before 1960, say, and certainly much further refined than in Dr. Alzheimer's time about a hundred years ago. The fact remains that error in diagnosis may be made, even though the chance of error is within reasonable limits. Physicians look forward to the day when they can have the same assurance about diagnosing Alzheimer's that they have about such conditions as heart disease.

Treatment

When you are diagnosed with some disorder or disease, you expect to have that condition treated so that you will recover. If you are told that the illness is untreatable, you are faced with the question of what the future holds, that is, what is the prognosis? Physicians, under these circumstances, will tell you what their experience and research has indicated. You are then in the position where you can anticipate and plan, no matter how painful that reality may be. The key is the ability to treat, at best, perhaps with the ability to cure, at least, with the chance to arrest the progress of the illness. At the very least, treatment can offer some reduction of suffering and pain while you live out the remainder of your life.

With dementia, there is no treatment for the cause at the present time. There will be no attempt to cure, no way to arrest the progress of the dementia. There is now a possible (but not probable) way to reduce the effects of memory loss, though not of confusion and disorientation. It is true that several drug companies are currently attempting to find other means to ameliorate (improve) functioning of memory in patients.

The Food and Drug Administration (FDA) has approved a drug that may be prescribed by doctors to help improve patient's memory function. This drug, known as tacrine and called Cognex in a copyrighted name by its developer the Warner-Lambert company, is known scientifically as tetrahydroaminoacridine (abbreviated as THA). Its action is to inhibit cholinesterase, an enzyme that breaks down a brain chemical called acetylcholine (ACh). ACh is needed for transmission of messages received by the brain for interpretation. When this neurotransmitter is not present, a person cannot remember effectively. ACh has been identified as the transmitter most often deficient or lacking in Alzheimer's patients. The drug is designed to keep the ACh level as high as possible. By suppressing the cholinesterase action, more ACh should be available for use by the brain. Theoretically, the memory function should be assisted.

Trials with the drug offered some promise. As a result, the drug company requested approval by the FDA to distribute the medication commercially. The drug is *not* (and is not intended as) a *cure* for Alzheimer's. The disease will continue to produce neurofibrillary tangles and neuritic plaques in increasing numbers of brain cells. However, many caregivers would be most happy if the patient could show more normal mental behavior, including better memory.

Even so, tacrine has its limitations. It appears to be most helpful to those in the earlier stages of dementia. Patients who have shown symptoms over a period of several years and who have severe memory loss are less likely to be helped at all. Even in those who have just been diagnosed, tacrine may not always be helpful. Its outcomes may be short-lived, so benefits are time-limited. It may produce liver toxicity so it must be carefully managed.

The above comments are not so much intended to be critical of the drug as they are to indicate the status of drug therapy for dementia. There have been several other drugs developed and tried over the years for similar action and effects. These include physostigmine, hydergine, and choline. Each has been largely unsuccessful. Under investigation and research at the present time are two other approaches. Nerve growth factor (NGF) is a protein that helps development of the sensory and sympathetic nervous systems (the part of the nervous system that arouses us for action and leads to production of epinephrine and norepinephrine). The assumption is that this protein will help prevent cell death, thereby preserving working neurons that might otherwise be destroyed by Alzheimer's. NGF might even reverse some of the destruction of dendrites on cells where the cell body has not yet been affected. A second effort is currently underway with a drug developed in Europe called acetyl-1-carnitine, which seems to work in the body by assisting in maintaining energy sources within the cell. The compound is a natural product in the body so the procedure is to stimulate its presence and effects. Those scientists who are involved in research here believe that this compound can help retard damage to neurons and perhaps even reverse it. The proof of effectiveness for these two drugs must be collected before they can be approved by the FDA. From such efforts there is hope.

To be honest, however, hope must be kept under control when it comes to treatment for the behavioral effects of dementia. It is not cynical to believe that any great strides in this direction are far in the future. Even more distant is some intervention, drug or otherwise, that will actually affect the progression of Alzheimer's.

Yet doctors may prescribe drugs for dementia patients. When this is done, the drug is intended to treat some symptom that is associated with but not directly caused by Alzheimer's. For example, patients may become highly anxious about their condition, particularly if they have a history of anxiety. The doctor may recommend a small dose of an anxiolytic, a drug that helps control anxiety symptoms. Of course, the physician may prescribe a treatment for some condition that is separate from and unrelated to the dementia. Alzheimer's victims may have developed other illnesses that are treatable. In such a case, drug therapy is recommended, although there must be careful monitoring for side effects.

Research Efforts

Medical research into Alzheimer's has been very active in recent years. The nature of the disease, what produces it, what its components are and how they occur, and how it can be more precisely diagnosed are basic but essential questions to research. Since these are fundamental and elemental questions, the research endeavors are in various directions. Chief among these at present is research on amyloid beta protein and its destructive effects on neurons. At the same time, efforts continue to discover why aluminum is in such high concentrations in diseased cells, one of the first areas of attack in an attempt to find the cause of Alzheimer's. There are dozens of other investigative attempts occurring, all requiring patience. The course of research is often slow and probably will require great amounts of money. If you and others involved with the problems of Alzheimer's support such efforts, eventually the answer will be found. Hopefully, it will be soon.

Medical science is just as concerned about the practical, daily meanings of Alzheimer's. How can caregivers be given assistance in understanding and dealing with the dementia produced by the disease? Are there interventions to use with patients so that they present muted rather than exaggerated problems? What are the effects of drugs prescribed for other disease processes? What dimensions of care are most suitable for the patient and caregiver?

There are many more questions today than there are answers. This is in part because awareness is so much greater than ever before accompanied by a desire to help end the destructive effects of the conditions that produce dementia. Only when questions are asked can answers be sought. Without knowing when or in what form, you can expect increasing focus and resolution, almost on a daily basis.

The Status of Supports

Most of the "supports" that you will need will come from professionals in disciplines other than medicine. There will be some specific skills and techniques available to each of these disciplines that require considerable training and expert administration. At the same time, many of these operations will dovetail with each other to assist you in your effort to maintain yourself at the same time that you must provide what is needed by the patient.

Psychological Supports

There are a number of subdisciplines in psychology, most of which will have little to offer for the problems of dementia. Primarily, then, those psychologists of importance to you will come from the clinical fields and associated areas. Some may be therapists, others may be psychometrists, still others may be gerontologists, but regardless of their background each will have something to offer as a support for you.

At the time of diagnosis and periodically after that, the effects of dementia on the patient in terms of competencies remaining and those lost need to be determined. This information can help the caregiving task by encouraging the patient to continue to do those things of which he or she is capable. Such determination of abilities requires both informal and formal measures, often requiring considerable training and practice. Psychologists are essential to this process because they have developed the appropriate tools.

Since memory loss is a major effect of dementia, you need to know what the memory status of your patient is. Psychologists are qualified and expert in this regard. There are some simple tests now used that may seem childish to you. In the hands of a psychologist, however, information can be gained on the general level of memory function and some of its specific expressions. For example, there is the measurement of the ability to retain material for use in the immediate future. This kind of memory loss is particularly implicated in Alzheimer's and represents a severe loss in functioning. If you cannot remember what you are supposed to do in the next few minutes, you cannot effectively control your own life. The psychological tests can indicate how much this form of memory has been impaired. The psychologist may then suggest to you ways to anticipate some ineffectiveness by the patient and steps you will need to take to keep him or her performing. Let's say that you involve your patient in setting the table for a meal. It may be necessary for you to hand the patient two plates and supervise their placement. On the other hand, the patient may still recognize that you each need a fork and spoon and can get those and put them on the table. A *general* memory loss may be present without meaning that every skill or ability requiring memory is no longer present. The psychologist is a resource that you can use for such mundane but important decisions.

As part of the diagnostic procedure, psychologists can furnish the doctor with information on the patient's intellectual abilities. The performance by the patient on tests of mental ability can disclose both remaining strengths and limitations now imposed. Neuropsychological tests can furnish information on brain integrity and skills available. Overall, this area of competencies and deficiencies is important for understanding the current status of the patient. Occasional reevaluation to determine any changes will be necessary.

"Treatment" has a different meaning for psychology than it does for medicine. There is, of course, a clinical intervention with psychological problems like depression and anxiety. Since these conditions may occur in both patient and caregiver, the need for a therapist may be present at any point in the course of the disease. Clinical psychologists are eminently qualified for this source of relief because of their training and experience. A variety of memory assists (called mnemonics) can be used to help retention of material. However, their use with patients may be limited by the fact that the patient does not encode or store the effective steps even as they are taught. As a result, the devices may not be successful, even though they should be tried.

The technique of reality orientation, which was developed to help patients remain in contact with reality, may be used in the home or an institution. It may be recommended that you use this technique in an effort to keep the patient oriented to reality for as long as possible. The progress of the patient's confusion and disorientation may be slowed by the effort.

Psychological research in the past has focused on the identification and meaning of the memory loss, confusion, and disorientation that characterizes dementia. More recently, efforts had been directed at specific questions. Since there is memory loss, what are its dimensions? As an example, Alzheimer's patients show problems with certain aspects of general information. It is important to know that the *names* of common objects may not be remembered while their *function* may be. The psychologist may point to a chair and ask what it is. The patient may reply, "It's what you sit on." The psychologist may agree but ask again, "What is its name?" The patient simply cannot recall and may even confess so. This loss in what is called "semantic memory" is more than an oddity; it is important to the functioning of the individual. Psychologists can identify such losses (and changes in episodic memory as well) and are seeking ways to explain it *and* to correct it.

There is continuing psychological research on the short-term and long-term effects of dementia in order to add to the knowledge base and to develop appropriate interventions. Means of adjustment that might be more effective than those already known are being investigated as well. Ways to cope with burdens and stress are available but efforts to increase the number of such techniques and to improve them goes on.

Social Supports

Whether or not advances occur medically and psycho-logically, the need for social supports will remain a major element. Because the daily impact of dementia is ever present, there can be no escape from the demands. Social workers and gerontologists, along with nurses, are the professionals particularly concerned about such matters. It would be unfair, however, not to mention social service directors, nurses' aides, paraprofessionals of various kinds, and activity directors since they are involved in the most direct contacts with patients and caregivers.

One essential element in the provision of social supports are governmental and community agencies. At the federal level, there is a unit within the National Institute on Aging that is concerned with dementia and its causes. Monies appropriated to this division are provided for major research projects, dissemination of literature, and sponsoring meetings and conferences. At the state level, there will be a division on aging that also will include personnel who are primarily concerned about the well-being and support of dementia patients and caregivers. Although these federal and state offices may seem removed from the needs of sufferers from dementia, they are important in the sense that they represent the social conscience. They are funded to help, and they release these funds for those projects that are approved because they are demonstrated to be worthwhile. How effective they are depends on the funding provided.

Additionally, and importantly, there is the Alzheimer's Asso-ciation. This organization publishes newsletters and pamphlets as information sources on everything from current research to legis-lation. Funds raised each year support research into the cause and nature of Alzheimer's as well as its effects. The organization is actively involved in the legislative process at the federal level to bring more supports and increase knowledge about dementia and its causes. There is sponsorship of workshops and seminars for professionals and laypersons.

At the local level are both governmental and private sources of social supports. There are offshoots from both federal and state agencies with personnel trained and qualified to administer the programs funded by the government. The private sources often depend on grants and donations for their existence. Chief among these are the Alzheimer's Association chapters. The chapters sponsor support groups and provide them with speakers and literature. In fact, a major provision of the local chapter is the educational function of pamphlets, books, and videocassettes about Alzheimer's and its influences. Local chapters can also provide information about professionals, including physicians, who have a particular interest in the disease. Fund-raising projects involve many caregivers, patients, and volunteers as a means of educating the public.

The tools of social supports have been developed over a number of years and come from various settings. These ideas and techniques have now been applied to the interaction between caregiver and patient whether in the home or institution. They may include techniques from psychology (such as reality orientation and counseling) as well as identifying resources in the community available to those affected by dementia. Social workers often are the liaison between physicians and caregivers, both immediately following diagnosis and throughout the disease's progression.

The research in social supports comes from both sociologists and social workers. They are particularly competent in the field of attitude surveys and have increased knowledge and developed ways of dealing with problems that have been disclosed. The effects of group characteristics on individual behavior is an interest of social research. The dynamics of interaction within groups and between individuals has been better understood because of these efforts.

Political Supports

The politics of dementia have their base in some major legislation passed and funded during the 1960s and particularly during the Johnson administration. In 1965, Congress passed the Older Americans Act and funded it adequately so that many programs that came out of the act were realized. Many of those efforts on behalf of the elderly are still functioning, though with lesser funding from federal budget to federal budget. Still, the positive effects of providing governmental support for the elderly are still major.

As a result of some of the agencies provided in the Older Americans Act (e.g., the National Institute on Aging), an increasing awareness developed of the detrimental effects of dementia on the aging population, which stimulated direct action that was extended to state and local sources. The result was the provision of programs specifically designed to support the effects of dementia. Now, public policy is a concern of both the Alzheimer's Association and its chapters. Legislation is sought on behalf of victims with each session of Congress. The record at present is not great, but the efforts continue and may eventually yield effects. Politically, only as legislation is developed, passed, and signed into law by the president will a permanent impact be felt.

The costs of dementia are heavy. Few persons are rich enough to pay all the expenses, and many caregivers experience major changes in their financial status. Even bankruptcy may occur, and although this may lead to provision of Medicare for the basic needs of the patient, there is no help for the caregiver. Medicare, the principal source of medical payment by the elderly, does not cover the costs of care for mental illnesses. Dementia is defined as a mental illness so that expenses are out of pocket if they are paid at all. There are efforts to expand the legislation of Medicare to cover the mental conditions but so far these efforts have been unsuccessful.

The Congress has sustained monies for research into Alzheimer's and other dementia-producing diseases. In 1993, the subsidy for this cause was $400 million. This seems like a large sum but it is small compared to monies provided for other conditions. In fact, there needs to be many times this amount if an answer to Alzheimer's is to be found soon. In a time when the economy is struggling, such funds simply cannot be made available without depriving other worthy causes of their income.

At present, then, the picture of dementia is spotty. There are more questions than answers and progress is irregular. We know a good deal about the effects of dementia behaviorally but very little about why those effects occur. Further, there is no clear picture about the reasons for the appearance of some behavior changes in some patients and not in others, nor why there are lesser effects of a behavior change in one patient and greater effects in another. Means to intervene for patients and caregivers are limited and of doubtful validity. The loss of talent economically for the society has not been assessed and must be compounded by the loss of viable life of those directly involved with dementia. We have come far, but there is far to go.

Dementia in the Twenty-First Century

Any attempt to forecast the future can be dangerous. Having all the facts necessary to evaluate the present is difficult enough, and the future does not necessarily follow present trends anyway. It is important to speculate, however, because an agenda is established. Perhaps that agenda will show changes in emphasis as time goes on or even prove to be in error in some respects. Still, if you remain open to the need to adjust your program, the gains will exceed the limitations. What follows is a personal suggestion, less prediction perhaps than hope.

The Future Status of Medical Training

If, like me, you have a yearly physical, you may have noticed an increase in the proportion of older persons in the waiting room. The reason is twofold: older people are subject to more severe health problems and there are an increasing number of older individuals in our society. Physicians are increasingly aware of that change as well. Among other things, they are attending symposia and taking courses that focus on geriatric medicine. Included in these efforts are exposure to Alzheimer's, to dementia and its effects, to treatment and therapy for patients and care-givers, and to surveys of medical research findings. It is probable that doctors inform the medical schools from which they gradu-ated or with which they are associated of the need for more exposure to geriatrics. In some instances, they will advocate additional coursework in gerontology and geriatrics. Some will support the recognition of the discipline of geriatric medicine as a specialty for medical students.

Since these factors are already at work, I feel secure in predicting that the twenty-first century will bring changes in medical education and training toward geriatrics. There will be courses required of all students in the characteristics of older persons (gerontology) and the physical and mental changes that accompany the aging process. Deviations from the normal devel-opmental patterns (better understood by that time) will be em-phasized so that doctors will see patients without the biases of past generations. The specialty of geriatric medicine will have taken its place alongside internal medicine, pediatric medicine, and so on, as a full-fledged and accepted discipline. It is possible that the concept and practice will be so popular that the total caseload of geriatric physicians will consist of people over age 60 or so. Indeed, there will even be those who accept only patients over age 85, while others will see individuals who are under that age but over age 65.

A significant part of the medical education in geriatrics will focus on the characteristics, diagnosis, and treatment of condi-tions that lead to dementia. It will be routine to investigate the possibility of Alzheimer's or other dementia-causing diseases when symptoms and complaints indicate the need for accurate determination. (This state is already beginning, although there are still some doctors who dismiss complaints on the basis that the patient is only growing older and has to expect such things. In the twenty-first century, such a statement will be taboo.) Physicians will be better educated and more understanding of the fact that it is not enough to find what is wrong. There will be an attitude that a doctor has a responsibility for the emotional states and needs of patients also, including especially those who must face dementia and its consequences.

Of course, I could be very wrong. Perhaps by then, the research will have paid off and preventive measures will have been found, making Alzheimer's a disease of the past. I hope that is the case. At least, perhaps by then, research will have disclosed a cause for the disease and efforts will be underway to eliminate that cause in future generations.

The Future Status of Medical Diagnosis

If the future of medical education occurs as I have predicted, diagnosis of Alzheimer's will be one beneficiary. There should be not only more universal recognition of the disease but more accurate elimination of conditions that might mask as Alzheimer's (such as depression or the effects of infection).

Knowledge of Alzheimer's

The result of the changes from improved medical education will ensure more accurate and complete knowledge about the disease by physicians. Geriatricians will be particularly well grounded in the expressions and meanings of Alzheimer's. Accuracy of recognition of the disease should be greater, not only because of increased awareness but also because the means to recognize the basic characteristics are known. In addition, doctors will be more attuned to the personal element, the effects on patients and caregivers, than some of them currently are.

Labeling and Diagnosis

There will have been considerable improvements in the diagnostic process. Perhaps the principal one will involve the information gathered from brain scans. Although the CAT and PET scans will still be used for gathering data about integrity of the brain, the MRI (magnetic imaging resonance) scan should have been improved and more fully developed. Since the MRI uses neither X rays (as CAT does) nor radiation (as PET does), there is less intrinsic danger attached to the procedure. Cost should be reduced in the next century, and the combination of safety and reasonable expense will contribute to its popularity.

There is an even more important reason, however. The potential of the MRI for depicting the status of the brain has barely been touched at this time. There will be increasing sophistication in the ability to interpret the images produced so that greater accuracy and wider utility will result. As significant as this fact may be, there is yet another element of considerable importance. The evolution of the hardware presents the possibility of examining the brain at the cellular level. Although a few scientists are already talking about this likelihood, most are more reserved on the issue. Still, the potential seems more than just a pipe dream.

If MRI turns out to be as capable as I predict, future patients and caregivers will benefit greatly. When the doctor who reads the scan can see the quality of individual neurons, it will be possible to diagnose with almost 100 percent accuracy. Destruction of cells and position of plaques not only will signify Alzheimer's, but the relation of damage in given areas to behavioral outcomes will also be plausible and usable. Perhaps just as important will be the ability to identify accurately other causes of dementia symptoms. Indeed, it should be possible then to recognize when Alzheimer's is not implicated in the behaviors.

It would not be surprising if even more sophisticated and accurate computerized sources of analysis of body systems will be available in the future. Indeed, that is likely. If costs are reasonable, there will be even greater benefits to the medical profession and to society.

Treatment of Dementia

Several drugs intended to help memory function have been tested. As mentioned earlier, one (tacrine) has been approved by the Food and Drug Administration. Others are being developed or tested, and they may eventually find their way to market as well. There is the possibility that within five years, and certainly ten years, there will be several medications that doctors can prescribe for the treatment of specific symptoms of Alzheimer's. This could even mean that you and your patient will receive some help.

If these drugs are safe in the sense that they do not have serious side effects (such as toxicity to some of the body's organs or increasing the intensity of other symptoms), they will be a great stride forward. The focus has been on memory retention because caregivers have most often listed memory loss as a major concern. The ability to retain a message long enough to carry it out (short-term memory) would relieve a number of burdens felt by caregivers. Patients could take greater responsibility for their actions and well-being, giving the caregiver greater relief. This may not be the major problem that you experience, but success here does imply that other symptoms will receive attention as well. This would mean that, at some point in the next century, the "universals" of dementia (memory loss, confusion, and disorientation in time and space) could be effectively reduced and handled. At the same time, treatment without side effects for personality changes may be available. No doubt medications used as tranquilizers, antidepressants, and the like, will also be more effective and safer. The term "treatment" will have achieved a significant meaning when these changes occur.

The treatment of discrete symptoms of a disease is necessary but hardly sufficient. What is most needed is treatment for the disease itself so that the process does not continue. At the minimal level, this would mean that the progression of the disease is arrested—things will get no worse. Better still, it could mean that the development is reversed. Patients could show improvements in behavior to some degree and, ultimately, to a significant degree. The sooner this step is taken the better for you and other caregivers. Realistically, research efforts are not directed this way at the present, so such a result seems to be well into the twenty-first century.

Ultimately, the objective must be to ensure that no person (of whatever age) is faced with the prospect of dementia, which will require both finding the cause of Alzheimer's disease and developing a preventive. It is not likely that a *single* cause will be found. Genetic mutation may be one cause. In this case, genetic engineering will have to be used if a person is to escape the ravages of Alzheimer's. In other instances, the disease may result from chemical abnormalities or imbalances (such as in neurotransmitters). Some means to correct the abnormality or improve the balance will be necessary. In still other cases, the culprit may be a disorder in a body system that will progress to dementia if not discovered and treated properly. Whatever the eventual truth about the cause of Alzheimer's, major decisions will have to be made by the medical profession, by society, and by individuals who are affected by the consequences. Overall, however, there seems much to be hopeful about, particularly when we consider the current status of treatment for dementia.

Research Efforts

Obviously, if the kinds of changes predicted above are to happen, there must be extensive research in both the immediate and distant future. Primary research at detecting the cause of Alzheimer's, already underway in many directions, will continue and expand. Some areas of investigation will prove to be dead ends, leaving more promising areas to be pursued even more vigorously. Eventually, the answer will come.

Coexistent with research to find cause will be research to identify a "cure," even though it may be restricted to improving symptoms rather than changing the disease process itself. Most of this research will be conducted by drug manufacturers so that doctors can have a medication to dispense. Many caregivers at present are hopeful that this result will come soon, and there are encouraging signs that it is happening. Once achieved, caregivers will become more insistent for a means to reverse present states.

Eventually, and to the benefit of all concerned, medical research will put physicians out of the dementia business!

The Future Status of Supports

Until such time as Alzheimer's no longer exerts its debilitating effects on people, those professions working with the day-to-day consequences will continue to do so. Their roles will remain much as they are but the tools and techniques they use should be refined and improved.

Psychological Supports

Psychologists will continue to be responsible for evaluating the mental status of patients diagnosed with Alzheimer's. Many of the tests currently used will continue because they are simple, quick, nonthreatening, and reasonably valid. These will include particularly the evaluations of memory, confusion, and orientation where patients must show that they are in contact with reality. There may be improved ability to correlate the results more specifically with brain function and integrity, but that would not change the benefits of knowing the status of patients' awareness and of the competencies remaining to them.

In some tests there will be improvements of considerable importance. Individual measures of intellectual ability is one area needing such improvement. An important part of the diagnostic process, the test most commonly used today is the *Wechsler Adult Intelligence Test-Revised*. The instrument is far superior to any other examination available and its utility has been proved over many years. There are some limitations, however, that should receive attention in future, or the test may be replaced by some other one. One of the major problems is that the scores are not normed for persons above age 75. As our society ages, there are more and more persons over that age, some of whom will need to be examined for their intellectual competence. A new revision is needed to correct for this deficiency by using those over 75 as a source for norming as well.

A second problem with the Wechsler that will be corrected in the future is the content of the test. A separate form of the test (or even a separate scale) should be developed to ensure that the content is appropriate for older persons who take it. If the publisher does not do so, another should undertake the effort. Currently, the same content (items) is used for persons age 16 through 75. In renorming, it seems reasonable and justified that more appropriate material for persons over the age of 60 or so can be inserted. There could even be a form for age 75 and over, with its own items and norms. Psychologists will then have a more accurate and valid measure to use as a part of the diagnostic procedure.

With investigation and experience, there will be better evaluation of skills required to carry out activities of daily living. This will come through the increased awareness of what older persons as a group can perform and at what level. Comparisons with the behaviors of young adults, or even middle-aged ones, will no longer be necessary. Eventually, psychologists will be as informed about normal development in old age as they are about normal development of infants and children.

Such events will impinge on the efforts of assisting patients and caregivers in dealing with the problems of dementia. There will be more suggestions that can be tried as well as a more precise understanding of the outcomes of efforts. This will mean less need for vague and general proposals.

Psychological research will continue into functional behaviors such as communication. How to ensure that a message is understood by the patient will be more explicit and relieve some burdens on the caregiver. The meanings of statements that seem unreal currently will be better realized in the future. In effect, psychologists will understand the reality conceived by the patient and not just the reality that those without dementia perceive. This will permit intervention in a way not currently possible.

Social Supports

In the future, there will be decreased need for governmental agencies to supervise social programs. This will happen because there will be increasing acceptance of responsibility at the local level along with greater development of such units as the Alzheimer's Association. Social programs have required government supervision to date because there has been a lack of experience and acceptance for the changes brought about. Society will be better educated about such issues and more willing to deal directly with the problems rather than leaving it to the government. A "social conscience" will be one of the hallmarks of a more mature society than has ever been known in this country.

Professionals involved in social supports (principally social workers and gerontologists) will have more tools for intervention available and be adept at using them. The kind of accuracy projected for psychologists is pertinent here also. Geriatric social workers will be widely found, whereas today they are present only in small numbers. This means they will bring better understanding of the elderly as a group and those affected by dementia in particular.

Research efforts will focus on the dynamics of caregiving, a thrust already taking place. As a result of the continued achievements, social workers and gerontologists will be able to help caregivers be more consistent and capable. This will reduce burdens and give the caregiver greater feelings of worth. The increased understanding of patient behaviors will allow communication with both the patient and caregiver. The ultimate gain will be that caregiver and patient relationships will be improved.

More effective outcomes from support groups will be found also. Where now the caregiver often takes little or nothing away that influences behavior at home (even though each may say that help was received), the day will come when there will be specific skills and knowledge that are translated into action. The principal outcome will be more meaningful and rewarding relationships between caregiver and patient. Caregiving will be seen as less of a burden and there can be a more viable life even where dementia is found.

Political Supports

The social conscience described above will affect politicians as well. Future members of Congress will see the need for protection of citizens from the ravages of Alzheimer's. Legislation to provide this protection will be a major priority. At the same time, the involvement of governmental agencies will be reduced so that a considerable portion of the funding can go directly to the source needed. There may even be funding provided to private agencies so long as the evidence is clear that the monies are used in a beneficial way. As needed, research that helps to reduce the adverse effects of Alzheimer's will be supported as well.

Summary

During this century, and particularly in the past 30 years, knowledge about Alzheimer's disease and dementia has increased significantly. The behavioral effects have been recognized, and diagnosis and some interventions have been developed and tried in medicine and in the helping professions. The picture still is one of a great many questions and few answers. An assessment of the present status in each of these areas has been made in this chapter. This evaluation was used to present possible developments in the future.

Among the factors considered are medical training and diagnosis. The current state of psychological, social, and political supports is surveyed as well. Finally, what the future may hold for each of these elements is considered.

Bibliography

Alzheimer's Association (1993). Research update. *Newsletter*, 13 (2), 4–5, 7.

Alzheimer's Association (1988). *Special care for Alzheimer patients*. Chicago, IL: Alzheimer's Association.

Bandura, Albert (1982). Self-efficacy mechanisms in human agency. *American Psychologist*, 37, 122–147.

Beck, Aaron (1976). *Cognitive therapy and the emotional disorders*. New York: International Universities Press.

Burns, David D. (1980). *Feeling good: The new mood therapy*. New York: Morrow.

Edwards, Allen Jack (1993). *Dementia*. New York: Plenum Press.

Morycz, Richard K. (1985). Caregiving strain and the desire to institutionalize family members with Alzheimer's disease: Possible predictors and model development. *Research on Aging*, 7 (3), 329–361.

National Institutes of Health (1987). Differential diagnosis of dementing diseases. Washington, DC: Consensus Development Conference Statement, vol. 6, no. 11, July 6–8.

Index